A Man Made of Elk

Stories, Advice, and Campfire Philosophy from a Lifetime of Traditional Bowhunting

A Man Made of Elk

Stories, Advice, and Campfire Philosophy from a Lifetime of Traditional Bowhunting

By David Petersen

Foreword by
E. Donnall Thomas, Jr.

Original cover art by
Thomas Aquinas Daly

Cover design by Sean Daly

Also By David Petersen

Postcards from Ed: Dispatches and Salvos from an American Iconoclast
(editor)
On the Wild Edge: In Search of a Natural Life (memoir)
Cedar Mesa: A Place where Spirits Dwell
Heartsblood: Hunting, Spirituality, and Wildness in America
Elkheart: A Personal Tribute to Wapiti and their World
The Nearby Faraway: A Personal Journey through the Heart of the West
A Hunter's Heart: Honest Essays on Blood Sport (editor)
Ghost Grizzlies: Does the Great Bear Still Haunt Colorado?
Earth Apples: The Poetry of Edward Abbey (editor)
Confessions of a Barbarian: Selections from the Journals of Edward
Abbey (editor)
Racks: The Natural History of Antlers and the Animals that Wear Them
Among the Aspen
Big Sky, Fair Land: The Environmental Essays of A. B. Guthrie, Jr.
(editor)
Among the Elk: Wilderness Images
Going Trad: Out There with Elkheart

Dedication

This book is dedicated to all sportsmen and women who strive to uphold the ethics and dignity of traditional-values hunting ... doing more with less, and doing it with honesty, humility, and respect.

Contents

Part I: An Elk Hunter's Almanac

Part II: Woodsmanship: How I Do It (and how I try not to)

Part III: Campfire Philosophies

Foreword

Like all of the few "outdoor" books that truly deserve to endure, *A Man Made of Elk* is, well … different. That's logical enough, for the same can certainly be said of its author.

A former Marine pilot and current backwoods intellectual, idealist, iconoclast, and, yes, hunter, Dave Petersen defies categorization as adroitly as his terrific prose. "Hook-and-bullet" writer? Forget that. While Petersen can entertain and inform with the best, his prime mission is to challenge the reader's assumptions about what it means to be a hunter … and a citizen of the planet Earth. Expect to face that challenge in the pages that follow. Readers in search of outdoor pap are looking in the wrong place.

The text that follows divides into three sections and it's no accident that "An Elk Hunter's Almanac" comes first. Early on, Petersen writes: "I become the animals I hunt." While readers will enjoy vignettes describing encounters with a number of game species, it's obvious that the writer spends most of his "woods time" as a wapiti.

I know deer hunters, bear hunters, and sheep hunters, but I don't know anyone else who identifies as completely with one species of game as Dave Petersen identifies with elk. This book's title goes beyond metaphor; the guy is made of elk. While Petersen's almanac of elk hunting tales doesn't spend much time wallowing (my deliberate choice of verbs) in traditional outdoor "how-to," a hypothetical hunter from the East Coast planning a first western elk hunt will find more genuine elk lore here than in most volumes devoted exclusively to the subject. Nonetheless, the reader will quickly note that Petersen, while all for killing elk with his homemade bows, views them as icons of wild places and traditional values, as much as he does sources of meat or antlers.

The book's second segment, "Woodsmanship: How I Do It (and how I try not to)," seems a somewhat unexpected effort to tell just that. Indeed, the reader will learn some nifty tricks about everything from ambush and calling tactics, to efficient means of field dressing game, to making elk jerky. By its conclusion, however, I can't avoid the impression that the author is as much concerned with why we should do things right in the field as he is with how to do them that way. Somehow, I doubt that Dave will be offended by this admission.

Who should read this book? Bowhunters to be sure, and traditional bowhunters especially. But its most important audience may well be non-hunting friends and family who need someone to walk them through the intangibles: the regard for tradition, the willingness to limit one's means of take and eschew technology, and above all the reverence for all things natural that devoted traditional bowhunters experience when they take to the field.

Let's hope *A Man Made of Elk* reaches them.

E. Donnall Thomas, Jr.

Passion

As my wife will cheerily tell you, I am a real slow learner.

For example, only recently did it dawn on me — and I'm a professional word nerd, remember — that the terms *passion* and *suffering* are closely related in meaning. Biblically, passion and suffering are synonymous, as per the twelve passions of Christ. But in everyday usage as well, the two words, and the feelings they represent, often go hand in glove, no matter how opposite they may seem. After all, doesn't passion connote pleasure (sexual and otherwise), while suffering denotes pain? And unless you're a masochist, a Marine, or a serious hunter, how can pain be good?

What broke the code for me was discovering that "passion" shares the same Latin root as "patience." From there, I'll let you make the stairstep connections, as this ain't no stinkin' English class. And what in blazes do passion and suffering, related in meaning or not, have to do with traditional bowhunting?

I am here to propose: everything.

Adventure isn't always fun when it's happening. Without some modest suffering — sleep lost, cold endured, heat and bugs, lung-burning climbs, knee-twisting descents, mind-numbing exhaustion, stumbling around in the dark semi-lost — it's impossible to know the bone-deep passion that drives a total hunting commitment. Without extraordinary effort, how can we expect, or think we deserve, extraordinary rewards? Without an eager willingness to work hard and swallow a bit of suffering, we are merely tap-dancing on the surface of far deeper possibilities, and learning little — about life or ourselves — in the process.

Recreation, yes. Passion, no way.

No pain, no gain. No sacrifice … no passion.

And yet, most of the mainstream outdoor industry today, through the glittery gizmos and "the faster and easier, the better" message and products it peddles, strives to minimize such heart-deep essentials of hunting as concerted practice, exceptional effort, stoic endurance, skills development, nature knowledge, patience, tenacity, responsibility, empathy, individuality, character, and honor. Why struggle for months and years to learn to shoot a stick accurately at a mere twenty yards, when you can line up the sights on a store-tuned compound and instantly be twice as accurate at twice the range? Why walk when you can zoom around on an ATV? Why master such basics of woodsmanship as wind direction and scent control, when you can wear a scent-proof camo suit and a bunch of chemicals and be as sloppy as you like (or so the ads infer)? Why, in other words, waste time and energy actually *hunting* — with all the sacrifices that true hunting demands — when a warehouse full of bright and shiny shortcuts are as close as the nearest sporting goods store or catalog.

Having a personally satisfying answer to all such "whys" is the mark of the true traditionalist, who frankly is not interested in minimizing the effort, skill, or commitment invested in shooting and hunting. Quite the opposite; we traditionalists want to broaden, deepen, and enrich our overall hunting experience. We don't want to shoot game at greater distances; we want to get closer! We choose to hunt "the hard way" precisely because it is the hard way!

Process *over* product.

In a life well lived and a hunt well hunted, the trip *is* the destination.

Many today, sad to say, seem to view hunting as little more than an excuse to buy and play with a lot of expensive toys that promise "success" in the sickly guise of making more kills with less skill, effort, and time invested … blissfully unaware that such shortcuts are robbing the would-be hunter of the greatest joys of hunting in the process.

Occasionally, even some would-be traditionalists are tempted by today's dizzying barrage of commercial hunting hype. But the unbending demands of traditional bowhunting quickly sort things out. You either enjoy the exacting practice required to achieve consistent stickbow accuracy, or you resort to less demanding tools. You either cherish developing the patience to sit motionless for long slow hours on stand and to sneak quiet as fog through the woods, or you resort to expedients. You either welcome the challenge and exhaustion and occasional pain of walking long miles and packing meat out on your back, or you limp along on mechanical crutches. You either try and try again to stalk within rock-tossing range of hair-trigger prey, or you opt for gear that can kill from afar.

We're either traditionalists at heart, because we want to be, or we're not.

In case you haven't noticed, I'm fiercely proud to be an ethical traditional bowhunter. It's a title I claim based on half a century of unwavering commitment. (I am sixty-one at this writing, took up archery at age eight, and started bowhunting at fourteen.) And yet I don't believe I'm better than anyone else based solely on choice of equipment. As Don Thomas frankly puts it: "Anyone can go out and buy a longbow." It's not so much a case of "us" versus "them," right versus wrong, sticks versus wheels, or smart versus dumb. It's a matter of how we as individual hunters and humans view and choose to live our lives. Some of us want passion. Others seek practicality. Some invite challenge and chance. Meanwhile, insecurity craves predictability. America, so far as I know, and with recent political erosion acknowledged, is still a free country.

Traditional bowhunting, like no other hunting I know, challenges us to experience palpably — actually *feeling* in our guts, lungs, legs, and hearts — the little sufferings and big satisfactions of going that extra mile, literally as well as metaphorically. No shortcuts asked or taken.

And that's what this book attempts to explore and evoke: one hunter's passion. Half a century of passion for traditional archery; half a long lifetime of passion for elk, elk country, and elk hunting; and a lifetime of passion for ... passion.

Confession: In a lengthy and honest, if hardly illustrious, career of thinking and writing about wildness — wildlife, wild places, wild people, and wild ideas — I've never sought or considered myself to be an "outdoor writer" in the usual sense of the term. In fact, I've dodged every such opportunity that came my way, and in the early years, there were many. I just didn't want to be pigeon-holed. What I did want was to be read both within and beyond the hook-and-bullet community. I wanted to be considered a hunting natural history writer, a "literary" writer, a truthful and at least borderline philosophical writer. Consequently, my previous books — while spinning out a few "Me and Joe" hunting yarns to illustrate and enliven my more serious apologias about our proper human relationship with the rest of creation — generally approached hunting from historical, biological, ethical, and philosophical angles. Where this book differs from those dozen that came before, is that it seriously and concertedly *goes hunting*. Certainly, I've included some campfire philosophizing (somehow, I got wired that way long ago, and though it gets me

In trouble constantly, I just can't help myself). And there's a substantial "how to" section as well, offering hunting tips and advice based not on a mere review and paraphrase of what other hunters and writers have said, but on my own long and ongoing learning experience of successes and mistakes.

Even so, I'm proud to say that the bulk of *A Man Made of Elk* just goes hunting.

Which is all I've ever really wanted to do.

Thank you for your indulgence.

Acknowledgments

In assembling a book from a collection of thematically connected but individually written pieces tracking fifty-some seasons of traditional bowhunting, the challenge is to arrange the parts so as to create a sonorous sense of flow and connectivity, striving for an organized herd moving smoothly in a common direction, rather than a wandering gaggle. Inevitably, after countless trips through the maze of words, stories, and themes — updating, revising, high-grading, culling, trimming, correcting old mistakes, adding new info and insights, and puzzling all the pieces together — you begin to lose sight of the individual animals within the mobile mass. At this blurry point, you need some help. At least I do. And so I consulted my personal physician, elk hunting companion, bow-building guru, and fellow campfire philosopher, Dr. Dave Sigurslid. Reading the manuscript in an early incarnation and offering careful advice was a generous and time-consuming act on Doc's part, and his healthful prescriptions infuse these pages.

Since this is my first book focusing purely on traditional bowhunting, intended to entertain as much as to teach or to preach, I wanted to do-it-up right by surrounding myself with some of my heroes in the traditional archery world. Toward that end, I aimed my arrows of request with precision at a select handful of targets ... and bagged the grandest of slams, to wit:

New York traditional bowhunter, bowyer, fisherman, farmer, and painter, Thomas Aquinas Daly, in my opinion, is the finest sporting artist working today. As my postscript tribute to Tom recalls in some detail, we once spent a week chasing elk together. Calling on that friendship, I recently gave Tom a call to explain this project and what it means to me, and to ask if he might have a painting that would be suitable for the cover. I described the book's themes and my desire for a moody, thoughtful, and darkly luminous cover scene that clearly evoked not only the looks but the feel and mood of serious elk country, with aspens and dark timber, and wherein a lone longbow hunter informs the scene as a small but significant element of nature, rather than the dominant theme. Moreover, only this faceless longbowman (thus, a stand-in for all longbowmen) sees the elk lurking back in the shadowy depths. Viewing this complex scene, you and I know the game is there only because we can read that information in the hunter's body language. When I finally shut up, Tom said, "You know, I *like* this idea. Tell you what: I'll paint you an original."

And just look what we got! *Dark Timber* is a masterpiece of traditional bowhunting art. If nothing else, this book can take credit for having inspired its creation. Endless thanks and respect, Tom.

Artful talent runs in the Daly family, and Tom's graphic designer son Sean produced three exciting design options for the cover, forcing me to choose. Thanks, Sean!

And what more artful, credible, and respected outdoor writer could any traditional bowhunting scrivener hope to have write a foreword than Dr. E. Donnall Thomas, Jr., our own Don Thomas. (Ironically, my years of ever-warming friendship with Don began in a heated argument. Were Don not the open-minded, tenacious, and good-humored soul he is, it could have ended right there, before it even began. But that's the proverbial 'nuther story for another day.) Don also volunteered to give these pages a final close look before going to press, and "cleaned me up" a good deal in the process. Much thanks, amigo.

And let me tell you how grateful I am to have had the original version of this book published by *Traditional Bowhunter Magazine*, which single-handedly rekindled and has steadfastly carried the torch that has, in recent decades, guided traditional archery, traditional bowhunting, and traditional bow-making out of the once-obscuring and near-fatal shadow of inappropriate technology and back into the limelight, where it damn-well belongs. As icing on the TBM cake, *Traditional Bowhunter* is the only national hunting publication I know of that refuses to accept ATV or other hunting-harmful, hi-tech advertising. And this no matter that publishers T.J. Conrads and the late, great, and still beloved Larry Fischer could easily double the publication's very modest profit, or more, by selling out like all the others. I admire and applaud such rare and self-sacrificing dedication to the core values of traditional fair-chase bowhunting, have long been proud to be a part of TBM's extended family, and am doubly proud to have TBM publish this book.

And finally, I wish to thank Robin Conrads for so cheerfully and competently stepping in at the last minute to help prepare this second edition of *A Man Made of Elk* for publication.

That said, now it's time for me to make like a cautious old bull at the peak of hunting season, and fade back into the sheltering woods, where security, unknown adventures, and personal discovery await.

* * *

Benedictio: Let us hunt with brains, legs, lungs, and heart, remembering always that quality, satisfaction, and true success rarely ride on quantity, and never on an ATV. Traditional bowhunting is a challenging adventure best taken by foot. Where is the hurry? The process is the product. May we shoot straight and often, think for ourselves, and defend bravely all obvious truths, so that our hunts will earn healthful meat, honorable friends, and happy memories always.

—David Petersen
San Juan Mountains, Colorado

Part I

An Elk Hunter's Almanac

David Petersen

Chapter One

Farts in a Hurricane (A Pronghorn Prelude)

L ate summer, late day, midlife.

With archery elk season — the apogee of my year — still two weeks away, I'm biding my time, dodging work and other "real life" responsibilities in favor of honing my stalking skills and hardening my legs and lungs with a few days of chasing pronghorns in Colorado's San Luis Valley, a hundred miles east of my Durango-area home.

For the past half-hour, a dozen of the wily prairie goats have been grazing carelessly in a grassy bowl a quarter-mile below me, courageously close by that stand-offish species' standards. Just moments ago, a score or so more appeared on the southern horizon, half a mile out, feeding fast as caribou toward the base of the long, narrow knoll where I'm sitting in plain sight, binoculars in hand.

Watching this swelling swarm of prongies, including several mature bucks, it's tempting to add one last stalk to the day. But the sun has sunk too low, as have the odds against me. And I'm just too damn tired.

I was already pooped an hour ago when I sagged into camp after a long, invigorating sneak-and-peek that took me to within thirty-five yards of a beautiful buck. Following a fruitless morning spent sitting in ambush over a natural pool in a nearby creek, and just after a rowdy midday thunderstorm, I spotted the animal from so far away that even through eight-power binoculars I could see no horns. Moreover, from that great distance the prongy looked small and pale, so I dismissed it as a doe. Then the sun winked out briefly and a jagged black line extending from horn tip down through bulging eye and cheek patch flashed like ebony — a legal buck.

After abandoning my ambush and moving close enough to assess the trend of the buck's stop-and-go grazing and to contemplate the corrugated terrain ahead of him, I contoured half a mile more in the animal's direction then leaned into the climb, hugging to the bottom of a rocky arroyo. Every hundred yards or so I'd creep to the lip of the shallow swale, peek over, and search until I relocated my quarry, adjusting the next leg of my route accordingly.

The closer I got, the shallower the arroyo and the fewer the trees, until at last I was on a level with my prey, with just two bushy little piñon pines between us. The tree I was hunkered behind stood fifty yards from the buck. If I could only sneak from there to the final pine and lean out around it without being busted, I'd have a twenty-yard shot. Peeking through parted limbs, I noted with reassurance that the buck had bedded, broadside and looking the other way.

From habit, I flicked my Bic to check the wind direction. Some experienced hunters claim that pronghorns pay little attention to scent; as my biologist hunting buddy Tom Beck phrased it, "Your basic prongy is a whole 'nuther critter from your basic deer or elk." And so true, as the two are related by neither taxonomy nor disposition. *Antilocapra americana*, the American "antelope-goat" (in fact it is neither antelope nor goat), has no close relative anywhere in the known universe. Yet, I know from hard personal experience that prongies do at times listen to their noses, scent-spooking even from hundreds of yards away. Besides, after a lifetime of hunting, it's become compulsive habit — reading and heeding the wind.

This time, the wind was with me and so was hope, so unto the breach I went — out and around the penultimate piñon, my heart booming like a timpani … slow, slow, keeping always that last critical bushy tree aligned exactly between my prey and me, taking one baby step at a time, careful of the crunchy volcanic pebbles underfoot. Fifteen exhilarating, exhausting minutes passed as I closed the gap to within ten paces of my goal—a tree so dense I could not see through it. And just beyond, lay my napping prize, wholly unawares.

Even as I was allowing myself to think, Good grief, man, you actually might pull it off this time (stalking a pronghorn to within stickbow range is arguably hunting's most difficult challenge), and with my fingers already tightening on the bowstring and my mouth watering in anticipation of oak-smoked antelope backstraps—the predictable bad news arrived, special delivery.

Wheeeee! The dread alarm-sneeze sounded. The buck was up, rigid, and staring arrows at me. I became a statue, but too late. Wheeeee! With rump hairs flaring electric white he was going, going ... I watched in awe as this most graceful of American mammals sailed birdlike over the rise and disappeared into the realm of bittersweet memory.

Oh, to be a pronghorn — to fly flat-out and never stop!

Well, I'd really expected no better. As my eloquent biologist friend Beck would say, "Trying to stalk a prongy to within stickbow range is about as productive as chasing farts in a hurricane."

Granted. Yet, like youth and lust and other fleeting pleasures, it sure is fun while it lasts!

And so, here now I sit here on this spectacularly lovely, somewhat lonely evening, content just to watch as a growing convention of pronghorns mill below, aware that I am here but sensing no threat. As usual at such times, I lapse into meandering meditation.

Being merely middle-aged, I find it disconcerting to admit that I'm already slowing down. Five years ago I'd have made a go for those 'lopers down there — no hesitation and to hell with approaching darkness and fatigue (of which I'd have felt far less). But time changes us all, not just in body but in outlook as well. While a young man fears that to go too slow is to risk missing something, an older man knows that to go too fast is to risk missing everything. If not disturbed, pronghorns don't travel much at night. Chances are good that come dawn they'll still be down there, waiting for Godot.

For now, armed with a deliciously filthy cigar and a cup of good Irish single-malt (whose label democratically proclaims: "Every man should have his Dew!") I'm content just to be here now in this vast empty place on this balmy August eve, alone but no way lonely, doing nothing but feeling everything, watching a good day die.

Watching, that is, as pulsing, shifting curtains of orange and lavender clouds — like a slow-motion aurora borealis — shroud the setting sun. And listening, as distant coyotes serenade a ripe rising moon and pronghorns sneeze in nervous reply. For all of this and a whole lot more, I am a grateful man. The key to contentment, I'm learning as I age, lies in maintaining an attitude of gratitude.

Not long ago, writer, artist, and desert rat Ann Zwinger — a thoughtful friend who knows and respects my boundless passion for wild nature and difficult hunting challenges — told me of touring a European museum where she paused to admire a hand-blown glass jar dating from 3rd century Cologne. It was, she noted, beautifully etched with a hunting scene and the epigraph *Vita Bona Fruamur Felices*:
"Let us fortunate ones enjoy the good life."

Amen Ann, and pass the Dew!

Life is good, or can be, should be, if far more fragile than most of us come to realize in time to make it really work. I'm lucky that way. This past spring, during wild turkey season, strange things started happening to my body. The first doctor I visited told me it was probably nothing to worry about, but that I "could" have bone cancer. That "could" became "do" in my suddenly paranoid mind, and let me tell you, compadres — it put me through some changes.

Most memorably, my life priorities — those blessings to be recalled on my deathbed with a happy tear — flashed through my head as big and bright as Las Vegas marquees: waking in the night close and warm beside my wife ... laughter-filled evenings in the carefree company of a few true friends ... and doing exactly what I'm doing this lovely lonely evening, being here now in the wild outdoors, whether anything is "happening" or not.

(Interlude: A hummingbird moth big as a B-52 just splash-landed in my booze. I shoo her away but she comes looping back for more. This time I let her be and she doesn't drink much before staggering happily off into the shimmering twilight. Which reminds me: My bowhunting buddy Milt Beens recently recounted having mentioned my name to some joker who responded, "Oh, I know him; he's that writer guy who likes to smoke cigars and drink whiskey." Well, yes, I suppose I do, especially at night beside the entrancing flaring flames of a backcountry campfire — drawn, you could say, like a moth. But always and only in moderation — that elusive key to a life of happy vice.)

Anyhow, so there I was, depressed and defeatist, convinced I was soon to suffer a miserable death, entertaining myself by composing my own eulogy. Eventually, after four more doctors and as many months spent wallowing in a purgatory of anguished self-pity, things sorted themselves out to the extent that I can say, like Mark Twain, "the reports of my death have been greatly exaggerated."

Too old to die young, too young to die old.

As a result of that mind-opening experience, I now make it a point not just to tell, but to show my wife how much I love her, every single day. The same with my little tribe of true-blue male friends, though quite cautiously with a few, so as not to embarrass the macho bastards.

And I've by-god doubled my time outdoors. More hunting and more fly fishing. More hiking and more camping. More muscle-powered careening around the backyard of beyond. More "doing nothing," much as I'm doing now. More honest living, while the living's good.

As the sun sets and tomorrow's patient prey fade to ghostly shadows, I retreat from the edge of the knoll to my modest camp among the perfumed pines, where I struggle to start a recalcitrant fire with wood still damp from the earlier downpour. Refilling my cup (one part filtered Old Woman Creek water, one part Tullamore Dew), I scoot up close to the smoky flaring flames and resume my mental perambulations.

What a strange and wonderful place is this. Not your typical horizonless sagebrush antelope flat, but scenic basin-and-range country: rugged and rolling, cliff-framed, darkly vulcanized, small-tree-studded, sheltering numerous verdant side-pockets grown hip-deep in yellow-flowering rabbit brush. BLM land, this: sublime by nature but too long molested by a blight of domestic sheep (those woolly maggots of the West). What else? A few stunted prickly pears. The occasional threatening display of yucca spears. Piñon pines most everywhere, though curiously not a one of their symbiotic sisters, genus *Juniperus*.

Withal — overlooking as best you can the glaring "wise use" abuse, including illegal OHV tracks scarring several hillsides — this is one of the most hauntingly beautiful places on Earth. A virtual window into our Pleistocene human-hunter past, as if the antediluvian mists had only this morning lifted. And only for a while.

Ah ... the ultimate inscrutability of time and nature ... the atavistic thrill of the unknown and ultimately unknowable.

Lazy minutes pass. The fire is burning low and so am I when the moon blinks on like a spotlight, leaping suddenly from behind a wall of clouds blacker than flaked obsidian. Lunatic that I am, I fumble for my binoculars and point the optics moonward, but can't bear the sight for long; the brilliance and mystery are far too daunting.

What was it you sang, brother Marley?

There's a natural mystic flowing through the air.
And indeed, there is, for those who aren't asleep.

But enough! Back to reality, such as it is. I drain the dregs of my nightcap drink, stand, weave across the rocky ground, through the inky dark to my bedroll, where I sit, remove my boots, and sprawl out on my back ... back to where it all began.

Two more days of pronghorn hunting, then time to head home to the mountains for a few frenetic days of playing catch-up at work. A few long nights of banking sleep. A nervously distracted interval to inadvertently gnaw on Caroline's nerves until she doesn't mind seeing me go again ... when beloved elk season comes.

But tomorrow and tomorrow, I will live for today.

Chasing farts in a hurricane.

Chapter Two

A Man Made of Elk

Recently, during a pre-season scouting hike, I was reminded that the most visible and lasting marks that elk leave in the woods — from frothy, mud-splattered wallows to skinned and broken rub trees — are artifacts not of everyday life, but of the annual rut ... that impassioned ceremony of elkish renewal that's reenacted every fall, bring us joy and challenge. Reflecting on this, it further occurred to me that as a traditional bowhunter, I too enjoy an annual ceremony of renewal, roped tightly to the autumn elk rut, during which, in many personally meaningful ways, I become the animals I hunt.

Motivated by this realization, back at the cabin I paged through my hundred-pound wapiti library in search of a rutting calendar — a scientifically certified timeline of what wapiti do before, during, and after their brief annual reproductive pageant, where they do it, and why. Surprised to find no such nowhere, I called on hunter and world-renowned wild ungulate biologist, Dr. Valerius Geist — and Val, as always, came through. What follows, offered purely for the fun of it, is Dr. Geist's summary overview (his words appear in italics) of the biological and behavioral stages of the Rocky Mountain elk's annual rutting ceremony — layered between my own rambling sketch of the perfectly parallel ritual that transforms me annually into A Man Made of Elk.

Late June: *It begins with the summer solstice. For elk, the daily decrease in daylight hours — as metered by the eyes and registered by the hypothalamus, which in turn is regulated by the pituitary — forecasts the hormonal cascade that initiates and directs the rut. Most notably, in bulls, the testes* begin to swell, fueling up for the action soon to come.

I too feel subtle pre-rut solstice stirrings, including a deep-seeded itch to renovate my backyard archery range (burlap coffee-bean bags stuffed with recycled plastic from the post office) and promote my arrow-flinging sessions from occasional to dedicational. And so begin, in elk hunter as well as elk, mysterious stirrings within; anticipation subtly building.

Early August: *Among Rocky Mountain elk, visible rutting activity begins now, just before velvet shedding. Until now, bulls have been social and relatively at peace, with aggressive behavior limited to the head-up hissing display. If there is a dispute, it's generally settled by striking out with the front legs, since velvet antlers are delicate and sensitive. The neck mane has not yet started to grow; that must await the hormonal changes triggered by velvet shedding and will not be completed until sometime in November. Consequently, the Rocky Mountain bull elk ruts with a short mane.*

Even as the bulls are anticipating their late-summer coming-out-of velvet party, Colorado's archery season is only a fortnight away. Now an attic full of hunting, camping, and meat-packing gear gets inspected, cleaned, and repaired as necessary. Fighting the urge to practice until my fingers fall off, I opt for quality over quantity by shooting just twice daily, a couple dozens arrows per session, at bean-bag targets the size of an elk's torso positioned strategically around my woodsy yard and moved often, uphill and down, none at measured distances, providing a variety of realistic shooting positions, shot angles, and natural obstacles. Additionally, on evening dog walks, I enjoy a bit of stump shooting — selecting at random such felicitous targets as rotten stumps and fallen leaves on soft dirt slopes.

With those happy chores done and antsy for more, I test-shoot my hunting arrows with two-blade broadheads attached. The five most consistently accurate of the lot, I ritually prepare by waterproofing the feathers with powder and — in an archer's approximation of a bull elk's antler rubbing — honing the broadheads until just glancing at them draws a spurt of blood. Finally, each head receives a light coat of Vaseline to prevent corrosion, then arrows go into quiver and quiver gets lashed to bow.

During these same endless weeks of anticipation, I read and think even more than usual about the magical wapiti, and map-poring becomes an obsession. But most gratifying of all pre-rut ceremonies is scouting, which not only provides essential on-the-ground information but also serves as an annual boot camp for legs, lungs, and civilization-dulled animal senses. Gifted as I am to call elk country home (in truth, I sacrifice a lot to live here, and even more to be the boss of my own time ... yet a gift it still is), I hunt the same local haunts each year, revisiting the best of them now under the guise of scouting. Old friends, as it were, quietly reunited.

As Wyoming mountain climber and meat-hunting Buddhist Jack Turner, in his thoughtful adventure chronicle Teewinot, poetically explains the spiritual significance of the scouting aspect of the scouting ritual: "A sense of place is a function not of space but of time, an accumulation of experience and memory constantly renewed. To return to a place remembered is to consecrate it with the rites of return. Ordinary trees, climbing routes, camping spots and fishing holes become natural sacraments, like bread and wine, yet always more."

Additionally, with the goal of discovering "always more" places to be hunted this year for the first time, then remembered and revisited in future years, early each August I explore new country, adding a ridge here, a rincon there, a new spring if I can find it, to my joyfully expanding wapiti world.

Mid- to late August: *With remarkable synchronicity, bulls now shed their velvet and become aggressive. Sparring begins immediately after shedding, and the first bugles sound. With the last days of August, bulls begin dispersing to their respective rutting grounds — places they're familiar and comfortable with from previous ruts, and where cows are known to congregate.*

By the final, dog-hot days of August—hallelujah! — I'm hunting again, happy as a bear in fermented berries. With a month of daily hunts stretching dreamlike ahead, I feel no pressure for quick "success," just as the elk feel no rush to mate. (Once, years ago, I killed a young bull on opening day. For the remainder of the month I was miserable and eventually turned to guiding other hunters for solace.) More important just now, for elk and elk hunter, is reenacting and rediscovering those palpable "firsts" that lend rut hunting its tangible magic: the first sapsticky antler rub on a thrashed Christmas tree ... the first tentative bugle ... the first eye-watering blast of pheromone-perfumed bull stench. The season's first wallow. From each such marker, each wild metaphor, plus tracks, droppings, and more, I deduce what practical information I can about the makers — their sex, size, diet, mood, and movement patterns — and fantasize happily from there, by now half elk myself.

11

David Petersen

Early September: *With the onset of bugling, bulls begin perfuming themselves with pheromones by self-urinating and wallowing. A related ritual, commonly called horning, involves thrashing brush and young trees with antlers. Horning generally occurs during vocal or visual inter-action with rival bulls, and serves to signal confidence and the intent to dominate. Preferred rub trees are conifer saplings two to four inches in diameter and seven to ten feet tall, from which bark is scraped, branches are stripped and the trunks occasionally broken. Dominant bulls also horn trees as part of the self-marking ceremony prior to wallowing; often, dark neck hair can be found on these mutilated victims of the early rut.*

Wallowing entails hoofing-out dry "scrapes," or, more often, churning mud or shallow water into a froth, urinating on belly, under-neck and ground, then rolling in the resulting muck. The object is to coat the neck mane with pheromone-laden urine and wallow mud, which is then trans-ferred to nearby "billboard" trees or other vegetation by neck rubbing. Also during early September, bugling increases and herding and courting behavior begin in earnest.

While not quite so bonkers as the bulls (I tried wallowing just once, many years ago, and can smell the stench in my mind's nose still today), by now I've been sneaking around or sitting patiently in ambush for a week or more, incrementally becoming, once again, a good attentive animal. And still my goal is not to "get it over with" but contrarily, to enjoy the act and effort of hunting while I can — process before product — coming and going each day in ghostlike anonymity, a secret sharer in the wildest workings of unfettered nature. Apropos, I do little if any cow calling, and leave my bugle at home.

Mid-September: *By now, dominant bulls are gathering and guard-ing breeding herds, all the while being harassed by off-prime, or "satellite" bulls, old as well as young. To maintain his herd, a harem-master must distinguish himself, through both advertising (bugling, bluffing, horning, ritualized antler displays) and valor, so that cows will cling to him as an island of peace, where less competent and therefore less desirable bulls don't dare venture. Even so, this is still the pre-rut, which technically continues until breeding begins, any day now. Now through early October, cows will come serially into estrus and seek to be bred by dominant bulls.*

12

Lesser bulls continue to be a bother to both cows and herd masters, even as the physical condition of active herd bulls gradually deteriorates.

If I were going to bugle, the time just now would be ripe. Without question, arguing with a bull who's in a foul and feisty enough mood to come at a swaggering trot to your vocal challenge is a peak experience; the most thrilling hunting I've experienced ... those growling, grunting, ear-piercing screams ... those pissy, belly-pumping chuckles ... that bullish hoof-stomping and calamitous tree-horning ... the cock-sure, head-swaying, rack-rocking approach of a puffed-up patriarch ... those bulging, rolled-back and bloodshot eyes, flaring nostrils, and grinding teeth ... that mad-dog foaming muzzle ... the cacophonous, rut-roaring pageantry of it all!

Alas, as I'll explain and justify farther along, I no longer bugle. (We have met the enemy and his name is *Excess*.)

As the lime-green days of mid-September brighten to leafy gold, and the breeding herds coalesce, I do less sneaking, no calling, and a lot more sitting — day upon patient day — in obviously elkish places: downwind of waterholes and wallows, alongside feeding and bedding areas, hard by busy trail exchanges and ridge-saddle crossings. After this dogged fashion, most of my winter's meat is made just about now, on the leading edge of the peak of the rut.

Late September: *While reliable data are scarce, wallowing should peak in late September and continue, gradually decreasing, through late October. By then, some exhausted herd masters may actually leave their harems in order to rest, abandoning unbred cows to younger males.*

According to the mandates of scientific wildlife management and common respect, just as the elk's breeding ceremony kicks into full-dress parade, archery season ends, at least here in Colorado. The elk now have two weeks free of direct hunter harassment during which to conduct the essential business of procreation. I have my meat (usually) or I don't (occasionally). Either way, I've had fun. Far more than mere fun, in fact. Every hour I spend out there among the elk makes me that much stronger, that much saner, that much more alive and glad of it. And when I come home under the weight of full meat bags, the elk's flesh becomes my flesh. Viewed in this light, in some semi-mystical way I guess I can see why a friend long ago nicknamed me "the man made of elk." (Though frankly, I'd rather be a bear.)

Although another year's hunt is history, the ceremony continues. Unlike those pooped quitter-bulls Val Geist speaks of, my own post-rut problem is an inability to stop. Or at least a stubborn unwillingness. While the herd bulls' constant activity — bugling, horning, herding, sparring, tending, breeding — has beaten them to mush, my own efforts have honed me hard as hickory, having lugged myself and a thirty-pound hunting pack up and down several mountain miles every day for nigh-on a month, concluding, most years, with a meat-packing marathon: three or four heavy loads of boned-out meat, which I often, and most proudly at my age, shoulder alone. And so it is, by hunt's end, that I've cinched my belt two notches tighter and forgotten what it's like to be short of breath or distracted by minor pain. Should I ever have to go a year without such therapy, I'd likely never recover. In so many ways, just so, elk keep me alive.

Early October: *As fewer and fewer cows remain to be bred, bugling decreases.*

My own preferred method for easing out of the post-archery season elk rut is to spend one October week guiding rifle hunters from a friend's wilderness horse camp. It's hard work but good, with some bugling still to be heard. Yet the recently blazing aspen leaves have gone to ground and faded there to brown. An unsettling silence shrouds the skeletal woods. Something utterly vital to the experience — the weight of a longbow in hand — is missing.

Late October: *By now, with rare exceptions, the rut is finished for another year. Cows regroup in winter herds, including calves and yearling bulls driven out during the rut. Bulls fall silent and become increasingly solitary, resting and feeding in an attempt to recover from rut exhaustion and battle wounds before the onset of winter. Many do not succeed, accounting for the high winterkill rate among prime males.*

* * *

November: *An icy wind buffets the winter-naked aspens beyond the cabin walls, rattling rudely round the door. The weather suddenly has grown moody, sullen and foreboding, foreshadowing the long cold time* *ahead. Put another log on the fire, little darlin' ... winter's a long time going, up this high.*

For the elk, whose winter habitat is increasingly being robbed and ruined by greed and human growth crassly called progress, the frozen months ahead often bring gut-shrinking starvation, bloody predation, and death. But for a man made of elk, winter brings a hunger not of stomach, but of heart and soul in longing. I suspect you know the feeling.

Chapter Three

A Lucky Day

The action starts around three on a Sunday afternoon, the last week of August, when I get a couple of miles up my favorite elk mountain and hear a distant bugle. I move cautiously toward the magical sound. As I'm approaching the edge of a deep, wooded gully, I hear a sharp snap of brush as a buck mule deer spooks from his cud bed among aspen saplings on the gully's far side. The buck's trajectory brings up the slope on my side, where he flashes by a few yards away. My assumption is that I spooked the buck, as so often happens when sneaking among bedded animals. Yet, the breeze is in my favor and I was making no noise whatsoever and if I was the spook, why did the animal flee *toward* me?

Even as I'm reflecting on this little mystery, I hear another snap from near where the deer had been bedded, then another and louder and faster than I can take it all in I'm surrounding by a band of fast-moving elk, including perhaps a dozen cows and calves led by a bullish 5x5. "Ah," I realize, "it must have been these elk that spooked the deer." I have no choice but to freeze in place, seeing no chance for a shot as the animals are almost running. The wapiti stream past me, stampeding down the same hill I've just come up, exploding through dense woods and brush. When they're past and it's safe to move, I creep along close behind and spy as they frolic like school kids at recess on an aspen bench sixty yards below — running in circles, jumping and splashing in a small spring-fed pool.

As I'm duck-walking and belly-crawling down the hill toward the elk, hoping to get close enough for a bow shot, the bull suddenly breaks from the others and goes galloping along the bench and soon is out of sight. When he bugles once, the others line out and follow. As the herd is cracking and clomping away, I cow call in hopes of bringing them back. But to no avail. These crazy critters have energy to burn, sights to see, and places to be. There is no stopping them.

After the elk are good and gone, I approach the spring pool, which I hadn't known about until the animals showed it to me. The clouded water is still quivering, and the hoof-waffled mud around the pool stinks with the exquisite, exciting stench of rutting bull. Hoping the herd's escapades might bring them back this way after a while, I look around for a hide. About fifteen yards downwind of the spring I spot a fallen log with a fir tree close behind, providing at once backrest, shade, and a background screen of drooping boughs to absorb my human form.

Not that I seriously figure to get any further action here today. After all, I've just been almost rubbing shoulders with a whole herd of elk, one of them a right handsome bull — more wapiti in one wad than I've seen throughout some entire bow seasons past. We should not get greedy in our expectations. Still, the herd might return. And too, having just found this promising place, I'd like to hang around. It's a pretty spot, and the sun is still a little too high to justify moving along to my evening ambush, half a mile from here. That must wait for the evening breeze to rise — or, actually, to fall, sliding cool down the mountainside.

So I sit, mentally re-viewing the elk swimming party, nibbling some elk jerky from last year's success, sipping sweet mountain water from my filter bottle and enjoying my great good fortune — as some sheet-wearing Harvard professor advised back in the '60s of my youth — to "be here now."

Suddenly — by George! — it begins again. From somewhere up the hill and not too far, I hear the sharp heavy crack of a breaking limb. And another. I take up my bow and slowly stand, leaning back against my backrest tree, hoping to blend in.

Another few moments and out marches a truly huge bull. Maybe the biggest bull I've ever seen (and of big bulls, I've seen a few). The antlers are 6x6 at a glance — tall, wrist-thick at their bases and broad as the hood of my truck. My heart throttles up and the little recurve, which suddenly seems weightless and fragile, trembles in my hands.

As if warned by some mysterious sixth sense, the bull hangs up behind a tangle of chokecherry brush, twenty yards away. Showing no sign that he has spotted me, the bull turns casually to glance back over his shoulder and he and I both watch as a second, even larger bull approaches.

Now I'm truly shaking.

The second bull stops directly behind the first, dwarfing his hefty companion in both body and headgear. I stare and stare and finally make out a seventh tine on the second bull's left beam. Could this be the same animal that dropped the pair of similarly conformed 6x5 sheds I picked up less than a mile from here two summers back? This is shaping up as an odd sort of day. First a wapiti wading party, and now two buster bulls acting like buddies even though the rut is on — still in its early stages, but definitely on. Moreover, they're standing right in my tracks where I circled the spring just a few minutes ago, yet haven't caught my scent. Not yet. But then, maybe that's why they're hung up and won't come the last little way to the pool, which I assume to be their goal. On the other hand, they don't appear nervous, just normally cautious. Surely, at any moment, one or the other or both will come forward to whiff the tracked-up mud around the pool, what with all that lovely fresh cow scent there. Then, by gum, I'll get my chance.

I wait.

But the bulls don't budge. Before long, they turn as one and plod away, back to wherever they came from. Flustered, I find the cow call and blurt out a couple of chirps.

The ruse works, sort of, with the lesser of the two big guys turning and angling out across an open-timbered bench to my right, circling the spring from a safe distance out — his intent obvious — to get downwind in search of the scent of that fishy-sounding cow he just heard. He's in the open now, but sixty yards away. And even that doesn't last when suddenly, for who-knows-what reason (he clearly isn't spooked), the circling bull stops, turns, and plods back toward big brother, who I assume is waiting someplace nearby, hidden from my view. I mew and chirp a couple times more ... and am answered with sullen silence. Both bulls are gone.

I sit and wait a few more minutes, gradually if grudgingly returning to homeostasis. Perhaps, I reflect, I should hang in here until dark. But soon I reconsider, bid a reluctant adios to this weird and wonderful new honey hole of a place, and slip off toward my evening stand.

Most September evenings, I like to hunt from one particular hide at day's end. I have many reasons for this preference, the least of which is because it's within sight of a game trail that climbs a short steep hill then meanders through half a mile of forest to an abandoned logging road that winds down the mountain to home and hearth. Easy to follow in the dark and makes for the quietest possible coming and going. Convenient. Familiar. Reassuring. And too, I dare to hope now as I creep along, some of the same wapiti I saw at the new spring might show up at this neighboring pool tonight.

My evening stand here at Hillside Spring is the usual: another downed log to sit on, another big tree behind to recline against, another screen of brush. And plenty good enough for the simple-minded likes of me: Nothing to buy and lug along, and no sickly sense of cheating with technology.

Eighty yards above my stand, a seep spring patiently fills a shallow pool that overflows and trickles down toward me, pooling up again in a hoofed-out two-gallon wildlife watering hole, no doubt a former wallow, before dissipating in a cattail muck. This lower pool is just thirteen stepped-off yards away — my kind of bow shot. The entire length of the trickle bisects a narrow lane through the aspens, like a long green hallway, grown up high in grass and sedge, gorgeous and lush. It's a place I visit frequently the year 'round, simply because it's beautiful, tranquil, unspoiled, with no livestock, logging, roads, human-made trails, houses, or other such annoyances anywhere nearby. For all the same reasons, it's also a favorite of wildlife. I could spend eternity here, and if it can be arranged, someday I just might.

I've been sitting here for half an hour, occupying myself by guessing at species of unseen birds by their calls, when I hear the Zen-like sound of one hoof crunching. This wake-up call comes from a spot along the lane where elk frequently emerge, about forty yards above me. The down-slope breeze, as always on quiet evenings, is solid in my favor.

A few seconds more and a bull appears. I recognize instantly and without disappointment that he's not one of the two monster bulls from the other spring, but a big three- or modest four-by: your basic "raghorn." And now, close behind him, comes a near twin.

After a good long look around them, both bulls step out into the open lane, teasing my hopes ... only to turn away and mosey up toward the spring pool. And there they languish for a good ten minutes, taking turns keeping watch, drinking and horning nearby saplings. All that done with, they indulge in a half-hearted spar. As one pushes the other, then the other pushes back, they work slowly down the seep lane toward me, antlers tangled and clattering, totally off their guards.

Suddenly and for no reason apparent to me, one of the pair seems to sense trouble lurking, breaks away from his sparring partner, turns and rudely stares — straight at me. How can he know? The breeze hasn't shifted and I haven't moved or so much as farted. For a moment the nervous bull appears indecisive, then trots into the edge of the woods, where he stops and stares some more. The second bull seems confused, standing his ground and gawking around, searching for what has spooked his buddy. After a bit, still seeming befuddled but opting for caution, he steps into the trees to join his pal and they move off together.

The proverbial deja view.

Since it's getting on toward dark and there's little to lose, I chirp once on the cow call and both bulls stop, turn, and mince a few jittery steps back toward the open lane. I chirp again. They inch ahead. It takes nearly ten minutes, but I finally work one of the youngsters (the befuddled one) forward to almost the exact spot where I arrowed my elk last year.

Almost, but not quite hardly, since a single protruding aspen limb handily blocks his chest. So close, with both bulls now locked solid on the source of the invisible chirping cow, I have no chance of changing my position to gain a clear shot window ... and so I simply sit.

Finally, the cooperative pair grows weary of this slow game and crunch away, still apparently none the wiser.

After all this wonderful afternoon's excitement, I'm tempted to say thank you and enough, and head for home a few minutes early, sneak-hunting as I go. But there's half an hour of close-range shooting light left — prime time for game to come to water. So I relax again ... and promptly hear a limb snap. Since the sound came from back in the woods on the opposite side of the lane from where I last saw the raghorn duo, I assume it's another elk and once again make ready.

"Another elk," I say. Such cock-sure confidence! But the wacky way this afternoon has gone, I've come to expect every forest noise to herald an approaching wapiti, and that every approaching wapiti (or at least one in every group) will be a bull. Presumptuous, superstitious thinking. But now and even so, out of the woods walks ... a cow? Come *on* now. Surely there's a bull back there somewhere.

A few more seconds and, as if the thought alone were enough to make it happen, a fat-racked five-by appears, trailing leisurely behind the cow. Bull, cow: As an equal opportunity carnivore, either is welcome in my freezer. I ease my bow up to vertical and make ready to draw the moment either animal comes close enough for a shot. Licking her nose as she walks, the cow heads my way. The bull, meanwhile, hangs back at the edge of the woods, allowing the cow to walk point. But as she nears, I see that the cow's pelage is scruffy, her face is drawn and scarred and ribs are showing through. An old gal, her. Cow elk can live twenty years or longer in the wild, and this one looks easily that old. No thanks. It's the prime-time bull or nothing. At the puddle in front of my hide, the geriatric matron lowers her long thin neck for a leisurely drink … and I find her oddly lovely. What wild places, what dangers and joys and adventures she surely has known!

With the bull momentarily forgotten, I watch and listen, rapt with awe, as the cow sucks water in through her teeth, exactly like a horse. Ms. Manners would not approve.

Meanwhile, the bull keeps watch from just inside the trees. No shot there. Yet hope remains. If this pair behaves typically, they'll switch places soon so the bull can drink while the cow stands guard. Having little by way of choice, I anxiously watch and wait.

Finally, the cow's robust thirst apparently quenched, she rejoins her escort and the two dissolve into the darkened woods, shadows fading into shadow. I guess he wasn't thirsty.

My luck.

Now, regrettably, it *is* time to leave.

I collect my various junk and stuff it into my daypack, stand, wrestle the load onto my back, take one last longing look around, ease the few steps over to the game trail, and huff up the slope and out onto an open ponderosa flat, moving quietly, as always, although I'm no longer really hunting … and meet face-to-face with a fat 4x4 muley buck, still in velvet, staring from twenty yards. There he stands, quartering on, looking bemused. I have a deer tag in my pack and the season is on. But I'm tired, and it's getting too dark to play this demanding game any longer today. The last thing I need now is an iffy twilight shot at an alerted animal … a difficult blood trail to follow by flashlight … maybe get turned around (never say "lost") in the process … be out here half the night … miss my dinner … worry my wife.

As the rationalizations spin out, I move on. And so does the buck, bounding away in the bouncing, pogo-stick run distinctive to mule deer.

One more mountain ghost, fading into the night.

21

Safe back on the faint but familiar logging trail, as I coast down the mountain in full dark I reflect on this weirdly remarkable day. I've heard early season bugling. I've witnessed elk at carefree play. I've seen bulls, both young and supremely mature, still running together at a time when you'd expect them to be competing for cows. In all, I've seen two deer and nineteen wapiti, including six bulls among which two were rare great masterpieces of selective evolutionary art.

I may be going home without having drawn my bow, much less releasing an arrow, "empty-handed" as they say, yet I am one very happy camper. By any sane standard, this has been a lucky day.

Chapter Four

A Hunter's Heart

September. The most august of months hereabouts, high in the Colorado Rockies. The flies and mosquitoes are gone, most of them, as are the buzzing swarms of motorized tourists. Autumn aspens illuminate the landscape with an ancient golden light. Most days are sunny and t-shirt warm, nights crisp and spangled with stars.

And best of all for the feral likes of you and me, September is rut; mating season for wapiti, of which Colorado has more than any other state or province. The pungent incense of the bulls' fierce animal lust perfumes the mountain air, and the valleys ring with their bugles. It's an otherworldly music, the bull elk's bugle, like a calamitous crescendo of bluesy high notes blown on a saxophone, proclaiming a wildness we can only imagine.

It's still dark when I wheel my old Toyota pickup into a little-used trailhead at the end of a ragged dirt road bisecting a local parcel of land owned by the Colorado Division of Wildlife. As the sun rises, I buckle into my big backpack, gather my bow and other loose gear, lock the truck (oh yes, even here), and take the trail less traveled — that is, no motors allowed. My plan is to rendezvous with a young friend — a former student back when I was a former teacher at the local ski college. Lane, I trust, will be waiting at his hide-away hunting camp ... somewhere out there. The way from here to there is new to me and, Lane has forewarned, "real up." Once there, I'll have all the time in the world (so to speak) to enjoy the bugling elk, the gilded aspens, a seldom-seen friend's companionship, and as much mountain solitaire as I wish.

Onward.

Although this state-owned parcel is literally just over the hill from my frenetic, tourist-trampled hometown of Durango, the 6,900-acre foothill tract is home to peregrine falcons, eagles both golden and bald, wild turkeys, black bears, mountain lions, mule deer, elk, and a whole menagerie more. Deer and elk in particular, along with their predators, rely on this place and a dwindling few more wildlife refugia hereabouts to sustain them in these "progressive" times through the long and often-brutal Colorado winters. This fact being far from secret, I'm left in ongoing frustration, disgust, and barely stifled anger at the bicyclists and motorheads who have tried for years, in every legal way and some ways not, to get year-round access here for what they openly refer to as "playing." To hell with wildlife. To hell with quiet-users like myself. "We want what's ours," they clearly are saying, "and what's yours too."

Until a handful of years ago, the Animas River valley, anchored dead center by Durango, remained blissfully undiscovered by superfluously wealthy exurban yupsters, rapacious land developers, and real estate hucksters, retaining its traditional agrarian nature and providing elk and other wildlife with abundant wintering areas in low-lying ranch pastures, especially along the cottonwood-sheltered riparian corridor of the Animas itself. (*Rio de las Animas Perdidas*, "River of Lost Souls," and an apropos name it is, given the way things are going around here.) But discovered it eventually was, and every year more traditional wildlife habitat is transmogrified into obscene trophy houses, most of them part-time vacation retreats for the conspicuously rich and banal, redundant golf courses, tacky commercial and industrial parks, noisy natural gas fields that ruin peoples sleep, views, air, well water and land values, condos like cliff-swallow nests and seas of suburban subdivisions to hold a floodtide of urban refugees that shows no sign of ebbing.

The chamber of commerce calls it progress.

I call it death by ten thousand cuts.

Looking around me now as I hike through this severely stressed elk wintering ground, the signs of pending disaster are ubiquitous. The brushy little Gambel's oak, whose acorns and annual twig growth sustain a plethora of winter wildlife, have been cropped almost to their trunks. Not just here and there, but everywhere. Too many elk, not enough elk chow or browsing room. Prolonged drought greatly enhances the threat. Come the next killer winter (and come it will), this wildlife "refuge" will become a showplace of suffering and death. Progress.

But enough negativity. We're supposed to be on vacation here.

Slogging on under the agreeable weight of my pack, I eventually leave the state wildlife parcel and cross some rancher's "bob-war" fence onto a cow-burned corner of adjoining private land. An hour or so more of steady marching and I cross another fence, leave the cow pies behind, and enter the San Juan National Forest, where the faint cutoff path I've been following intersects a broad backwoods freeway known as the Colorado Trail. Were I to turn down-trail rather than up, the CT would deliver me in due course to one of the most popular trailheads for mountain bikers this side of the Land of the Moabites, at Junction Creek just north of Durango. As I head once again uphill, I know I'll be having company.

And sure enough, too soon here comes a tightly bunched pack of riders — three, four athletic young men — skull-capped and body-painted in Lycra, their legs distended with straining muscle from pumping like piston rods on toys worth twice as much as my truck. The trail is narrow and fringed with forest and I am blocking their way. Yet they give no indication of seeing me, though they must, and show no inclination to slow down and file by politely. To avoid disaster, as the last possible moment I'm forced to leap off the trail and into thick brush. or get run down. As the pack speeds past, I call out a friendly greeting and wave a middle-finger farewell.

Shaken and angry, I step back onto the trail and continue my upward journey, breathing deeply, rhythmically, invoking a respiratory mantra intended to cool my boiling blood. Trailside encounters between bikers and hikers (and horses too) don't have to be this rude, and it disturbs me that they often are. One potential source of friction, I suppose, is that so many mountain bikers tend to view themselves as competitive athletes, and consequently are focused on the performance of their bikes and bodies and their relative positions among their competitor-companions, than on the sublime natural surroundings through which they race in a myopic blur. This is one good reason I detest the relentless and spiritually ruthless *Outside, Backpacker, Men's Journal, National Geo Adventure* mindset of marketing nature as a post-adolescent playground into which really *cool* people bring all the *cool* toys mechanical toys they can acquire, and the glitzier the better.

Hikers and backpackers, on the other hand, are relatively uncool, generally preferring contemplation to competition, scenery to speed, simplicity to audacity, quiet conversation to exclamatory shouts. While they do have cool gear and some of it laughably over-teched — telescoping walking poles with built-in shock absorbers, hydration packs, map-reading GPS's and suchlike — none of it has wheels, gears, or motors to separate your feet and heart from the ground. The irony, I realize, is that a hiker one day may be a biker another and occasionally even a horse-back rider or motorhead. And each has a distinctive attitude. It's as if we allow activity and attire on a particular day to dictate our personality. Groupthink.

Time passes, as do the slow steep miles. The oak brush thickets and sunny ponderosa woods of the lower montane ecology gradually are supplanted by cool dark forests of subalpine spruce and fir bejeweled with flickering groves of quaking aspen. All around me now, millions of loose-jointed aspen leaves answer to the midmorning breeze, whispering sibilant secrets in an ancient alien tongue.

And with the aspens come frequent sign and occasional sightings of the wild menagerie that thrives among these shady groves' fecund under-story of ferns, giant cow parsnips, angelica, chokecherry, serviceberry, and a frenzy of bright wildflowers. Already this morning I've interrupted two conventions of blue grouse as they pecked for brunch among the forest understory and leafy duff. A little farther along I'm treated to the pigeon-toed prints of an adult black bear. The heart-shaped tracks of deer and elk are everywhere and the forest is alive with the happy chatter of birds and ... damn the luck, more people.

Fifty yards ahead, loping easily down-trail, talking quietly and laughing, come three brethren backpackers — no, it's one brethren and two sistern. This time I am not forced, as I was by the speeding cyclists, but freely elect to step off-trail to make way. The hikers see me and to my surprise, rather than offering greetings or maybe even a polite "thanks," simply fall silent. When they come abreast I smile and say good morning and am doubly confused when they keep right on marching, their replies limited to a subdued Hi and Hello from the two women — no eye contact — and a somber silent nod from the glaring man. A triple cold-shoulder. Not that I care.

Or do I? Granted, I'm getting older and am no longer so pretty as I once never was, but even so, I can't imagine that I'm in any way scary, and hikers are traditionally friendly.

The mystery is solved a few moments later when one of the women — they've rounded a bend and must think they're out of earshot — hisses, "*Hunter!*" hurling the word like a curse. After that I hear no more from these friendly folk, and just as well.

I should have known. Although I'm hiking in shorts and lugging a big brown backpack, I'm also wearing a camouflage t-shirt and cap and carrying a longbow and quiver of arrows. While in my mind, at the moment, I'm a backpacker, to others I'm a filthy "*hunter!*" Generalized, boxed, and discarded.

The more I reflect on this, the more it bugs me, notwithstanding that I harbor many judgmental generalizations of my own, most notably regarding motorheads. But out here in the motor-free woods, as hikers, bikers, hunters, fishers, horse people — we're all here for much the same root reason: to enjoy just *being* here, albeit each in our own way. Further, we frequently play musical outdoor-activity chairs. It's just too bad that our gear, clothing, companions, and mindset for a particular day's excursion so often seem to dictate not just the attitudes of others toward us, but the way we treat others as well. Protean role-playing.

Just as my topo map tells me I'm nearing the ten-thousand-foot contour, my legs demand a break. My stomach seconds with a growling reminder that it's way past lunchtime. Today's midday menu (and tomorrow's, and the next day's): dried fruit, a big slab of hot-peppered elk jerky made with my own private recipe, a chocolate bar, and a quart of tepid water. I collapse in the shade, jettison my sweaty pack, eat, drink, and shift into mental neutral. A nap tries to ambush me, but there are unknown miles left to hike and the sun is past its apogee. So too soon I groan to my feet, saddle up, and stagger back out into the bright green heart of a perfect September day, rejoicing in my hard-won solitude ...

Which, before long, once again is interrupted by yet more human traffic. (This unrelenting, unsolicited *society* is starting to wear mighty thin.) It's another mountain biker, apparently alone, catching a free downhill ride from gravity. I brace for another brusque encounter, but this day is made for surprises and the young man brakes to a stop several yards up-trail and waits.

"Hi," he says as I approach, smiling big and real. "You must be Dave. I'm Bill. Lane told me to watch for you."

Now what the heck ...

Though Bill is dressed in *de rigueur* biker black, I see now that he too is a hunter. A short compound arrow-launching device (as a traditionalist, I just can't bring myself to call these hi-tech gizmos bows) is strapped across the handlebars, while bundles of camping gear lump out all around. Bill tells me that he's just come from two days of camping and hunting with Lane, my host. Now it's back to Denver and to work for Bill, while Lane ("that lucky SOB") stays on for a full vacation week. Lane had advised me that a friend of his would be leaving camp the same day I'd be arriving, but I hadn't expected a biker.

With no further ado, Bill offers to ride back up the trail with me — "It's just a couple of miles" — to set me on the obscure elk path (just one of hundreds bisecting the interminable Colorado Trail) that will lead me, after a mile or so of bushwhacking, to Lane's cloistered camp. I protest: "Too much trouble for you." Bill counters that I'll never find it on my own, then dumps the bulk of his gear alongside the trail, wheels around, pushes off, and pedals slowly, almost effortlessly back up the mountain. I follow at a fast, heart-pounding shuffle, feet hot and legs aching, bemusedly aware that this blows hell out of my bikers-as-buttheads stereotype.

When we arrive at the invisible cutoff, Bill points the way, wishes me good luck, and disappears. I leave the busy trail without remorse and follow the serpentine, blowdown-clogged game path until it peters out on a narrowing tongue of wooded ridge, where I glance around and spot ... nothing.

No camp in sight. As prearranged, I take a small plastic disc from a shirt pocket, place it against the roof of my mouth and blow, producing a mewing sound like some lost kitten.

Silence.

I repeat the elk herding call and this time receive an in-kind reply from the shadowy forest below. I stumble down that way and right into Lane's little camp.

For what little is left of the afternoon, we two old friends catnap and talk. Come evening, we boil pure Rocky Mountain spring water to rehydrate our desiccated dinners and make tea. As dark approaches, the temperature drops in synch with the sun, prompting Lane to kindle a campfire I feel compelled to comment is "pretty thrifty."

"Well," Lane defends, "I usually camp cold when I'm elk hunting. Don't want to scare away the critters, you know. But you're right, it's pretty chilly tonight, so what the heck, I'll build it up a bit."

28

I'd have said, "what the hell," but Lane is a born-again believer and almost never swears. I too am religious, but in a radically different sense, so that our philosophical diversity leads to some fairly high-flown, at times high-tension dialogue. ("Nature," muses Lane, "is God's grandest creation." "Nature," I counter, "*is* God.")

Over tea (he) and whisky (me), we cuss (me) and discuss (he) my day's perplexing trail encounters. The macho young bikers, we agree — well, boys will be bullies, especially when running in packs; and to hell/heck with them. More difficult to figure, and far harder to comprehend, is the sullen behavior of the trio of hikers. I'm sure, I tell Lane, that my meeting with them would have been warmer had I not been carrying a bow and arrows. "Why do you think that is, ole' buddy?"

"Well," says Lane, "maybe they've had some bad experiences with hunters in the past. Hunters are people, and a lot of people are slobs in everything they do, and its human nature to draw negative generalizations from a few bad individuals."

Right you are, professor. I consider my own biases — against mountain bikers, public-lands ranchers (a coagulation of scoundrels), New Mexico drivers (the only requirement for an operator's license there is a prefrontal lobotomy), motorized morons ripping around the backcountry, rape-and-run politicians, and other groups with whose members I've had unpleasant run-ins. "But what," I abruptly offer, inserting a high-flown non sequitur in hopes of justifying my unjustifiable prejudices, "what of Sartre's *le pour-soi* and *l'en-soi*? What of *that* little distinction, eh Lane, my philosophical friend?"

"Nor," continues my wise young friend, cleverly ignoring my incomprehensible dodge and steering us back on track, "nor does the negative image of hunting that's put out by the news media help things any. In their view, only slob hunters, wildlife criminals, and animal-rights fanatics are newsworthy."

"Seems like it," I grant, recalling a recent National Geographic TV documentary called "Hunting in America," which I was led to believe would be honest and objective and in which I appeared and by which I was disgusted, embarrassed, and angered by the producers' cheap-shot sensationalizing, dismal ignorance of the subject matter, and stubborn refusal to employ any thoughtful discussion of hunting's pros and cons, favoring instead typically out-of-context sound bites. And so on.

"But it's not only the news and nonhunting media who distort hunting," I now suggest. "Just as bad are *Outhouse Life* and all the other hook-and-bullet rags who've sold their souls for advertising dollars, and the anti-wilderness NRA and U.S. Sportsmen's Alliance and other industry-sponsored, self-proclaimed 'hunters' rights' propaganda groups with their long histories of half-truths, entrenched denial, and paranoid right-wing ranting about "the antihunting threat." With a very few sterling exceptions, notably *Traditional Bowhunter Magazine*, the outdoor rags are so far right they make Limbaugh look left. How do you expect a nonhunter to react when she sees such trash on the supermarket shelf?"

Feeling macho and growing mad as the proverbial hatter, I gulp another slash of Dickel, torch a Backwoods Natural cigar and blunder on with my rancid rant.

"The greatest threat to hunting isn't external, Lane; it's internal, arising from our collective failure to police our own ranks and morals, and to distance ourselves from negative industry and advertising influences. There's a lot wrong with hunting today, and I don't mean just illegal activities like poaching. The root problem is the hunting community's hardheaded refusal to admit that some things some hunters do, even when locally legal, are ethically indefensible: baiting, rich man's globe-trotting head hunting, guaranteed 'hunts' on fenced 'game ranches,' rampant littering, arrogant OHV abuse, road 'hunting,' contest killing, space-age cheater technology, dead animal parts conspicuously displayed on vehicles to disgust the general public, alignment with the no-compromise anti-government anti-environment far-right radical militia mentality, and a general care-less-ness in our behavior afield."

Lane moans and nods in reluctant agreement.

"Increasingly," I drone on, dangerously tipsy now, "these sins are dividing our ranks, forcing some ethical hunters to become nonhunters, converting nonhunters to antihunters, lowering the recruitment of young people into our ranks, and providing powerful ammunition to the rabid hunter haters. What was it Mark Twain said? 'Ain't we got all the fools in town on our side, and ain't that majority enough anywhere?' Hunting today, just like the mother culture, is fat with fools; it's a built-in flaw of democracy that any idiot can do any damn thing he wants, just so long as it's legal somewhere. Modern hunting is badly in need of a good internal bullshit filter. We need ..."

"Now just wait a *darn* minute," says Lane, feigning (I think) outrage. "You know danged well there's a powerful political lobby of loony-tunes animal-rights nuts out there, urban innocents who fantasize a perfect world where all predation, human and animal, is eliminated, where mountain lions lie down with fawns and wildlife populations are kept in balance via human-administered contraceptives. These turkeys have sworn to stop *all* hunting, not just the bad bits, and seem unable to distinguish. And most of them are so blissfully ignorant of how the natural world works, they couldn't tell a deer from a steer if it was standing on their Tevas. More often than not, their arguments are biologically naive, pragmatically unworkable, and ecologically immoral."

All right, Lane! Suddenly on a roll, my bright and earnest opponent stops just long enough to fortify himself with the dregs of his tea, then bulls ahead.

"What the fanatical animal-rights types refuse to acknowledge is that humans evolved as predators, and nature needs predation, especially these days. Hunters didn't design the system, and now, with most of the big natural predators wiped out to make the world safe for domesticated livestock and domesticated humans, we hunters, as ironic as it may sound to the uninformed, have become wildlife's closest allies."

No argument. I think of those state wildlife lands down the mountain. If it weren't for money extracted from hunters through license fees and special taxes on sporting goods, that land would be just another subdivision, apartment complex, or used car lot. Overcrowded and overgrazed it may be, but at least it's there, thanks entirely and exclusively to hunters. And yet, such pragmatic justifications of hunting fail to bear on the opposition's primary complaints, which are ethical and philosophical, not utilitarian.

Musing along these lines, I recall a story related to me by Dave Stalling, writer and former western field organizer for Trout Unlimited's Public Lands Initiative. While backpack bowhunting in the Idaho wilderness, Stalling encountered two day-hikers. The men identified themselves as attorneys for the Sierra Club, out to enjoy some of the wilderness they worked daily (at West Coast lawyer wages) to protect. Across the next half hour, these gentlemen derided, berated, and verbally excoriated Stalling with a fierceness only barristers, preachers, and other ideologues can muster. For what? For being a "a hunter." Dave says he attempted to answer their charges calmly and reasonably, but they would hear none of it; their minds were made up and shut tight.

Finally, tiring of the game, Stalling wished his critics a good day and walked on. "Wait a minute!" one of the pair called after. "Listen, we're kind of ... well, *lost*; can you tell us how to get out of here?" Dave, a former Marine Corps force recon ranger, pulled out his topographical maps and showed them the way.

I doubt I would have been so generous.

Lane's chintzy little fire flickers, flares, and fades to glowing embers. Likewise, our lively conversation has given way to silent introspection, and we never even got around to the real meat of the matter, the hardest questions of all: the apparent hypocrisy of taking pleasure in an activity whose end goal is death, while claiming to care deeply about the same grand animals we work so earnestly to kill.

But ongoing campfire philosophizing will have to wait for other evenings, other fires, if not other camps. Lane and I rise sluggishly and stagger tentward. With no bugs or Bubbas buzzing about to annoy us, we decide to sleep with the tent flaps tied back and our heads poking out, the better to enjoy the sparkling firmament.

"I should probably warn you," says Lane as he zips into his sack (Oh no, I'm thinking, he's going to say he snores!), "There's been something hanging around here the last couple of nights, making the weirdest noises. When it came last night, Bill and I got up and shined our flashlights all around, but it went quiet and we never saw it. Sort of spooky."
I haven't a clue to offer.

Sometime after midnight, I'm awakened by a sharp jab to the shoulder. "It's back. Listen!" I listen, and sure enough, before long comes a loud, ethereal keening, like some demented demon's-spawn in need of a diaper change. And close.

"What the hell *is* it?" whispers Lane, forgetting for once to not cuss.

The banshee wails again, this time in stereo, and suddenly I know. "Porcupines," I say. "Making love."

"Well," says Lane, "I'll be ..."

Thanks to the amorous porkies, we oversleep, waking only when the sun slaps our faces. In penance, we bolt jerky and creek water for breakfast, grab our bows, and strike off for parts unknown to me. This entire huge basin is terra incognita to me, and Lane has generously volunteered to conduct a morning tour.

During several hours of quiet poking around, we find where elk have recently foraged and where their big cloven hooves have sunk deep in the mud of a spring seep. By examining their droppings — the older (hard and sun-bleached) spoor are formless lumps, like dwarf cow pies, while the fresher (soft and shiny black) scats are acorn-like pellets — we determine that the big herbivores are already shifting from their spring and summer fare of moisture-filled grasses and forbs to a fall and winter diet of woody browse.

And such other bits of natural history that only biologists and veteran hunters generally bother to notice.

The high and low point of the morning scout comes when our noses lead us to a fresh wallow carved into a muddy spring seep, proving that at least one mature bull is lurking about, probably shaded-up somewhere nearby even now, chewing contemplative cud and watching, listening, nostrils alert for danger. I drop to my knees for a closer reading of the sign.

The story is clearly writ: Some sex-crazed bully boy has hoofed the spring seep into a quagmire, urinated into the mess, stirred it all around, then rolled to cake himself with the funky muck — the wapiti way of dressing for a hot date. Nearby, a forlorn spruce sapling has been stripped of its bark and lower limbs by the hormone-enraged bather's aggressive horning.

As long ago became my habit when hunting, I put my face down close to the reeking muck and inhale deep of its pungent, pheromone-laden fumes, prompting my wiseacre friend to quip: "Why don't you just roll in it and experience the real essence of elkness?"

As we walk on, I don't bother mentioning that I've already done that, back in my formative years as a shameless elkoholic. A staggeringly stupid error I have no desire to repeat.

It's early afternoon when we sag back into camp for lunch and brief naps. Afterward, we fling a few practice arrows at a makeshift target, check the sharpness of our broadheads, and otherwise make ready for a serious evening hunt.

Lane plans to climb a nearby promontory and bugle. Any rutting bull within hearing (so the theory goes) will interpret the calls as a challenge to his territorial dominance and answer in kind, revealing his location.

Might even come a-running, hot for a fight. Most often, though, a harem master will simply herd up his cows and run away (to live and breed another day). But even a retreating bull will sometimes bugle when bugled at, granting the priceless gift of hearing him sing. Bottom line: you never know; sometimes the magic works, increasingly more often it backfires, even in a semi-remote backcountry place like this.

Lane invites me to join him. I decline. For me, playing the silent, solitary predator is the quintessence of the big game bowhunting experience; companionship and conversation are best saved for the evening campfire. We exchange good lucks, and Lane strikes off uphill. I go low, headed back to a grassy little glen at the bottom of a nearby canyon where we cut fresh sign this morning and where food, water, and wooded seclusion — the Big Three of quality wildlife habitat — are abundant. There, I'll lie (in fact sit) in ambush, and elk or no, it's a room with a promising view.

Time passes quickly, and less than an hour of light remains when I hear a high, clean, distant call that rises in steps through three octaves, sustains briefly, then comes crashing back to earth. Lane is nearly a mile away as the arrow flies, but sound carries well in the rarefied subalpine air. No sooner has Lane's realistic fake bugle faded away than I hear, much closer, a low grunt and the brittle crashing of limbs. Adrenaline surges; my heart slams into overdrive. The sounds are coming from a wooded plateau directly across the little canyon from me, and I don't have to see the noisemaker to know who it is and what he's up to — a wapiti bull, infuriated by Lane's vocal challenge, is venting his excitement by stomping around and antler-thrashing some unfortunate tree.

When Lane bugles again, the real bull answers immediately. The animal is close enough, just a hundred yards or so, that I can hear not only the higher notes of his call but the deep, eerie, underlying growls as well. Lane sings a third time and the bull, by now as hot as a teenager on a date, replies with a series of three rapid, braying grunts ... *Yo mom-ma!*

And here I sit. I could enter the fray with a bugle or cow chirp of my own. That might bring the bull out of hiding and into stickbow range. Might also, most likely, scare him off. My only other active choice is to try stalking up the hill toward him. But only lovers, inexperienced hunters, and other impetuous fools rush in. Moreover, if I move as slowly and painstakingly as I should, I'll run out of daylight before I can get there.

Rather than take a chance on blowing this bull smack out of the neighborhood, I place my bow on the ground beside me and lie back on the cool, leaf-cushioned earth to enjoy the sunset concert. Short of a miracle, there will be no killing this night, though the hunting could hardly be better.

Why do I bowhunt? It's a lot to think about, and I think about it a lot.

I hunt to acknowledge my evolutionary roots, millennia deep, as a predatory omnivore.

To participate actively in the bedrock workings of nature.

For the atavistic challenge of doing it well with no hired help and a minimum of technical assist.

To learn the lessons, about nature and myself, that only traditional bowhunting can teach.

To accept personal responsibility for at least some of the deaths that nourish my life and lifestyle.

For the glimpse it offers into a natural wildness we can hardly even imagine.

Because, done right, sneaking through the backcountry with stickbow and wood arrow in hand provides the closest thing I've known to a palpable spiritual experience. I bowhunt because it enriches my life and because I can't help myself. I was born with a hunter's heart.

David Petersen

Chapter Five

Close to Home

Weminuche Wilderness, San Juan Mountains, Colorado.

Cupping my hands over my mouth to fake a megaphone, I take a deep breath of crisp alpine air and grunt out a crude approximation of the territorial mating call of a bull moose in rut: *Oo-Wah! Ooo-Wah! Ooo-WAH!*

Even before I've finished the chorus, a cow moose appears from the timber's edge, a hundred yards away. Gangly and muddy brown, she is headed straight for me. Trying to ignore her looming presence, I call again — *Ungh! Ungh!* — challenging any bull that might be lurking about to come out and retrieve his bride. Or at least to answer in kind.

But instead of a mature bull, I get a paddle-horn, tall and black with bulging shoulder hump. Emerging from the forest at a trot, the young bull deftly inserts himself between the cow and me and herds her back into the woods. No doubt, the seven-hundred-pound adolescent felt threatened by my overly confident calls, rightly concerned that his one-girl harem was looking to jump to a bigger ship.

While I could legally take the little bull — assuming I could maneuver to within selfbow range — I am here for something else. According to local legend, somewhere near this remote willow flat at 11,400 feet lurks a bull with antlers spanning fifty inches or more, a trophy by Shiras standards. This is my first morning here. I have a week's supplies in camp and am encouraged that if I keep at it, I can find that dream bull and bring him home for a winter's worth of meals, a lifetime of memories. You can hardly take a step in this place without kicking fresh moose droppings.

By day's end, though I've gotten no shots, I've seen four respectable bulls, if not the fifty-incher of local myth.

So why do I feel so uneasy as I slouch back to camp in the dark?

36

And why, come morning, do I pack up camp and head home, 150 miles away?

A worrisome pattern has clearly formed. The previous week, after setting up camp four miles from a trailhead where I left my truck, I grew inexplicably morose after just two days of hunting, thus decamped and headed home. And before that, an outfitter friend had offered to pack me into the wildest heart of the Weminuche Wilderness, the haunt of big bull Shiras, only recently opened to moose and never before hunted. Yet, as the time for that weeklong adventure approached, I backed out, not wanting to be gone from home that long.

And even at the best of times, while hunting and seeing moose, I've felt oddly detached, distracted by conflicting desires. So I run home, hunt elk for a few evenings, then take off on yet another wild moose chase. I'd become an emotional yo-yo.

It is written: Be careful of what you wish for. Eighteen years. That's how long it took me to draw a coveted Colorado bull moose tag. So why was I acting so impetuously, throwing it all away?

Because, between the time I started playing the moose lottery, age forty, and when I finally won it, age fifty-eight, I had fallen so passionately in love with local terrain and bowhunting local elk, that to miss even one day has become unthinkable. Or so I thought.

Nor are my precious homeboy hunts generally all that exciting. No heart-thumping calling contests or exacting stalks. Rather, each afternoon I hike up my backyard mountain to one or another tiny spring-fed pool in an aspen grove — and sit there like a statue until dark. Most hunters would find it boring. For me, it's the epitome of what Thoreau called "soothing employment." Across those quiet September evenings I see elk, deer, bears, and more, without them seeing me. I slap the summer's last mosquito and feel the first nip of frost. I hear hundreds of bugles, near and far, and watch the aspens go from lime to brass. One year I killed a gorgeous bull on the first day of September — and suffered the rest of the month.

And moose season — here's the rub — overlaps and therefore competes with elk. To go for either one, means to forego the other. Consequently, forced to a choice, elk won out over moose, no matter how hard I fought it.

In the end, after four aborted tries, feeling spineless and mercurial, I gave in to my heart and finished the only Colorado moose season I will ever know sitting at a local spring ... and never even saw an elk.

Passion unfolds in mysterious ways. Does the lifelong whitetail hunter, in love with his local woodlot, read with aching heart the exuberant stories of other hunters' adventures in exotic, far-off lands, vowing someday to do the same? Many surely do. But some do not, having found contentment in smaller pleasures, in familiar places and routines, at peace with themselves and their place in hunting world.

Could it be that we homebodies are the truly lucky ones?

Chapter Six

Wapiti Wisdom

H *ippy-hoppity, here comes the wapiti.*

Just a silly kiddy-ditty, you bet, but an easy way to remember the correct pronunciation of the oft-mispronounced proper name of North America's second-largest deer. Not *wa-PEE-de*, but *WOP-it-tee*. While the word is Shawnee for "white rump," "beige butt" would be more apt. The familiar name "elk," meanwhile, appears to trace back to a case of mistaken identity, when early immigrants—farmers and tradesmen, not naturalists—misidentified the wapiti, a new and unfamiliar species to them, as *elch* (German) or *elg* (Danish and Norwegian), their native names for the moose.

By any name, the elk is today the most popular big game trophy in North America. And for good reasons: It is huge, averaging five hundred pounds for mature cows and seven hundred pounds for 6x6 bulls, netting about two hundred pounds of choice red meat, which, to my palate, is on par with whitetail and notably less "gamey" than mule deer. And of course the wapiti wears massive, ornate antlers, bugles magnificently during early fall archery seasons and haunts some of the loveliest wild places on the continent. And thanks to the heroic efforts of the American hunter/conservationist and scientific wildlife management communities, elk today are numerous and widespread. At least a million wild, free-ranging wapiti currently roam twenty-six states and all eleven Canadian provinces — putting a "hunt of a lifetime" within the reach of anyone with healthy lungs and legs and the price of a tag, a tent, and a few tanks of gas.

About 1.3 million years ago, early in the Pleistocene epoch (the most recent great ice age), elk emerged as a distinct genus, *Cervus*, in central Asia, having split from the sika deer lineage. From their likely origins in the foothills of the Himalayas, ancestral elk spread west into Europe, adapting to their new surroundings to become the red deer (*Cervus elaphus elaphus*). At the same time, another branch of the primordial *Cervus* clan drifted east, adapting to the hard winters, high mountains, and open steppes of Mongolia and the Siberian Uplands. Descendants of this second group continued to disperse across the Chukchi Peninsula and, eventually, onto the low-lying "mammoth steppe" of Beringia, a.k.a. the Bering Land Bridge. And there they remained for hundreds of millennia, adapting to this harsh, half-Asian, half-American landscape to become the modern wapiti we know today (*Cervus elaphus canadensis*).

As the last Ice Age thawed (called the *Würm* in Europe, the Wisconsin in North America), sea levels rose and Beringia began slowly to "sink" — an inundation that concluded only about ten thousand years ago. Forced to higher ground, some Beringian wapiti were isolated on the Siberian side, while others were "stranded" in Alaska. And so it is today that wapiti on both sides of the Bering Strait look the same, sound the same, behave the same, even stink the same. They *are* the same. From Alaska, wapiti dispersed to occupy every habitable niche throughout the continent … and then went extinct as Alaska grew colder again, though they've recently been reintroduced there as island populations.

Wapiti rut from late August through mid-October. During this time, bulls employ both vocal and visual advertisements to attract females. Those same bugles and antlers serve secondarily as threats to intimidate competing males. In a balanced population, a rutting hierarchy evolves that allows the fittest mature bulls to enjoy most of the breeding and thereby pass their superior genes on to future generations. In all deer species, antlers are biological "luxuries." No matter how genetically blessed a bull or buck may be, only after the animal's primary nutritional and health needs are satisfied—bone and muscle growth, the healing of injuries and infections — will "leftover" nutritional resources be channeled into exceptional antler growth. Thus are big antlers indicative not only of good genes and longevity, but also of an exceptionally efficient foraging strategy (good habitat helps). This synergetic combination of "nature and nurture" explains why romantically inclined cows seek out big-antlered bugle boys to father their calves. Likewise, big, symmetrical antlers serve as signposts of comparative vitality among competing males. Only as an evolutionary afterthought did antlers come to serve as sparring weapons during the rut.

If we add to the cows' instinctive attraction to big, balanced antlers the fact that older bulls are more experienced and efficient in the delicate art of courting, we begin to understand not only why, but how a single mature bull can attract a harem of as many as several dozen cows, while lesser bulls get none.

Alas, the best laid plans …

Queering this whole elaborate arrangement is the modern craze for trophy hunting. The situation we have today, where industry and ego have teamed up to prod all hunters to try their best to kill the biggest males they can, often as they can, rubs hard against both natural selection and elk social harmony. When the number of mature bulls in a given area is unnaturally depressed by focused trophy hunting — as is the case across most of elk country today — younger, relatively inexperienced males are left to do an unnatural share of the breeding. And generally they do it poorly, leading to stressed cows, late and failed pregnancies, smaller and later-born calves the following spring, and higher calf mortality come winter.

Thus, in the long and prudent view, our passion for killing trophy bulls is biologically reckless and works against the continued availability of trophy bulls down the line.

Most cows begin breeding in their third autumn and produce one calf per year throughout their long reproductive lives. Calving season is mid-May through mid-June, peaking around the first of June. At birth, healthy calves average about thirty-five pounds. Weight gain is rapid, with youngsters adding more than a pound a day throughout the summer. By September, a healthy calf will be as big as an adult deer and can fend for itself should Mom meet with an arrow. Cows can live twenty years or longer in the wild, while males are lucky to make it past three years, the age when they become legal game in most states as "raghorns." (While nobody seems to know the origin of this slang term, it is used by biologists as well as hunters in reference to young, branch-antlered bulls and is neither pejorative or complimentary, nor accurately descriptive of anything.) Beyond the security of national parks and deep, road- and motorized trail-free wilderness, precious few bulls these strange days live to attain the prime antler-growing ages of six to twelve years.

I've hunted wapiti for twenty-six years. Yet I wouldn't dare to assert a single best way to go about it. In my experience, "best" is always relative. Relative, for instance, to terrain and vegetation, rut stage, hunting pressure, local game populations and gender ratios, weather, and so much more — including the individual hunter's personal preferences and priorities, woodcraft and naturalist skills, physical stamina, and, let's face it, bank account.

For the initial few years of my elking career, I eagerly took the first legal animal I got a clean crack at. With experience, "any elk" became too easy and my interest shifted to killing, just once, a representative "nice" 6x6. I spent the next four years pursuing that goal. With a "record book" head finally on my wall (but in no record book, thank you), I settled back into meat hunting, generally killing young bulls as they tended to be the first to present themselves. In recent years, I've evolved into what I only half-jokingly refer to as a trophy meat hunter, selecting for young fat cows and "spoon meat" calves, since these two classes are the most biologically expendable while providing the finest meat. Almost comically, in my quest to kill a calf I have so far failed, already investing more seasons trying than it took me to bag a trophy bull.

Although I've never experienced more thrilling hunts than those that conclude in a screaming, brush-bashing, close-quarters bugling duel with a testosterone-drunk bull, such explosive action is scarce as fur on a fish these days, at least for us average Joes and Josephas. I no longer use a bugle, as the technique has been so massively abused it rarely attracts bulls any more, but frequently shuts them up and scares them away, while molesting the hunt for other hunters and disrupting the natural workings of the rut by silencing bugling bulls. Cow calling remains unpredictably viable, though far from magical, and is rapidly is going the way of bugling as it, too, has been greedily marketed and amateurishly abused.

Most of the elk I've killed in recent years have been ambushed at close range over secluded spring pools in dense forest, a long hike from the nearest road, ATV trail, cow pie or call-tooting nimrod. But I'm lucky in that regard, since such oases of wildness are increasingly hard to find on our increasingly over-logged, overgrazed, over-roaded, motor-infested public lands. And public lands, for most of us, are our last best hope. (How any serious hunter can *not* be a conservationist — a purely self-serving and utterly essential stance — has long eluded and troubled me.)

In sum, my advice to freshmen elk hunters is to be suspicious of gadgets and magazine ads claiming to provide an "easy" way to kill elk. There *is* no easy way, and if there were, it should be illegal. Rather than roaming the woods blowing on toy whistles or driving the roads hoping to spot pot-shootable game, far better to strive to become an old-fashioned woodsman. Learn all you can about the lives, needs, and behaviors of your quarry, its preferred habitats, and the greater ecosystem of which it is a functioning part. Stay on your feet (unless you're sitting on stand) and well off the roads. Studies confirm that elk numbers and daylight activity dramatically increase beyond a half-mile from the nearest public road, motorized trail or clear-cut. And rather than searching for any single "best" way to hunt elk, stay tactically flexible in order to take advantage of every ethical opportunity that presents itself.

"Yes," exclaims lifelong hunter and world-renowned elk biologist Val Geist, "I'd rather eat meat taken from the wild forests with skill, toil, and sweat. It keeps one honest in our culture of fancy illusions."

David Petersen

Chapter Seven

"Come On!"

Come with me now, back to a recent yesteryear, when I still hunted for horns and before the delicate art of bugling to rutting bulls had been ruined by greed, overuse, and stupidity, most certainly including my own — back when the magic (occasionally) still worked …

The month-long Colorado archery elk season is half done before my old good friend Milt Beens (say "Benz") and I manage to wrangle a day of elk hunting together. I've been at it for two weeks of evenings already, seeing a record number of cows and calves and enjoying one stinky-close encounter of the raghorn variety. But nothing yet worth ending my season for.

Milt, as usual, has been working too much. He's a talented potter and painter, and moonlights full-time at Wildcat Canyon Archery, a home-based business on the outskirts of Durango, where he crafts graceful, self-nocked, artfully stained and hand-detailed wood arrows. He's also a natural-born teacher and mentor. In winter it's skiing (Milt trains instructors). The rest of the year it's traditional archery. It's on Milt's obstacle-course 3D range that I hone my shooting skills on lifelike targets in lifelike surroundings early every August. What else? As an enthusiastic recreational philosopher, Milt is lively and stimulating campfire company, especially after a couple slashes of Maker's Mark. He is, in sum, a man of diverse talents, good humor, and rare selflessness.

Today, I hope to give a little something in return by helping Milt kill his first stickbow bull. Which is not to say he's a wapiti virgin, having long ago put elk meat on the ground with rifle and compound arrow-launching device. But no big antlers adorn his wall, and he's yet to kill a wapiti with traditional equipment. After a decade of frustration, he's starting to feel jinxed, reluctant even to continue trying.

44

So a lot rides on today. Milt is toting a lithesome longbow made by his friend Jerry Barr, and a quiver of woodies Milt hand-split from an old stair step and fashioned into elegant shafts fletched with feathers of wild Canada goose — naturally waterproof, if a bit sibilant in flight. My bow is a custom recurve I bought used from Milt some years ago.

It's still black-dark when we rock-hop across a shallow river and angle up through a big national forest pasture overgrown (as too many public lands pastures tend to be these days) with thistle, searching in the dark for an unsigned trailhead. On the path at last, we lean into a long, steep climb, bound for a ridgeline along which we hunted grouse together last fall — a place where the sweet, heavy perfume of rutting elk enticingly lingered, like the scent of a lovely woman.

Excuse the purplish prose but it's quite simply true this morning: Dawn blooms pink as a hothouse rose. Autumn's first hints glint like puddles of liquid gold in a lime-green sea of quaking aspens. The mountains stand tall and clean, uncluttered by fog or clouds. The sky, as it lightens, acquires the blue-green sheen of turquoise. No other hunters in sight or sound, and no boot prints ahead of our own. Cool but not really cold. A steady down-slope breeze. Elk sign everywhere, and much of it fresh. Heaven on Earth. (And where better to enjoy a palpable paradise, than where we are right now?)

Topping out on the eastern rim of a densely wooded canyon, steep and deep, Milt and I are rewarded with a verdant panorama of logging-scarred but otherwise blessedly unspoiled wildness all around. We stop to suck at the thin mountain air, slow our hearts, and listen. After five minutes of depressing silence, I uncoil my grunt tube, venture a single prospecting bugle and — holy *molé*! — I get *two* bugles coming right back, one from each of two feeder forks in the canyon ahead. Thus awakened, the wapiti get right down to business, bugling and chuckling tit for tat, talking among themselves. My own bugling having happily become superfluous, I put a lid on it, the better to remain anonymous. The hunt is on and away we go, hell-bent for adventure.

We keep to the hiking trail for another quarter mile, where it hooks into a small cloistered park grown waist deep in native grasses and forbs, whiskered through with aspen saplings and an occasional white pillar of an adult. This might just do it. The starboard bull is still a half-mile out, maybe more, but the fellow up the left-hand canyon is closer.

Milt moves forward and kneels in the tall grass a few yards down-wind of the intersection of the hiking trail and a game path angling up from the canyon fork. Staying back, I also plop down in the grass and make ready: head-net on, calls near at hand, check the breeze, arrow on string in case a cautious bull should circle and approach us from behind.

I open the vocal bidding with a few herding mews and chirps, loud enough to carry, yet calm. The two bulls' reactions are immediate, identical, and profound: They both shut up. Very well. Bending my grunt tube skyward, I squeak out a brief, wimpy bugle — brash, but with an overtone of uncertainty, like a precocious spiker or raggy—then drop the tube and make with another brief series of cow calls. Milt chimes in with more of the same, just one of the girls. The more distant bull sings with gusto. The nearer animal contains his response to a braying burst of chuckles.

And so it goes, for fifteen noisy but fruitless minutes. I bugle small and cow call big. Mr. Right grumbles and roars. Lefty merely laughs. Nobody budges. Time to up the ante.

Following the game trail now, we pussyfoot down off the ridgeline, headed for the bottom of the canyon at its junction with its twin feeders. Lefty should be close ahead and a ways up the opposite slope, though he's fallen silent. Left to sing to himself, Mr. Right keeps belting 'em out every couple of minutes.

About forty yards below the canyon-bottom Y, and half that above the tinkling brook that defines the canyon floor, we stop to test the waters. I cow call and Lefty bugles immediately — so close and thundering that I almost swallow my diaphragm. The conifer forest on the bull's side remains shrouded in morning shadow and is so dense and dark with old-growth evergreens, you'd be lucky to spot a neon elephant within. I whine again, and big limbs crack. He's moving, and now sounds to be almost directly across from us, maybe eighty yards.

Show time.

We whisper a hurried plan that sends Milt to the canyon bottom, where he backtracks downstream and downwind a ways, and dissolves into the scenery. I stay put, hunkered behind a clump of brush. With real *good* luck, I can entice the bull out of the timber and into the open-wooded canyon bottom where he'll hit the game trail, head my way and provide Mr. Beens with a close broadside. With real *bad* luck, the bull will circle downwind before coming off the hill, dramatically increasing his chances of smelling two rats in the woodpile. The greatest likelihood, of course, is that he'll simply shut up and sneak away, denying us even the small thrill of counting his tines.

All is ready. I chirp once. Lefty bugles. I bugle back. He clams up. Deciding to apply some pressure, I bugle and cow-call interchangeably, building gradually to an electric excitement.

From below left comes one sharp *crack!* I strain my eyes into the trees and get my first glimpse of our boy. A stout five-by, maybe even a six. Standing, staring. Hung up, or merely cautious? I blow a prolonged chorus of passionate, bent-note whines and by George, here he comes. If he turns downstream before crossing the creek and gets past Milt without picking up his scent or his arrow, and steps into a small clearing directly below me, I'll take the shot, though I hope not to get that chance.

No worries. Even as I think the thought, Milt's spunky little longbow whispers *Thut! Sssszzz!* hisses the goose-fletched missile. *Smack!* announces the heavy wood shaft. *Thud-thud-thud!* responds the retreating bull.

Hoping to turn the stampeding animal back toward Milt, I bugle again.

Silence.

After a while, Milt appears in the game trail below and gives a smiling thumbs-up. The man is absolutely beaming. He walks up to join me as I struggle to light a shaky smoke (an old and filthy post-shot tradition; part celebration, part unwinding, part superstition, part addiction, and wholly self-indulgent).

"Good hit?" I ask in a whisper.

"*Real* good!" Milt booms back.

"Let's just sit here — quietly — and give him a few minutes to lie down and die in peace."

"No need," says Milt, loud and proud. "He's already down and dead ... right over yonder." He points and I look. "See those four big black legs sticking in the air?"

I follow Milt down the trail. Just before crossing the little creek he stops near a big aspen. "Right here," he says, "is where the bull was standing when I shot." The story is clearly written in hoof scuffs and sanguine liquid splotches on the ground. "Wait here," commands my ecstatic friend as he dodges around a clump of snowberry brush and stops in front of a huge ancient aspen tree. "And I was standing here."

47

"Standing?"

"Standing, so I could shoot over this brush. Couldn't be more than eight, nine steps between us, eh?"

Thrashing through the brush, attempting to forge an arrow-straight line from me to he, I pace off seven yards.

"And check this." Now Milt steps away from his ambush tree backstop to reveal the most enigmatic aspen carving I've ever seen. At head height and scrawled in big capital letters all swollen and black with age is the exclamation "COME *ON!*"

"Come *on!*" says Milt, impatient to get on with it, his excitement mounting by the moment. And who could blame him? I'm hardly bored myself.

We jump the brook, take a few steps more — and there lies the splintered feather-end of Milt's artful arrow. "Looks like maybe fifteen inches penetration," he observes. "Enough, I guess."

I guess, given that just thirty yards from where the deadly splinter struck home, the bull lies in awkward repose. A gorgeous animal, his antlers are stocky and dark as old oiled oak. Five tines to the side with a small fork topping the right main beam, just big enough to count, were anybody scoring.

"Six-by-five," I pronounce, confirming the obvious.

Milt sags to his knees and strokes the giant deer's flaxen side. "He's so beautiful! And so big! I never dreamed ..."

I agree absolutely. He is both beautiful and big. And cooperative to boot. In all my years of hunting elk it has rarely happened as perfectly as this. We've been blessed with extreme good fortune this magical September morning.

But now the party's over. It's time to get to work.

Carefully, we wrestle the hefty Lefty off his back and onto one side, take lots of pictures, attach validated carcass tag to antler, and struggle to sled the mammoth cervid downhill a few yards to a somewhat level spot. Several minutes later, probing cautiously into the steaming chest cavity, Milt retrieves the business end of his arrow, which indeed has penetrated both lungs, coming to rest against an off-side rib.

Conversation lapses as we bend to the bloody chore. But the hunt is not yet over, after all. Mr. Right, a real go-getter, has just tuned up again and is bombarding us with outraged bugles. As the excited animal works gradually closer, Milt entreats me repeatedly to "Go *get* him!" Reckon I should. But frankly the idea of attempting a same-day double strikes me as, well, maybe just a little too ambitious? With more than fifty years of living under my belt, I can't get too excited about the possibility of having two horse-sized animals on the ground at the same time, so far from the nearest road. Don't want to have too much fun all at once.

All that notwithstanding, and with the bugling bull and Milt bugging me nonstop, I eventually acquiesce and agree at least to try to get a look at the braggart; take it from there. Using grass to wipe the worst of the gore from my hands, I grab my bow and my calls and follow a track-churned game trail up the brushy canyon bottom toward the source of all the heckling. Stopping often to look and listen, then weaseling forward a few more baby steps at a time, I'm able to maneuver with thirty yards of the frenzied beast. Trying to get closer would be foolhardy. May be too close already.

Assessing my limited options, I back into a thorny clump of wild rose brush growing behind a blow-down fir trunk lying just off the game trail. After observing a few moments of silence, I give it a go. In response to my mewing, Mr. Right redoubles the ferocity of his bugles — earthshaking at such close range — but makes no move to come. I bugle. He bugles back but stands his ground. I chuckle. He bugles and chuckles but does not move. Hung up. Just like a springtime gobbler. My doubts about the advisability of this little enterprise return, and after a couple of minutes more I slip away and hurry back down the trail to my partner and what's left of Lefty. A strange feeling, this — running away from a bugling bull!

Only a few minutes pass, engrossed again in visceral matters, before the bull's nagging, combined with Milt's persistent encouragement, prompt me to give it another go. Again I wipe my hands, sheath my belt knife, collect my gear, and go tiptoeing unto the breach. This time I'm more restrained with my dialogue and manage to coax the bull to within twenty yards, where he stops, entirely hidden behind the forest wall, and rakes a tree. A feckless hunter is a reckless hunter, and next thing I know I'm raking right back.

Silence.

I wait, also in silence.

A minute later I hear hooves splashing through the creek, then a rock comes rattling down the far embankment. That scoundrel — he's circling downwind, hoping to get a whiff or a glimpse of the talkative but invisible elk herd. And next thing I know, he's standing broadside in an opening directly across from me and barely out of range; we spot one another at the same instant.

Can't say what he makes of me, but I see a handsome fiver, though not nearly so big as his ego. His antlers are perfectly symmetrical and gracefully curved, but like the rest of him, skinny; not much meat on those lanky bones. This early in the season, this far in, with one elk on the ground, I think I'll pass. I stand and walk away, prompting the bull to promptly depart.

Back at Milt's kill site, after a very few minutes' respite, the unspookable Mr. Right approaches yet again and resumes his verbal harangue. This time we pretend to ignore him. Finally, he circles close downwind. A piercing alarm bark rings through the canyon and that, at last, is that. What a wapiti's eyes and ears may occasionally miss, his nose knows instantly.

"Good riddance," I quip.

"Sour grapes," observes the resident philosopher.

And he could be right. It occurs to me that had I been serious about killing that bull, I'd have sneaked up the trail in silence while Milt mixed occasional calling with his meat cutting. Chances are, the recklessly curious young fellow would have pranced right down the trail past me, homing on Milt, providing a shot opportunity even closer than Lefty's knee-knocking seven yards. Maybe.

With the woods now emptied of sound and temptation, I ask my pal to fill the vocal void by recounting the morning from his point of view.

"Ironically," Milt begins, "today almost didn't happen. Last night I was still unsure; almost called you and canceled. My experience in a decade of bugle hunting has been that I enjoy the social aspect and the exercise and all, but nothing ever happens. I've rarely even gotten to see an elk, and when I have, I've never had a shot. I'm not the kind who has to kill frequently in order to enjoy hunting, but after so many years of nothing, it gets kind of hard to justify the time taken off work.

"So I got up and drove to your place this morning feeling pretty ambivalent. And sure enough, the hike in, stumbling around in the dark, the deafening silence at first, it was shaping up to be just another day of fresh air and war stories. And even after you bugled and the bulls answered, it was like, hey, I've been here before; we may hear 'em, but we'll never see 'em. Seeming to confirm that likelihood was that initial set-up: We called, they answered. Exciting, but as usual, nothing came of it.

"Even when we moved down here in the canyon and you called and Lefty answered right away, I was still doubtful. Then, right after I got settled into my ambush spot and you started really working out, I heard a limb crack and there he was, standing in the open maybe sixty yards out. At that point I realized we could hardly have picked a better set-up—the wind was perfect and the possibility existed that things could go right.

"As the bull moved slowly closer, I could see he was a good one and I felt my first twinge of hopeful excitement. On he came until he was almost in spitting range, then he stopped behind a fat little Christmas tree. I could see him through the limbs, but I couldn't shoot. His body language was incredibly calm, like, 'I wonder who that is up there carrying on?' Hardly a hot bull. Next thing I know he dips his head, yanks up some grass, and starts to chew!

"At that point I wouldn't have been the least surprised to see old Lefty bed down and go to chewing cud. But then you called again and he stepped out from behind the spruce and started toward you. A moment later, while his head was passing behind that first aspen I showed you, I came to full draw, silently chanting—I kid you not, and I hadn't seen the carving yet—'Come *on!*'

"Two more steps and he was completely in the open, broadside and close. And then, incredibly, he stopped. I wish I could say that I picked an exact spot on his chest to aim for, but I have no memory of it. You know how it is. The adrenaline kicks in and you go on autopilot and have to depend on instincts developed through long practice.

"When I released, it was like seeing an elk shot from a cannon; he swapped ends in midair and was out of there. You bugled, and that slowed him to a walk. When you bugled again he turned and started back. I went to nock another arrow but before I could, he coughed, took a couple more steps and collapsed. The whole scenario lasted less than a minute, with Lefty traveling maybe forty yards total after the shot, going and coming."

Taking a break from his story, Milt lays aside a detached hindquarter, grunting under its weight. Smiling and shaking his head in happy disbelief, he concludes on a note of gratitude, allowing as how "After all those years of disappointment, I can't believe how easy this morning went, how perfectly it all worked out. This bull was a gift."

"No way!" I feign to argue. "You hunted this guy, in effect, for ten years. You tune your equipment like a musician and shoot hundreds of arrows a month. We scouted this place and planned our strategy like battlefield generals. We made the right moves at the right times, calculating a killer set-up just so. You kept your cool when the action got hot and released a perfect arrow. You know your stuff and you paid your dues. Your karma is good. You *earned* this bull, my friend!"

After a long bit of silence, Milt says again, with heightened emphasis: "He was a *gift*."

"Yes," I say, finally getting his point, "indeed, a *gift*."

"Well then," orders my bloody good friend. "Come *on!* There's a lot of work left to do."

Chapter Eight

The Same Elk Twice

Happy days! Another archery elk season rises with the sun tomorrow. But even as I pack a lunch (mashed chicken in a can, a big crooked carrot, and a chocolate bar), my anticipation is burdened by concern.

Each autumn, while official counts tally more elk than ever before, elk country becomes a little more crowded and suburbanized, a little less peaceful and wild, a lot noisier with the annoying whine of ATVs and dirt bikes, the elk pushed a little higher, a little farther away, onto private land prematurely, forced into an unnatural silence. And it breaks my bloody heart — like being forced to watch, helpless, while someone you love is slowly tortured, and few but you who give a care. No evil "antis" at work here, just the insidious onrush of gluttonous growth, physical sloth, and technological addiction we euphemize as progress.

But then, I can hardly blame land developers and trophy-home builders and "landowner rights" fanatics for the weather, another source of my concern for the upcoming hunt. It's been an exceptionally soggy summer here, pushing up plenty good elk chow high and low, water standing everywhere, encouraging wapiti to wander near and far. Mostly far I fear.

We shall see.

A restless night — then at last *Reveille!* Out of bed and back up the mountain, running full-tilt boogie on first-day adrenaline ... but, alas and alack, it would seem I'm the only one awake up here.

Hearing no bugles and finding no fresh spoor low down, I opt to invest the day in uphill scout-hunting: get the big picture; play it from there.

Throughout an idyllic late-August day, I haunt the flickering shade of lime-leafed aspens, edging around hidden meadows flecked in five shades of purple with harebell, aster, larkspur, geranium, and monkshood, the warm midday breeze thick with the aromatic exhalations of ponderosa pine, subalpine spruce and fir, and Douglas fir (not a true fir, but close enough for the elk and me). At play in the fields of an earthy Elysium, heaven enough for me.

But in all the day's hours, all my ups and downs and miles around, I see, hear, or smell not one sweet stinking wapiti. Nor do I find much in the way of fresh sign.

Not, at least, until I've closed the day's loop to back where I started from — and luck into a ponderosa sapling thick as your wrist with the hide skinned off. The moist green cambium and sticky wet sap attest to the rub's freshness. Well, well ... even though, by all appearance, no elk have been eating or drinking or wallowing or walking or bedding or bugling or even making poop on this mountain of late — ghostly though they be, they be here. At least, one horny fellow is shagging about. And one is a real good start, so early in the rut. Others will follow. They always do.

Midway between the rub-a-dub tree and a small spring pool, I find a dandy natural blind; the usual for me — a blowdown log to sit on, a dense bushy fir behind — and settle in to wait.

A dismally tranquil evening ensues. The Steller's jays and ravens, chickadees and nuthatches, pine siskins, flycatchers, and others who normally animate this quiet quakie grove are staying away in flocks. Ditto the squirrels. Odd, what?

An hour grinds by and my bony butt is starting to ache. With the evening just coming prime, right when I should be on highest alert, I catch myself lighting a filthy smoke, a sure-fire sign of semi-acquiescence. Here I sit on my lumpy log, fuming and fidgeting, daydreaming of Mexican beer and Cuban cigars and Caroline back home and ... hold everything! A huge dark shadow has just floated into view, and out again, now back in; an amorphous apparition gliding ghostlike across a wooded rise just above me.

I drop and smash my smoke beneath a boot, grab my bow, swivel around to face the hope ... and wait.

A minute passes. Where is that shadowy sucker? And *what* is it? Two minutes. Comes a crispy crackle of dry aspen leaves, then out from behind a fat young spruce steps a fat young bull. Fifteen yards and the breeze is in my hairy face. As the animal grazes around the tree's grassy perimeter, he presents an inviting left-facing broadside — busily chowing down, recklessly relaxed.

But is he a legal bull? Submersed in a deep pool of shade, antlers tangled in amongst a confusing backdrop of boughs — four-by, maybe. But precision is essential here: Colorado law requires at least four points on one side—or one brow tine five inches long. That's it: The one brow beam I can see clearly, clearly is closer to ten.

Shoulder muscles tense, fingers tighten against string ... but wait.

This is all too much, way too fast. Do I really want to compress a whole month of hunting into just one day? Then what? Sit home and suffer with envy, that's what; nervous as a preacher at Mardi Gras. Meanwhile, out there, out here, the wapiti sing on with mounting lust and the aspens go slow gold and the air smells like Eden and "unsuccessful" hunters continue playing the sacred game, having the time of their lives. Is that what I truly want?

Last time this happened, I'd hunted for a week and the animal I brought home was no lanky adolescent, but a big burly boss bull, the biggest I've ever killed — and even then, I was restless and irritable the remainder of the month. That was when it all came clear for me: the *hunt* is what I most love. And with a one-animal season, killing kills the hunt. In a normal four-week bow season, hunting mostly evenings, I can look forward to several such exciting close encounters as the one I'm enjoying now — with elk, mostly, but also deer, bear, and more.

I lower my bow and go with the gold of this moment — not merely watching, but close enough to hear (the ripping-up of grass, the grinding of teeth, an occasional rumble of stomach, one slow quiet fart) and even smell (those funky fall pheromones, that ripe green eructation). The bull feeds on, oblivious, eventually working his slow way back around behind the spruce and out of sight. From there, I neither see nor hear him go, but gone he is.

As quiet returns and my heartbeat slows, I'm plagued by second thoughts.

Should have gone for it, I suppose. Get it done with. Meat in the freezer, more horns on the horn wall, and a full September to invest in something other than bowhunting. For once. Like work; earn a few shekels. There's still firewood to fetch, and the local trout are ravenous for anything fly-like that floats. And wouldn't it be swell to get up to Yellowstone to enjoy the grandest elk-rutting spectacle in all of nature's creation? Caroline, my long-suffering elk widow, would be ecstatic. And bottom line, in the words of that infamously eloquent hunting philosopher Thomas D.I.

Beck: "Young bull eats *good*."

Should have gone for it.

Ten minutes pass and I've just torched another frustration-fighting smoke, when without so much as a howdy-do, a compact five-by appears from behind the very spruce that so recently swallowed the raggy. It's as if the first bull stepped behind the tree and was touched with a magic wand that gave him bigger antlers. But no time now for voodoo philosophy. Young bull eats *good*.

Feeding left to right, the fiver stands just ever so slightly forward of broadside, head twisted back over right shoulder, nibbling — no, he's whiffing — spruce needles, one huge unseeing eye pointed right at me. I wait ... down dips the big black muzzle to behead a poor helpless dandelion, and there it is — a great tan open patch of chest, albeit encircled by antlers. Under less optimum conditions, either that hovering halo of horn or the slight forward angle would be reason enough to pass. But at fifteen yards, with a kill zone big as a basketball, it seems foolproof to me.

My anxious arrow leaps away — appearing instantly and exactly at the point of aim. Which, due to the encircling antlers, is slightly higher than the low-chest/heart shot I prefer, yet well within the big ribby oval of lung.

As the bushwhacked bull ducks and spins and hits the deck running, what I see knocks the wind out of me — we've gotten only half-shaft penetration, if that. How can it be?

With anxious eyes and ears I follow the stampeding animal as far as possible, which isn't far — a brief drum-roll of hooves, a single crack of limb from atop the rise, a quick stony clatter in the gully beyond. Silence.

While I'm confident the bull is "as good as dead," I'm damned concerned about the limited penetration. Elk are tough hombres, and with a one-lung hit, the dying could take awhile — not what we want at all, for elk or hunter either. With the rapidity of mood-change that comes only in hunting, I go from higher than a start, to lower than whale crap. But it's going to take more than dime-store remorse to end this bloody business I've begun; we'd best own up to that. We are in for some work.

With less than an hour left of light and a head full of gloom, I scrap the wait and scuttle over to inspect the crime scene. No encouragement here: No arrow. No blood. No prints deep and sharp enough to have been cut by a running animal. No divots of hoof-churned earth. As I criss-cross the area, searching, hoping, the sky goes dark and raindrops tear my face. Damn. I lope up the rise and peer down into the big dry gully: twenty yards deep and twice that across, tapered to a V at the bottom. I trudge up-gully and down, finding nothing but gully.

Stupefied, I'm pondering my next move when a limb cracks loud from a broad wooded flat beyond the cut. Wapiti ... or squirrel? In either event, there's no way I can cross this rocky moat yawning before me without making as much racket as a platoon of Marines at route-step. With only minutes of light left, I see no choice but to back off for the night; get back on it in the morning.

From sad experience, I know what this desperate decision will cost me. On a cool mountain night, you can usually get away with leaving a dusk-shot deer unattended until morning. Not so with elk. Too much mass. Too much internal heat. Too thick a hide. Best insulated and thus first to sour is the prime rump meat surrounding the down-side hip joint.

But what choice do we have? Stumble around aimlessly in the dripping dark? Maybe spook the bull plumb off the planet? Better to let him bed in peace tonight, deal with it tomorrow.

Rain clatters irritably on the cabin roof; another interminable, sleepless night.

To help with the tracking and packing chores I've recruited my hunting and fishing buddy Erica, ever-ready for adventure. We hit the mountain just in time to watch a soggy sun heave itself into a sallow sky. The rain stopped two hours ago, recuperating, no doubt, for another go later. Arrived, little sister Erica and I spend three hours carefully combing the wooded flat in the vicinity of that final teasing snap last night. No go. In our time remaining together—my stewardess (I mean "flight attendant") pal has a plane to catch midday—we concentrate on the gully, scouring it down and up, across and back, busting through its brush-choked bottom. *Nada*.

As noon nears, Erica wishes me luck ("Looks like I'll need it," I admit) and silently flies away. I expand the search — wider, higher, faster, using physical exertion to stave off despair.

Erica has the eyes of a young hungry eagle. And after a lifetime of hard practice I'm no slouch on a blood trail myself. But there is no blood to trail. This is the dark side of hunting (not just bowhunting). It doesn't happen often, but even once is way too much if you have a heart in your chest. If you've ever been in such a fix, you know how hot burns the heartache. "If only," we whine in retrospect regret, "If only I could call back that arrow."

Two days more of cruising and losing. I've taken by now to scanning the skies for feathered scavengers, listening at sunset for the full-bellied yodeling of well-fed coyotes, tasting the breeze for the sickly sweet flavor of carrion — searching for something, anything, on which to hang my tag and my guilt. But the skies remain empty, the twilights silent, the air sweetly fragrant.

I've searched every acre of the entire south slope of a pretty big mountain, stopping only at the apogee, where the earth dives cliff-like down a black-timbered slope — a foreboding shadowy world I can see no gain in probing. I've looked low as well as high, but remain convinced the bull went up, as down, two miles or so, are river and road and people and dogs and all manner of civilized peril.

Granting myself a moment of fantastic optimism, I reflect that if the bull had the spunk to get himself off this mountain — which, unless he's sitting in a bird's nest or hunkering in a bear's den, he appears to have done—he could still be alive. This thought, no matter how wild, offers a glimmer of hope. And hope, that thing with fur and feathers, is all I have right now.

Either way — dead and lost or alive and lost — I can't fight free of the nagging self-indictment: I did something wrong. But what? When you hit where you aim, using gear that's served you well for years — who or what do you blame? More important, what do you change to make certain it never happens again? The bull elk, others have written, is old Elk-heart's personal spiritual totem. Taking one of these grand beasts each autumn, killing quick and clean — to bring his great strength into my body and his crown into my home, to keep his fierce wildness alive in my heart — this is meant to be. Must be. The food of life is death, nor is it all one way: my day will come, and the worms will laugh last. But wounding and wasting — I could not bear to keep hunting if that became the norm. Or anywhere near it.

Thus do I harass myself with largely unanswerable queries: Was my broadhead sharp enough? (Sharp as I could get it.) Is my sixty-four-pound recurve up to the job? (Same bow, three years ago, drove a shaft slick through both lungs of a much larger bull, splitting a rib going in.) Did arrow nick antler, spoiling its speed and trajectory? (Not that I could see or hear at the time.) Should I have held off and hoped, all or nothing, for a full-broadside, low-chest, double-lung/heart sure-shot? (No doubt about it!)

Seeking moral support and advice, I take a morning off the search to visit Milt Beens at his home-based Wildcat Canyon Archery. How, I beg of my wise friend, short of going to a heavier bow, which—given my increasingly ancient age and a perpetually painful right shoulder — would mean switching to training wheels (the horror!), how, Milt, can I assure that I'll never ever again make a "perfect" shot on an elk, only to watch the animal flee, half-shaft flying, never to be seen again?

Recapitulating my own thought processes, Milt asks first about my choice of broadhead.

I name a popular and proven glue-on.

"Was it sharp?"

"Sharp as I could get it."

"Arrow weight?"

"About 540 grains including a 125-grain head."

"For heavy game like elk, you need a heavier arrow."

Later, back at home, I phone my outfitter pal T. Mike Murphy. Mike concurs with Milt, repeating the "heavy arrows for heavy game" chant.

Before hanging up, I ask Mike to repeat a story he told me some years ago. He obliges, the gist of which is this: Mike was guiding a compound shooter who made a spot-on chest shot on a big five-by, but for unknown reasons got poor penetration. In two days of searching, they found no arrow, no elk, and next to no blood. Both men returned home heartsick. More than a month later, that same bull was killed by a rifle hunter. The animal had traveled eight miles and was bugling and otherwise acting normally bullish. In one lung, it still carried a section of aluminum shaft with factory three-blade attached, encased in a "weird growth" of protective tissue.

Another Sisyphean push up the increasingly painful mountain. Another big fat zip in my efforts to find the wounded elk, or what remains of him.

After more than a week of hard hiking enlivened by wind and rain and hail and lightning (all of which I accept as well-deserved karmic punishments), I would bet my best bow there's nothing dead on this mountain. No stench of mortal flesh, no flocking feathered morticians, no singing coyotes or gooey, stinky, hair-packed bear scats. Where to from here?

As if on cue, friend Michael McCarty, a black-powder man, invites me to come hunt from his backcountry horse camp, four miles up a local mountain valley. Hankering for a break from my toils and craving the smell of fresh scenery, I accept.

Next morning, I drive in pounding rain to the designated trailhead, cinch myself under a bulging backpack (I am my own horse), and start up a steep switch-back trail eroded deep by decades of horse and elk hooves and flowing now in a boot-sucking surge of mud and liquefied equine flop. What do we care? At this point, this year, shit is my name, penitence my game.

I hunt three days out of Mike's camp and never even see an elk—a blessing thinly disguised, sparing me the painful last-second decision of whether or not to shoot another elk, having already, almost certainly, killed my moral limit for the year. (Ah yes, but we do lust after that sweet pink meat, don't we?)

I'm hardly surprised to return to my backyard mountain and find no fresh sign at all. After three weeks of smearing my man-stink around like peanut butter, I doubt there's a wapiti left within miles. But then, proving once again that miracles do happen, even to the undeserving, on my way down and out and right at dark, I'm blessed with an omen so wonderfully weird that I vow to keep it to myself. But resolve is weak, and later, over dinner, when Caroline asks after my day, my childlike excitement wins out.

"Heard a couple of bugles," I say, playing it cool and coy.

"So?"

"So, well, they were the first bugles I've heard up there all season and the weirdest I've ever heard — eerie, ethereal, almost scary, breathless, restrained, almost like ..."

"Like a spike bull?"
"No. Like ... a one-lunged bull."

September 18. This evening, rather than bulling up the mountain as usual, my plan is to hang low, near where I heard last night's haunting elk music. Things get fun fast when I find one big fresh elk print in the silted bottom of a spring pool. As thrilled as if the elk that made it were still standing in that print, I find a suitable hide nearby, and dissolve into the woodwork.

I've been hunkered in my root-crater blind for half an hour when a pair of ravens, a quarter-mile down the slope, start chanting a hoarse-voiced mantra that gets my full attention. Having heard this agitated, repetitive, three-note call many times before, I know that it's possible, even likely, the mischievous birds are harassing moving elk.

Sure enough, even as I'm yanking on my daypack to chase the big black birds, the corvine elk alarm is confirmed by an outburst of cow calls. I scurry ravenward, slowing as I draw nearer, gearing gradually down to full-stalk mode — sniffing the breeze for rutty bull stench, scanning the forest for movement, tracking the ravens like radar.

More mewing, which I peg as coming from across the gully, out on a wooded flat. Confident the animals are headed my way, I hurry over and plop down on a lumpy log with good cover behind and a broad view out front.

As anxious minutes pass, my raven guides tire of the game and fly the proverbial coop. No matter; there's still stimulation enough to keep my heart hammering in my ears: periodic cow chatter, an occasional heavy crack of limb, and every few minutes, a nearby ghostly bugle.

Such are the moments of a lucky life.

About half-past six—within minutes of the time I loosed the ill-fated arrow, ironically, while sitting on this very log and three weeks ago tonight—a bull appears in silence atop the rise, poses there in regal silhouette for long slow seconds, then lowers his head and comes loping straight in. Oh my ...

On comes the elk at a jaunty trot, dark and sleek and wearing an expression I can only describe as cocky. He's coming head-on and fast and I can't see his side to confirm my hopes and suspicions, yet I sense that I'm seeing a miracle in motion.

61

As often happens when a herd comes to drink, the bull seems determined to reach the spring first and suck up his fill before the others arrive to muddy the waters. Before dropping his head to drink, he peers all around and, for one neon moment, locks eyes with me. Thirteen yards! I squint my peepers to hide their bloody whites (I'm wearing a face mask, of course) and the bull appears to relax. If only a little.

A bowhunter's dream, this — except that the animal is standing front-on: an unthinkable, immoral, moronic shot angle that even I would never consider. And time's a'wasting; once the herd arrives, my job becomes a whole lot harder, maybe impossible.

Like some overgrown pronghorn, the nervous bull feigns to drink — then jerks his head quick back up, water cascading from his chin, his eyes boring holes in my camo. Now, sweet as angel-song to my ears, comes a chorus of herd chatter. The bull swings around broadside to look ... and there it is: a black-red wound no larger than a quarter, dead center the starboard chest.

Well, where have you been, old friend?

Now comes again the bowhunter's blur: The bull returns to his evening cocktail, remaining broadside, and I draw and anchor and pick a spot low and forward — just so ...

The spring pool erupts like a geyser as the bull explodes into flight. This time, I note with bottomless gratitude, he's taken the shaft to heart and fletch-deep. Dead elk running.

And dead elk don't run far. Plenty noise all the way, climaxed by a crash and a cough at the bottom of the gully. Fifty yards. Fifteen seconds start to finish. Silence.

I sit for a while and tremble, then rise on wobbly legs, walk to the spring and take up the trail: bold and bright and beautiful. I know just where he lies and could beeline there — but after three physically and emotionally painful weeks spent searching for just one drop of this bull's blood, I've worked up quite a sanguine thirst.

Somewhere out in the shadowy forest, a lonely cow elk cries.

Twilight fades from purple to pink as I kneel to stroke the big golden beast. Truly sorry for the pain I put you through, brother. And now, it appears, you get the last laugh. The bull has conspired to expire in the sharply V'd bottom of the gully, belly-up, wedged in tight, thick brush all around. I have to chuckle. After all we've been through together, we wouldn't want this final bit to be too easy, now would we?

Getting a good look at the antlers for the first time, it all comes clear: Not only have I killed the same elk twice, I've killed both the bulls I saw opening evening — the (this) five-by I shot and wounded, and that (this) raggy I declined. What we have here is a 5x3.

As I withdraw the undamaged arrow shaft, a gentle rain begins.

Well, we have a real job of work on our bloody hands now. In addition to the usual drawing-and-quartering, I'm anxious to inspect the ribs and lungs for damage, retrieve whatever might remain of the woebegone first arrow, try and find the fault.

But in death as in life, the bull proves intractable. Try as I might, I can't wrestle him off of his back, wedged-in as he is. Guess we'll just have to take it as it lies. I withdraw my old Schrade Sharpfinger (my favorite until I discovered Helle) from its sheath and set to work.

Right at dark, I hear a small noise above me. Thinking "bear," I look up to see a big leggy calf standing at the gully's rim. Apparently, the wee wapiti has detected the aroma of bull rising from this breezy ditch, approached to check it out and, seeing my movements in the murky dusk, mistakes me for the bull it smells. I drop the backstrap I'm holding, stand and say "Hello there." The calf cocks its head—and starts down! Fearful of being trampled, I wave my arms and shout "Git!" The calf gits.

Two hours it takes me to do the job, the second hour in mineshaft black with a metal mini-flashlight clamped in my teeth, a cold evening breeze sailing down the gully, and a slow steady rain. From cap to boots I'm soaked from the drizzle. From boots to knees and from fingers to elbows I'm a mess of blood and gore. And so tired I could lie me down on the nice warm meat pile and instantly be asleep.

And this, I reflect, is exactly as it should be. I sure as hell know where my meat comes from, and at precisely what costs to all involved.

So here I stand, if only barely, astraddle a skinless, limbless, headless and unbackstrapped carcass still wedged downside up and still with the innards in. If it weren't for the precious tenderloins, I wouldn't have to gut it at all. But those two tender loins are like twin veins gold in this meat-mine, so I open the belly, scoop out the gurgling viscera downstream of the diaphragm, and make the four long cuts by Braille, my hands submerged in pooled blood.

OK, all that's left now is the "necropsy." Yes, quite so. But if I stay out here in this rain much longer, they'll be necropsying me. Dead tired. Dangerously close to hypothermia. Couldn't determine much of anything anyhow in this dark and that mess ... to hell with it, we're outta here.

I wipe and resheath my knife, wrap the mountain of meat in my Space blanket — minus the backstraps and tenderloins, which, mindful that bears are about, I stuff into my hunting pack — stagger up and out of the gully, and down the mountain home.

It's nearly a week — handsome little rack on cabin wall, freezer and belly both bulging with fresh elk meat — before it enters my feeble mind that the scavengers will have long since finished and gone, and if any part of the first arrow remained in the elk, it should be there, somewhere, in the bottom of the gully.

And so I make the familiar climb yet again. And when I get there, there it lies: seven inches of shaft broadhead, still "shaving-sharp."

And that's how you kill the same elk twice.

I hope you never have to.

Chapter Nine

One Perfect Arrow

After a night's seamless sleep — aided by two, *maybe* it was three celebratory shots of old friend George Dickel — I hit the mountain at dawn. With me I have one sturdy young friend and two pack frames, all the better to retrieve my family's winter's meat. (No stinking ATV needed or wanted.) By leaving the hide and head behind, we'll have the bone-in quartered bull down in just two physically demanding yet personally gratifying trips.

As we approach the killing spot, a riot of ravens flares up from the gut pile, flapping heavily, screaming their objection to our interruption. Already, the word is out. The single pair that circled impatiently last evening, as I raced against dark and dying flashlight batteries to get the bull skinned, quartered, and bagged, has grown overnight to a dozen. With more, no doubt, headed this way. Ravens just can't keep a secret.

While we search for the lethal arrow, I recount for young Dan (and myself) the high points of the hunt — how I hunkered in evening ambush as the spooky 5x5 cautiously came to water, then sent him an arrow from fourteen paces. The bushwhacked bull made it only thirty yards before bulldozing into a tree and crumpling, dead.

As I'm reminiscing, Dan finds the arrow perched improbably atop a snarl of brush: full-shaft blooded and slightly bowed, but still in shooting shape — that good old hickory wood. While deconstructing the bull last night, I noted with grateful amazement that the slender, single-blade broadhead had slipped in neatly between ribs, deflated both lungs, slashed the aortic arch atop the huge heart and severed an off-side rib on exit. And now, after all of that, I've only to wash away the blood, straighten the shaft, retouch the head, and refletch — and she's ready to hunt again.

With Dan's help, the pack-out goes quickly, assuring that before another sunset this generous gift of meat will be cut, wrapped, and stashed somewhere cold and dark.

Certainly, this isn't the biggest bull I've ever bagged. But that wasn't my goal and measured by what counts most at this self-reflective point, so deep into my hunting life — clean kills and honorable memories — he is the best.

Looking back down my long bowhunting trail, the way is littered with error and pain. No worse than most hunters and better than many, yet, my kills have not always been perfect and a nightmarish few, as we have seen, were the farthest thing from perfection. This bothers me a lot. Consequently, just one perfect arrow — arrow after arrow, kill after kill, year after year — *that's* the trophy I'm stalking these days.

A "perfect" arrow, by my lights, is any arrow that kills fast and clean. A perfect arrow of course presumes perfected personal shooting skills — form, range estimation, timing, anchor, aim, release, follow-through; all those picky little puzzle-pieces that come together only after hours and years of devoted practice — plus solid judgment and saintly self-control when the heat is really on.

Yet a perfect arrow also mandates a perfect *arrow*. Perfect, that is, for the bow, the shooter, and the prey. In searching for arrow perfection to suit my particular needs — killing elk fast, with a medium-weight recurve or longbow at close quarters — I've talked to countless fellow hunters, studied the opinions and formulas of sundry techsperts and, most important, paid good heed to what has and has not worked for me in the woods.

But the influence that ultimately led me to my personal perfect arrow was my bowyer friend Milt Beens, whom we've already met, It was Milt who made and convinced me to shoot Old Hickory, 738 steel-driving grains of near-instant death. In its first use, in a rib-hit young bull, death came in just five seconds. That bull enjoyed a far quicker end than many I've seen hard-hit with rifles — empirical confirmation of our new motto: "Heavy arrows for heavy game."

My hope here and now is also to convince you that Milt is right. It's a controversial topic, to which some archers, feeling somehow threatened, react as defensively as if you'd called their kids butt-ugly. But for the sake of the suffering and lost game that can potentially be saved, let us run that risk.

For much of my early elking career, since moving here to the San Juan Mountains of southwest Colorado in 1980, my "tool kit" comprised a custom recurve pulling sixty-four pounds, slinging 540-grain arrows at 175 feet per second. Sometimes I used cedar shafts with single-blade (flat) heads; more often, since I didn't trust my sharpening skills, I went for screw-in replaceable-blade heads, mandating aluminum shafts. Thus equipped, I killed and recovered more than a dozen elk and as many more muleys. While I often got pass-throughs and near-instant kills on deer, no such luck with elk. It seemed that my fate was always to hit bone, prompting many blood-trailing nightmares and, damn me, two unrecovered bulls. Both of the latter began with perfect shot placement on close, broadside or quartering-off animals, but perplexingly poor penetration leading to one-lunged, strong-running elk and thin blood trails.

A one-lung hit is never fast, never pretty, and never certain. Double-lung penetration is essential to quick kills and ethical bowhunting. Double-lung/heart with pass-through is the perfection we are after. And the keys to deep penetration, I've finally become convinced, are precise shooting (forward and low, lung/heart), heavy arrows, and sharp flat heads. For years, Milt had praised the superior lethality of this combo. But, like most archers today, mesmerized by the glittering promise of high speed, low trajectory, and their collective advantage of a few extra yards of accuracy, I didn't really listen.

Then came that fateful "Come *On!*" morning when Milt arrowed a reluctantly cooperative 6x5 bull from nine yards. The 125-grain, single-blade head — powered by a heavy fir shaft Milt had hand-carved from an old porch step — slashed through both lungs and the heart, lodging hard in an off-side rib. The bull never made it out of sight ... and you can't see far in an old-growth forest.

As we worked to convert elk to elk meat, Milt casually mentioned that the longbow he was carrying that day pulled "barely fifty pounds" at his draw length. Incredulous, I blurted out something rude, like: "If I'd known you were shooting a *toy* bow, I wouldn't have called in this bull for you." Milt just smiled, patted his elk and held up the broken shaft, stained crimson to its wild-turkey feathers.

"Toy?" my friend echoed back to me. "Certainly, I'd never use *less* than fifty pounds for elk. But compared to other considerations, draw weight doesn't mean so much when it comes to killing. *Penetration* kills. And the driving force behind penetration is *momentum*. And the heart of momentum isn't bow weight, arrow speed, or even energy, but arrow *mass*. A heavy shaft tipped with a sharp single-blade head, even when shot at relatively slow speed from a relatively light bow — *that's* your elk-killer. More bow weight is a plus, and so is more arrow speed. But beyond reasonable minimums, neither is mandatory. And without sufficient momentum, neither is enough. Heavy arrow, flat broadhead, close shot: that's the ticket."

Milt went on to bemoan the fact that so many of the replaceable-blade broadheads dominating the market today, propelled by muscular compound bows and fast, light arrows, tend to fail on impact with bone — component blades break, bend or come out, or head breaks off at attachment with shaft — reducing and often negating their penetration and killing power. "Single-lung hits are generally the best you can expect when heavy bone meets fragile broadhead. And the odds of hitting bone are always high."

Indeed, it seems today that the idea of the "extended-range advantage" of light arrows, fast heavy bows, low trajectory, and high energy has become more important than the reality of how poorly such zippy combos often perform on sturdy game and the senseless suffering they cause, especially when shot from the energy-bleeding extended ranges they pretend to provide. With thin-skinned, light-boned, small-bodied "big" game — such as pronghorn, deer, and even caribou — component heads and light arrows can be deadly. In fact, for all such lighter game I use lighter shafts. But such huge, heavy-boned, hard-to-die beasts as elk and moose demand and deserve something more. (The use of open-on-impact heads on elk and moose borders on pathological carelessness.)

Deeply impressed with what I'd seen and heard that day afield with Milt, I was hot to give heavy a go — until Murphy's law intervened. Thanks to increasing shoulder pain, I was obliged to drop my bow weight by a honking ten pounds — from sixty-four to fifty-four. My VA docs called it "degenerative bone disease." By any name it's arthritis, and it hurts.

After selling my old bow to a friend, I asked Milt to order a sixty-inch takedown recurve from custom bowyer Pat Ley, whose Sleybows have no equal in my experience for smooth draw and lack of stack or hand-shock — three critical advantages to a sore-boned old traditionalist. But since I'd lost so much bow weight, and notwithstanding the lighter Sleybow shot ten feet per second faster than its heavier predecessor, I was afraid to add more arrow weight to the mix. Besides, I rationalized, the 540-grain shafts I'd always shot were hardly lightweights, at least compared to the 350-grain graphite darts so popular with the speedhead crowd. Maybe, I dangerously dared to hope, the increased speed I'd gained, alone, would turn the tide and lessen my wounding rate.

With a couple of weeks no-shooting rest, a reduced practice regimen, and the lighter bow — inscribed "Elkheart" by Pat — the shoulder calmed down and I found myself staring at a broadside raghorn the very first evening of elk season, calmly feeding at thirteen yards. But as had so often happened before, the arrow hit a rib going in, limiting penetration to half-shaft. The speed I'd gained hadn't, it seemed, helped at all when a rib got in the way. Fortunately, aiming low and forward, I'd pricked the heart as well. Even so, I was forced to watch as the bull, after running only a few yards, stopped, stood his ground, swayed for a while then fell, having stoically bled to death. Tragically, a follow-up shot was impossible (you'd best believe I tried to arrange it). But the end came fairly fast and the animal seemed more confused than pained while waiting, flicking his ears at flies and looking around. What a roller-coaster ride of emotions!

To some, I often fear to most hunters, any dead animal equals a successful hunt, no matter how hard it dies. To me, on the heels of the previous and far more painful "same bull twice" episode, this slow death was gut-wrenching. I don't need that kind of hunting "success." I don't want that kind of memories. I can't stomach poorly killed meat. Something had to change ... and that something was me.

And so it came to pass that I finally took Milt's advice and went with heavy arrows and flat, 130-grain (and later, 145-grain) heads, which I filed to chisel-points (more inclined to slide off an edge-hit bone and less likely to bend than a thin-tapered tip), and then had professionally sharpened.

One perfect arrow, at long last.

By happy coincidence, a year after Milt had bagged his 6x5, and a year before Old Hickory and I finally teamed up, a series of articles was launched in *Traditional Bowhunter Magazine* that scientifically confirmed Milt's experience-based heavy-arrow convictions and a whole lot more. Allow me, in summary, to recap.

The author of the series was Dr. Ed Ashby, who had been personally involved in the most realistic and useful bowhunting lethality research ever conducted — the now-famous Natal study, carried out in the mid-1980s under the auspices of the Natal Parks Board, South Africa. Across two years, necropsies (animal autopsies) were performed and records were carefully compiled on hundreds of big game bow kills, ranging from hundred-pound African antelope to half-ton zebra, all taken in fair chase hunts using various broadheads, arrow weights, compounds as well as stickbows, and involving every conceivable shot placement and angle.

Additionally, Ashby and fellow researchers used heavy bows to pound the thirty-two then-most-common broadhead designs a total of 154 times into the scapulas of freshly killed, still-warm and whole animals—mostly zebra, which easily approximate the musculature and bone density of big bull elk — thus attaining the truest and most useful rating of relative broadhead strength-penetration-lethality capabilities extant. Here's a summary of several significant points arising from the Natal study:

1. "Replaceable-blade heads," Ashby reports, "are four times more likely to be damaged [on striking bone] than a rigid single-blade head." And "single-blade heads penetrate both soft tissues and bone better than any multi-blade head [component or rigid]."

2. With unintentional spine hits, the kill rate was "over 80 percent" for single-blade heads … as opposed to 0 percent for component/multi-blades.

3. Of ten rib (entrance) hits with flat heads, average penetration was 19 inches, earning 100 percent lethality … contrasted to 33 percent lethality for three-blade heads on a sample of three animals, with the deepest penetration only 14 inches.

4. For maximum strength and penetration, of all broadhead designs available today, Ashby recommends single-blade heads having a three-to-one length-to-width ratio (one inch wide by three inches long is optimal), constructed of high-quality carbon steel with a Rockwell hardness of 49 to

55 (softer tends to bend; harder is brittle and may break). And the heavier, the better.

5. Overall and in general, Ashby recommends 650 grains of arrow weight (combined shaft and head) as a minimum for heavy game.

6. To assure reliable lethality in the event of a bone (entrance) hit on big game, Ashby calculates that an arrow must deliver at least .57 pound-seconds of momentum. Bow-weight/arrow-speed combinations achieving that minimum include:

450 grains @ 285 fps
550 grains @ 234 fps
740 grains @ 161 fps

Compare that to your own big game combo. My old 540 @ 175 rig fell far short. Although Old Hickory and Elkheart, at 738 @ 159, just manage to cut Ashby's minimum pound-second mustard, they whack through elk ribs like straws, suggesting some leeway in the formula. (To suggest one possible variable here, it's unlikely that the stopping power of elk and zebra bone is identical.)

7. Because a slender shaft creates less friction passing through bone and flesh, Ashby urges using arrows no larger in diameter than the broadhead's ferrule and preferably smaller. In tests with all else being equal, shafts with larger-than-ferrule diameters achieved 33 percent less penetration than ferrule-diameter shafts, and 40 percent less than smaller-than-ferrule shafts. This is plenty enough to make the critical difference between one-lung wounds and double-lung kills. Restated: Avoid fat arrows.

Although the Natal study, per se, is history, Ed Ashby is still kicking, still hunting on three continents, and still on the cutting edge of arrow lethality research. In his most recent study results, he includes forward-of-center (FOC) shaft weighting as another element of maximizing penetration. While tapered shafts, footed shafts, and weighted inserts for hollow shafts all can be happily employed to increase FOC, the easiest way for most of us is simply to increase broadhead weight. For my part, with my mid-weight bows, I now shoot 145s exclusively.

Hickory as an arrow wood is frankly an anomaly. I like it because it offers both strength and mass in a slender shaft: Old Hickory is an 11/32 x 5/16, tapered for FOC. Shafts of compressed cedar, maple, and other more traditional arrow woods offer similar slimness, but lack the density and weight.

We all "know" that arrows kill by bleeding. And true enough — when it comes to that. In fact, an arrow that kills by bleeding is a less-than-perfect arrow. Granted, countless elk and other big game have quickly met their end when a sharp broadhead pierced the heart or cut a major vessel. Moreover, death by massive hemorrhaging is not apparently painful (another argument for another time) and comes fairly fast. Problem is, in the realm of death-dealing, "fairly" fast is way too slow. In bowhunting, nothing short of double-lung penetration will do — low and forward, optimally with full-shaft pass-through, resulting in the instant collapse of both lungs and oxygen starvation of the brain. My five-second bull would never have died so well from bleeding alone.

"Heavy arrows for heavy game."

For all its superficial attractions, speed is a flawed and thus potentially cruel standard by which to measure an arrow's penetration/killing power on elk-sized game. One problem is that in calculating kinetic (moving) energy, arrow speed is squared, making speed appear far more important than weight ... and that's the lie that leads us astray. The weakness of kinetic energy is its ephemerality, dissipating fast in flight, faster in hair and flesh, and real fast in heavy bone. Conversely, in calculating momentum, speed and mass are equal partners, providing a far more accurate predictor of inertial tenacity and projectile sturdiness, thus of penetration, thus of fast death. Consider this analogy, as far-fetched as it seems:

Since bugling is a form of competitive advertising among rutting elk, the farther a bugle can be heard — let's call this feature "sound penetration" — the larger listening audience it will reach. Because the North American wapiti evolved in a largely open environment (Berengia), natural selection favored a high-frequency "whistle" that carries well across open terrain. Contrarily, the call of the European elk, or red deer, has been adapted for dense forests, where flimsy, high-pitched sounds are readily absorbed or deflected by the "meat and bones" of foliage and trees. Therefore, to maximize the range of its calls, the red deer stag evolved a lower-frequency "roar" that rumbles and rolls through all obstructions. The wapiti's whistle in this analogy, like a light fast arrow, can be said to have high kinetic energy. The red deer's roar, like a slower, much heavier arrow, has momentum. Each works well *in its intended niche*. Neither works so well out of context.

It's much the same in hunting, with bullets as well as arrows: For long shots on light game, speed and energy offer flatter trajectory and enhanced accuracy and thus predict success. But for close shots on thick-skinned, massive-boned, heavily muscled, hard-dying elk, moose, and suchlike, the magic's in momentum. To assure double-lung penetration on brutish game, we need brutish force, not bantam speed. We need heavy arrows, even at the cost of increased trajectory and decreased range of accuracy. Lest we forget in the face of all the high-tech hype: getting close is what traditional bowhunting is all about.

With the setup detailed here, by increasing my arrow weight 198 grains, I sacrificed only five yards of reliable accuracy. Considering the slam-dunk lethality and attendant peace of mind I've gained, that's one fair trade.

But enough. My ears are already burning with outraged protests, such as: "I've killed tons of elk meat with light arrows and component heads." Likely you have. And likely (a) your lethal arrows got lucky and didn't hit bone, and/or (b) your kills were not so fast and your blood trails not so short and bright as you might have wished, and/or/and (c) you're conveniently forgetting about those elk you hit and lost along the way. No one is proclaiming that clean kills on elk-sized game never happen unless you're following Ed Ashby's advice. But exceptions don't prove the rule and we are saying that clean kills on heavy game are far more likely when using the Ashby formula of heavy arrow, sturdy slender two-blade heads, slender shafts, and notable FOC.

And too, you might object, component broadheads have improved greatly since the time of the Natal study. Well, yes and no. Some test heads are no longer in production; others remain essentially unchanged; and new heads hit the market every year, bad as well as good. But no real matter when you recall that *no* multi-blade head, whether component or fixed-blade, and no matter the number of blades or "the presence or absence of any 'bone-breaker' tip" (Ashby), proved as sturdy or offered as much penetration as did flat heads in the Natal study. Moreover, Ashby's most recent and ongoing studies, using the most advanced and contemporary heads, reconfirm the Natal results right clean down the line.

Of course, that one clean pass-through and near-instant kill *could* have been an anomaly. Fearing the same myself, come the next elk season I once again had Old Hickory on the string — the selfsame arrow I'd used the year before, being one of a matched baker's dozen Milt had made for me. And sure enough, when finally I got my shot, things *did* turn out differently ... that is, even better. This time I let fly at a mature cow from eleven yards, getting precisely the same double-lung/aorta shot I'd scored on the bull, except this time the arrow severed ribs both entering and exiting. And this time, the animal made it only fifteen yards before stumbling, doing a rodeo flip haunches-over-head, and sighing her last, having literally never known what hit her. It took a whole *three seconds*. And most amazing of all, Old Hickory survived intact yet again. This fall, I hope to get my third pass-through with that same resilient shaft — though I can hardly hope for a faster kill.

In conclusion, it's an indisputable if not at all simple matter of physics. And physical rules are not defined by their exceptions. For deeper penetration, faster kills, shorter blood trails, and happier memories, The Rule — as writ by the laws of physics and confirmed by Ed Ashby's unimpeachable scientific studies as well as a massive body of direct observation by a growing number of trad bowhunters — is simply this: "Heavy arrows for heavy game."

Postscript: Since writing the above I've hunted a couple more elk seasons and talked to a lot more bowhunters. I have also — at long last and with the exacting guidance of my personal physician — started carving my own bows from Osage orange, hickory, and bamboo, hunting with them almost exclusively. The notably slower speeds of arrows launched from these all-wood bows have forced me to rethink my Old Hickory stance. Too much of even the best thing is still too much. I now believe that hickory poles as heavy as I was shooting from a very fast custom recurve at exceedingly close-range (fifteen yards and under) are likely a bit *too* heavy for typical traditional bowhunting needs requiring utterly reliable accuracy out to twenty yards. Depending on the bow and its shooter, arrows exceeding 700 grains frequently can't deliver the necessary accuracy. Yet an average twenty-nine-inch cedar shaft with 145-grain broadhead weighs 555 grains tops, which for elk and moose, given the likelihood of a rib entrance hit, is simply not enough *umph* to assure pass-throughs.

Given sufficient practice, any dedicated archer shooting a recurve or longbow of fifty pounds or more can accurately sling arrows in the 600-650 grain category, out to twenty yards. This year, after nearly twenty years of applying, I finally drew a coveted Colorado moose tag, and what I'll be shooting at that thousand-pound (or bigger!) bull is sixty-seven inches and fifty-seven pounds of Osage orange selfbow powering 655 grains of wood behind a 145-grain two-blade head. At twenty yards and under, this combo provides a workable compromise between a draw weight I can accurately handle, dependable accuracy, and lethal penetration.

If I prove myself wrong and survive the Great Moose Adventure to tell about it, I'll be sure to let you know.

Chapter Ten

Wallowing in It

At the base of a densely forested, east-facing slope, at a place I call Hillside Spring, a shallow pool of potable water sits hidden in afternoon shade. Since this bathtub-sized pond represents a third of all the water on Spring Mountain, it attracts elk, deer, bears, turkeys, squirrels, and more, plus their predators big and small, including sometimes me.

When groundwater is abundant and the pool's capacity is breached, the overflow trickles half the length of a football field down a narrow, green, tunnel-like lane beneath old-growth aspens, ponderosa pine, and fir, before sinking back into the ground to reemerge half a mile farther down the mountain at double-pooled Bear Spring. At the terminus of the Hillside seep lies a shallow depression that rutting bulls excavated years ago as a mud bath. I call it Big Wallow, and it's at the center of my wapiti world.

If walking into the breeze and not smoking a cigar, you should smell a recently used elk wallow well before you see it. And what you'll see when you get there is a shallow muddy depression perforated with cloven hoof tracks as big as a big man's palm and those tracks filled with oily-looking, funky-smelling water. Size varies wildly, though most elk wallows I've encountered here in Colorado are no larger than a single bed. While most hereabouts are secluded in dense forest, wallows also appear along the edges of secluded marshy meadows. The common denominator is shallow standing water or good juicy mud.

Examine the muddy edges of a fresh wallow and you'll often see detailed impressions of coarse neck-mane hair, where a bull has rolled and rocked, coating himself with muck. As to *why* they do this — until recently it remained a mystery to biological science, if not to experienced woodsmen. Old-time logic held that since most wallowing is done during the day and early in the rut — which runs mid-August to mid-October on average, peaking in late September depending on latitude — the heat-intolerant animals wallow primarily to cool off. An alternate theory posited that elk wallow to coat their hides with mud for protection from biting bugs. These remained popular myths for decades, no matter the obvious facts that elk have hair too thick for all but the biggest and baddest bugs to bite or sting through, rendering mud armor redundant, and that rutting bulls wallow no matter the weather, even if they have to break through a crust of ice.

Likewise, neither cooling nor armoring explains why only bulls wallow and only during the rut, nor why bigger bulls wallow more. Nor did either assumption address the greatest enigma of all: Why do elk foul their mud baths, and themselves, by urinating in the mess and rolling in it?

This final mystery, it turns out, suggests its own solution: The whole *purpose* of wallowing is to get good and piss-stinky. For anyone who's ever witnessed bull elk wallowing and smelled bull elk in rut, it seems there should be no doubt regarding the wallow-stink connection. Yet, even the father of modern elk biology, Olaus J. Murie, missed this critical link. In his 1951 classic, *Elk of North America*, Murie nicely updates and expands the then-traditional cooling/armoring beliefs when he writes of the wallow that: "Its purpose seems to be the soothing of the rutting fever, a cooling for the body, an outlet for pent-up energy."

And yet, no mention of the perfuming function.

Males of all five species of the North American deer family (caribou, wapiti, moose, mule and white-tailed deer) experience an annual puberty. Following the rut each winter, the testicles shrink to about half their rutting size — a defensive adaptation that bicycle racers and other male human athletes might well envy. As the rut approaches, testosterone floods the blood. This annual hormonal surge is timed by photoperiod, or seasonal daylight, as metered through the animal's eyes and reacted to by hormone-producing glands. Thus chemically stimulated, the testicles swell anew and lust again awakens. At the same time, the rutting bull's urine becomes saturated with pheromones — natural perfumes, as it were, ripe with information for rival bulls as well as estrous cows. As the rut progresses toward the mating finalé, the flaunting of pheromones becomes an impressively elaborate production, culminating in and maximized by the ritual wallow. Something like so ...

As the day begins to warm, the bedded bull becomes increasingly agitated. So early in the rut, the cows he lusts after aren't yet ready to mate — that must wait for late September and early October. Meanwhile, to be certain that no breeding opportunity is missed, mature bulls are gathering cows and monitoring them frequently for signs of approaching ovulation. As breeding time nears, both genders carry strong chemical messages in their urine. To "download" this information, a tending bull will stick his nose into a cow's urine stream and curl his upper lip so that sensory receptors in his palate can "read" the urine's aroma for an indication of the female's breeding status. In the process, the lip-curling bull exposes his teeth in a bizarre gesture known to biologists as the Flehmen grimace. (Other deer and horses do much the same.)

Meanwhile, with every passing day, the bull's testosterone poisoning becomes increasingly erosive to his mood. Bugling helps to vent the steam, at the same time advertising his confidence and mood to cows and rival bulls. Another steam-venting and advertising caper is "horning." This involves engaging his towering antlers — mature bull elk commonly attain four feet or more in antler length, another four feet in spread between main beams, with six long tines sprouting from either side — against young Christmas trees, debarking and killing the helpless saplings. But every now and again, nothing will do but a good pissy wallow.

As the bull nears his wallow, he vacuums the air with nervous nostrils, testing for any scent that might suggest the presence of danger — a bigger bull, a mountain lion or bear, you or me. Detecting no threat, the seven-hundred-pound deer plods deliberately to the edge of the pool, where he stops again and looks around — big ears swiveling to absorb every chirp of bird, every mousy rustle of grass or brush. Assured he's safely alone, he steps into the wallow and touches his nose to the mud then raises his head and bemusedly licks the muddied orb, contemplating some secret knowable only to his kind.

The wallowing ceremony formally begins when the bull proclaims aloud his presence and intent — though not always with a bugle. Bugling is a song best saved for times when the animal is undistracted and can be fully alert. Rather, for this special occasion, the bulls I've watched at wallows greatly prefer to open the ceremony with a staccato string of coughing, high-pitched chuckles, not unlike a mulish bray: *Unh-a-unh-a-unh-a-unh!* In other circumstances, this distinctive utterance may follow a particularly eloquent bugle. But at the wallow it's more often used alone. Why? My best guess is that a chuckle is lower both in tone and volume than a bugle, so it doesn't carry so far to reveal the bull's location to competing bulls or lurking predators, any of whom might well sneak in to rudely molest the wallower's privacy and security while he's distracted with bathing.

After the first good chuckle, the bull listens for a response, which (it seems safe to assume) he hopes is not forthcoming. After a while he lowers his huge, elongated head down between his front legs so that his chin is facing back and his antlers are almost touching the ground in front. Thus positioned, when he chuckles again, the rhythmic palpitations of his abdomen, which serve to power and punctuate the vocals, also facilitate a cadenced throbbing of the erect, front-pointing penis. So it is that with each chuckling vocal throb, the big rutter sprays a jet of pheromone-impregnated urine onto himself, coating belly, chest, front legs, and under-chin, with special attention to the luxurious growth of mane hair carpeting the lower throat, the dandiest of stinky-water sponges. Incredibly, the bull can even aim his stream hard left or right, assuring extensive coverage of his entire undercarriage. Once he's thoroughly soaked, with urine having dripped, dribbled, and been sprayed into the mud below, the bull flops down and rolls in apparent joy, legs kicking the air like a horse just unsaddled, methodically coating himself with the black oily muck.

This ancient pre-courtship ceremony may last from several minutes to an hour or more and generally includes stabbing at the damp soil in and around the wallow with antler tines, thus expanding the diameter of the wallow pond while coating his antlers with pheromone-laden mud and vegetation. For the grand finale, the rancid, dripping, crud-encrusted dandy stands, shakes like a wet dog—once you know what it sounds like, you can identify the loud and leathery *flop-slap flop-slap-flop* of wet slapping mane hair from a hundred yards away — then tromps to a nearby tree, hereabouts most often an aspen, and vigorously rubs his piss-muddy neck against the smooth-barked trunk—marking the wallow as his very private own.

On departing — no longer concerned with maintaining his wallowing privacy, but rather wanting to advertise his accomplishments — our boy can rarely resist offering up a long, satisfied bugle. That done, the cock-o-the-walk melts back into the sheltering forest to seek out a shaded day-bed and chew on a good wad of cud, awaiting the evening's excitement to come.

Chapter Eleven

Evolution of a Trophy Hunter

Across four years, many years ago, I was a dead-serious trophy hunter. The obsession lasted that long only because that's how long it took to get it done, thus out of my ego and off my back.

Which is not to say it wasn't fun.

Since the first rule of trophy hunting is not to shoot any animal except the trophy you're after — thereby ending your hunting and sending you packing home — the hunting is generally prolonged and, thereby, so are its challenges and rewards. Across those four superhumanly patient, bloodless autumns, I was rewarded with several close encounters with bears ... a bemused pine marten that let me approach to within a handful of yards as it sniffed up and down a hollow, half-fallen aspen snag searching for a way to get at the terrified rodent he knew to be quivering within ... the death squeaks of white-footed mice on a quiet cold morning when an industrious long-tailed weasel killed one after another of the plentiful rodents, packing each of the tiny corpses over a downed log at my feet, back to her hungry den ... ravens that twice and in no uncertain terms advised me of approaching game (a near-mystical experience I've enjoyed repeatedly but only on my backyard mountain and have yet to come fully to intellectual grips with) ... elk by the dozens within stickbow range, which I watched and contemplated rather than killing ... and the proverbial "a whole lot more."

"Incidental" encounters such as these account in good measure for my lifelong dedication to bowhunting, and help as well to ease the pain of blowing one self-styled "trophy" hunt after another.

David Petersen

For a memorable instance: In 1991, the year I declared myself a trophy hunter, having determined just once in my life to kill an elk with really big antlers (generally if not always, the meat's just as good), my friend Bruce Woods flew out from Ohio to hunt elk during the muzzle-loading rifle season, which runs for nine days smack in the middle of bow season here. Bruce arrived the evening before his season opened and I took him with me on my evening bow hunt. There, my one-man audience hunkered in the root crater of a fallen tree while I moved on another few yards and took a seat on a wooded hillside overlooking the little hidden pool I call Hillside Spring.

All was quiet until an hour before dark, when we heard a nearby crack of limb. I nodded at Bruce, pulled up the camo facemask that I wear like a scarf around my neck, and strung an arrow. A minute later here came a picture-perfect 6x6, headed in to water. But as the giant deer approached my shooting zone, he unexpectedly veered up the hill and started walking toward me along a prominent game trail, above which I had chosen to sit. The bull was coming fast and head-on, and everything was against me getting a clean shot. So I didn't even try. At a half-dozen paces the bull finally caught my ugly human scent, whirled and thundered away.

Bruce was elated. While he'd hunted from Alaska to Africa, this was the first wild elk he'd ever seen, and he'd almost seen it trample me.

Next morning, I left Bruce and his smoke pole to guard Hillside Spring, hoping last night's bull would return to quench his thirst. I then slipped along another quarter-mile to Wapiti Spring.

Two hours into the morning, growing drowsy with inaction, I heard a vigorous crashing of limbs and a rhythmic panting and looked up to see last evening's bull inbound on the trot. At the spring pool he splashed right in and began loudly slurping water. Here was one thirsty elk — and one badly rattled elk hunter. Convinced he would leave as abruptly as he'd come, I raised my recurve and jerked it back to full draw, causing the wood arrow to fall off the shelf and clank against the handle. The bull heard this tiny noise and couldn't have left faster if he'd been shot from a rocket launcher. Neither Bruce nor I ever saw him again.

And so it went. Another year passed, and most of another elk season, the final afternoon of which I spent waiting in ambush for a husky-sounding bugler, as yet unseen, whose movements I'd patterned (by ear) over the previous several days. Like so: About two hours before dusk each evening, he'd issue a peculiar sounding bugle from his bedding area — like a dog yawning — then start feeding down the mountain with his harem of cows, singing every few minutes, finding his voice as he went. About a hundred yards above my ground hide, he'd strike the lightly timbered rim of a low ridge across a dry gully from me, where he'd spend the rest of the evening marching back and forth, bugling almost continuously, while his girls fed and mewed nearby. Same timing, same ridge, same pattern every night.

But the stubborn fellow steadfastly refused to come down off his parade ground and cross the narrow gully to my calls. At the same time, crackly ground litter, fickle breezes, the approach of darkness and the impossibility of climbing up out of the gully undetected kept me from attempting to stalk him. Earlier in the season, while I still had the luxury of time on my side, patience had been my strategy. Now I was running out of both.

And so it came to pass, on the final afternoon of the season, that I climbed the mountain early, crossed the gully and scaled the bull's bugling ridge. There, I snooped around and found a hide that offered good concealment, clear shooting lanes, and a predictable descending evening breeze to carry my scent back down into the gully and away from the approaching bull. Who, if he stuck to his established routine, should pass within a dozen yards. Smug and expectant, I settled in to wait.

After a long quiet time and more or less on schedule, I heard the familiar dog-yawn wake-up bugle. But this evening, as the bull sang his way toward me, a second bugler sounded a challenge from not far up the mountain. No problem, I figured. This new boy could be expected to work his way down to my ridge to check out the resident bull, and I'd have them both in my lap and distracted by one another.

Of course, "stuff happened." Instead of the challenger coming to the champ, the champ went to the challenger, leaving me high and dry. With only half an hour of daylight left, I decided to run a stalk on the now-battling bulls, who I could hear screaming and snorting and clanking antlers in an aspen grove a quarter-mile up the way. As I neared, and just as I began to think I actually had a chance … an unseen sentry cow barked.

Once again and as usual, I walked down the mountain and home empty-handed, in the dark. So ended my second year of trophy hunting.

David Petersen

During the last week of August, 1993, Mike Murphy invited me to accompany him to his high-country elk camp. In return for my helping him get camp ready for the arrival of his first shift of archery clients, Mike said he'd find the time to show me some elk. I always enjoy horse packing and Mike's cheerful Irish company, not to mention his superb camp cooking and a promising shot at a big bull, so I pounced on the offer.

As it turned out, we wound up with just one evening to hunt. But *what* an evening! It was so early in the season that I had yet to hear the first bugle on my backdoor mountain. But altitude makes a difference and Mike maneuvered us into the midst of a veritable cacophony of rutting wapiti. I counted what I thought to be a dozen different buglers within hearing. But Mike, always conservative, allowed as how there were "probably only six or eight."

By any count, it was a real animal house, and we were in the bedroom. At one point, I feared we'd be trampled by a run-away cow and the bull that came stampeding down the hill to haze her back into his harem. There were so many bulls competing in such a small area that none would move off his little patch of ground to physically challenge another. Nor would any of them come to us, though it was Mike's expert calling that had started the riot and was helping to keep it going. For fear of spooking the whole lot, we couldn't risk a stalk. So we just sat there and enjoyed the concert until dark. As we were slipping out, a confused spike bull, apparently taking us for a couple of stray cows, dogged us close for half a mile, tooting his tenor horn all the while.

Next morning, Mike's hunters rode in and I rode out — back to my lonesome quest for the apparently unattainable.

And so had gone my trophy quest, for three consecutive years: thrill after thrill, failure after failure. Happily, I was always able to pick up a mule deer buck to keep the freezer from starving. But that was then, and this is now, year four of my fruitless quest, Labor Day evening, as it happens, and here I am, out and about and at it again.

Why — I ask myself this question every time I decline a close sure shot at a cow or young bull — how did I get myself into this self-denial business? And why have I stuck with it for so long? Perplexing questions, especially in light of my disgust for the egocentric species of hunter the tag "trophy hunter" too often describes. But of course I have my reasons

—much the same reasons, in fact, that prompt me to hunt with recurves and longbows. Some things in life — friendship and marriage, college, the Marine Corps, and hunting jump to mind from personal experience — some things *should* be hard, for in the challenge resides the reward, win or lose. The trip is the destination. The process is the product, frustration you constant enemy.

I've been hunting elk since 1981 and have killed my share. A few more than my share, perhaps, considering the normal success rate for bowhunters is less than 15 percent, including both sexes and those using compound arrow-launching devices with sights and training wheels. Each and every one of my elk was earned with sweat and pain, and all were taken at close range while hunting alone. But then, all to this point have been cows and younger bulls. So, these past four seasons I've been holding out for a personal trophy. Hunting more, killing less, subsisting on venison and post-season road-killed elk.

A blue-black raven appears suddenly overhead, cronking excitedly, its ragged wings moaning eerily with each deep stroke. I have learned what this often signals (for some reason, in some places and only during the fall rut, ravens like to follow and verbally harass elk), and am not the least surprised when, moments later, the woods come alive with the spirited chirping and mewing of wapiti on the move. From the sounds of it, a whole passel of the buggers are headed my way. And this time of year, surely there's a mature bull in the batch. With quiet joy I reenact the ancient primitive ritual of fitting arrow to bowstring.

The chatty herd is approaching from my left, maybe a hundred yards out, scattered among dense timber. Before the first of them comes into view, I hear a nearby resonant knock, like a horse's hoof striking a hollow log, sounding down from the hillside to my right. I shift only my eyes — wait —and there he is. The fruits of my prolonged quest are finally within grasp.

Maybe.

The next minutes play out as if I'd scripted them. The herd bull, traveling ahead of his harem, walks directly to the spring I'm watching and wades right in. He snatches a glance in my direction — I'm hunkered down just thirteen paces from his heaving chest — but fails to see my motionless camouflaged form. He takes one more step forward and his head disappears behind a thick-trunked aspen. His vision in my direction is now totally obscured and I am blessed with an unobstructed broadside target.

Strangely becalmed, I raise the bow and draw, concentrating on a spot low and behind the extended left front leg. As if acting of its own volition, the feather-fletched shaft flashes away and disappears into living flesh.

The bull explodes from the pool in a shower of mud and water. Within seconds he is out of sight, though I can hear him crashing around in a tangle of aspen deadfall nearby ... or maybe that's the rest of the herd in panicked retreat. I reach for the cow call dangling from a lanyard around my neck, squeeze out a couple of passionate bleats ... and low and behold, the bull comes walking back, casual as you please. I sneak another arrow from my bow quiver and prepare for a follow-up shot, but never get the chance. The bull stops, stands for a moment like a statue of himself, then jabs at the sky with his mighty rack of antlers, slumps to the ground, and is quiet.

After four long years of hunting, the killing has taken only a minute.

It's six in the evening with two hours of daylight left as I approach the monster bull. He is lying amidst a snarl of Gambel's oak brush just forty-two paces beyond the spring. For a long time I stand and stare, awestruck.

Looking around, I can find no blood whatsoever. Yet, when I draw my sheath knife and set to work, I find that my broadhead penetrated a heavy rib and went on to puncture both lungs, split the heart and lodge in an off-side rib. By dusk I have the bull eviscerated, excoriated, swaddled in cheesecloth (he requires three "deer" bags) and spread out on my survival blanket to cool.

My night's dreams are wild, fierce and free: ancestral memories from the glorious Pleistocene.

At daybreak I'm back on the mountain to quarter and bag the night-chilled meat, and am relieved that no bear has found it. By midmorning, with the help of a friend and two of Murphy's mules, I'm homebound with meat and antlers. The latter prove too unwieldy to top-load on a packsaddle, so I carry them out. Together, antlers and head must weigh close to fifty pounds, yet they ride light as angel's wings across my shoulders.

I've decided on a skull, a.k.a. European mount — an economical and primitively aesthetic alternative to an expensive and ostentatious head mount, which neither Caroline nor I want in our house. The bull's amber-swirled ivories, or vestigial upper canines, capped in simple sterling, will make elegant earrings for my lovely bride. Little will be wasted.

And so it goes. Within five days of the kill, with the aspens barely tinged in gold, my hard-won wall-hanger is hanging on my wall. The antlers are not only beautiful, they are unique — oddly beaded, sharply ridged, and mildly palmate where tines join main beams — indicators of a borderline post-prime bull. Like me, this old boy was one hoof in the grave but still with an eye for the girls. The cabin is so small and the antlers so huge that Caroline is forever banging her head on the brow tines, while I tend to poke myself with the second level, or bez tines. We can only laugh, calling it "the elk's revenge."

I've been asked by well-meaning friends if I intend to enter this bull — at 313, the first I've taken that qualifies — in the Pope & Young Club bowhunting record book. No thanks. "The book" is for a different sort of "trophy" hunter than me. While a detailed and accurate record of antler sizes, when and where, etcetera, is a useful tool for scientific and wildlife management use, the glory of an exceptional rack belongs to the bull who grew it, not the hunter who ended that bull's career. I have my memories and I have the meat and antlers, and that is plenty enough.

Far more important to me are the four consecutive autumns of hard and true hunting those lovely antlers embody. They were the best years of hunting — the most challenging, educational, and spiritually reward-ing — I've ever known. Maybe will ever know. And fair enough. Should I never kill another "book" elk, I am content. The four-year bull's flesh is now my flesh, and his antlers grace our humble home — not as hat rack or "trophy" in the usual sense, but as a work of fine art sculpted by nature from blood and bone and kept on display for the same reasons we value fine paintings and Caroline's pressed flower and butterfly collections.

And more: Those noble antlers, together with the skull of a large male bear (given to me by a game warden friend) that rests on the man-tle, comprise my personal shrine to a freedom wild and fierce — the elk's, the bear's, and my own.

That was back in 1994. I've taken elk most seasons since, but always for meat, never again for antlers. Yet I still trophy hunt. Only now the trophy I seek is a tender yummy yearling cow or calf: "spoon meat," a hunter friend calls it. Like veal, only without the cruelty attendant to veal production (which is why neither Caroline nor I will eat it).

Although the concept may grate hard against our parental sensitivities, killing calves is a good thing biologically and evolutionarily, thus ethically as well as gastronomically. Close to half of all elk calves (and deer fawns) born each spring will die before or during their first winter. Whether many or few are killed by hunters, studies reveal that the total number of cervid infant deaths changes little if at all, the slack being taken up by predators, illness, winter starvation and traumatic accidents (including collisions with cars driven by anti-hunters). That's the way, you could say, God planned it. Also, as my biologist friend Tom Beck, who refuses to kill big bulls, is wont to proclaim: "We need more prime males out there doing the breeding. They get the job done faster, better, and with far less stress on the cows. And because they've lived several years, they're the winners of the 'survival of the fittest' culling process, with proven good genes and instincts to pass along to future generations."

That sounds, and tastes, just right to me.

Even so, bull bugling, bull wallowing, and that good old funky bull stench beat at the heart of early season elk hunting. That's where the real excitement resides. Would I kill another big bull, should the opportunity arise?

What do you think? Ho!

Chapter Twelve

A Mighty Big Squirrel

O ut here in the elk woods, the strangest things can happen ...

So there we were, my long-haired hunting buddy and I, hunkered in hopeful ambush, waiting for a local elk herd to file past from their day-bedding area a mile above us, headed downhill for another autumn evening of drinking, browsing, and carousing. With good luck (for us, not the elk), they would pass close by our makeshift hide and upwind, along a freshly hoof-churned and encouragingly bull-stinky game trail. The evening sun was soft and low, casting long, eerie shadows across the elk-beige carpet of conifer needles padding the forest floor. Lost in concentration — watching, listening, sniffing the cooling breeze for scent of our prey — I didn't even bother to turn around and look, but merely nodded when Erica leaned close and whispered excitedly, "Wow, I can't see the animal, but if it's even *half* as big as its shadow, that's a *mighty big squirrel!*"

Moments later, when a nearby clump of oak brush began to audibly rattle and shake, I did turn and look. What I saw was a blur of burnt-brown fur, about two feet long and three feet above the ground, though the bulk of the fast-moving creature's body was hidden behind the brush. These San Juan Mountains of southwest Colorado are serious black bear country, notwithstanding a majority of the local blackies are brown, cinnamon, or even blond. Having across the years enjoyed countless close encounters with bears while hunting elk, mule deer, and turkey, intuitively I knew I'd glimpsed the curved rump of a fairly big bear as it moved behind the brush only ten feet away. Now it was my turn to lean close to Erica and excitedly whisper: "*Bear!* Do you have your spray?"

She did, and with the sudden confidence of a magnum canister of oleoresin capsicum hot pepper "bear spray" clasped tight in my right fist — aimed bearward, safety off, thumb on trigger — we sat in rigid silence, staring a hole in the shaking brush, waiting for the beast to reappear, virtually in our laps. And sure enough, moments later, out stepped ...

... a *pine marten*?

Yep. The agile, cat-sized weasel must have leapt from the ground into the tops of the brushy little trees just as I had turned to look, in pursuit of some fleeing prey, no doubt — a chickadee or a chipmunk maybe. The brownish arc of its back and brushy tail had registered in my paranoid mind's eye as the curve of a big bear's butt.

"Well," whispered Erica, snickering cruelly, "there's your 'bear.'"

Darned smart-alecky girl. Fighting to regain my composure, the blush of embarrassment flushing my white-whiskered cheeks, I fired right back in self-offense: "Yeah, and there's your 'mighty big squirrel' too."

"Touché," giggled my hunting buddy.

Out here in the elk woods, the strangest things can happen, even when the elk don't come.

Chapter Thirteen

Failure

Slouching homeward after what would be my last evening of elk hunting for another year, I felt like a shapeless bag of gloom. What rotten luck I'd had all month. Following three weeks of hearing no bugling, seeing few elk and none up close, and enjoying next-to-no action of any kind, I had located an exceptional bull — a big handsome nontypical with misshapen antler tines sticking out every which way. The unique beauty of this bull's rack made it a prize so tempting it caused me to weaken, waver, and re-experience the old trophy-hunting fervor I thought had long since died. While the rest of the wapiti world — including trophy record books, evolutionary biologists, and romantically inclined female elk — rate perfectly symmetrical antlers as the ideal, I feel precisely and strongly the opposite. Symmetry is sameness and sameness is, well, the same. Give me the diversity of variety. Or even the variety of diversity.

In any event, over the next three evenings I gave that bull everything I had — stalking in on his increasingly enthusiastic bugles with the patience and caution (though certainly not the skill) of a puma, then invariably having to back off just as cautiously when the wind or a sentry cow or some other vexing complication got in the way.

Finally, late the third afternoon of the pursuit, and the last day of the season I'd be able to hunt (that old devil work was getting in the way), a combination of luck and determination got me to within twenty yards of the browsing bull, my approach screened by a thick forest understory. He was oblivious: eat-and-step; eat-and-step. But consistent with the way things had been going for me, between the bull's slow movements and mine, we eventually wound up with only a brushy young spruce between us. Expecting the bull to feed clear of the spruce shield at any moment—one more step on his part would do it — and while his head was down, I muscled my sixty-pound longbow back to full draw.

Mistake.

Being no blind fool, the bull caught the movement, stiffened, and looked up. So there we were, my dream bull and me, only twenty yards apart and both of us, so to speak, at full draw. After several seconds of this cataleptic standoff, two things became painfully evident: First, the bull wasn't about to oblige me by stepping clear of the spruce. And second, my arms were trembling under the weight of the bow and about to fold. Something had to give, and pronto.

But what?

To attempt a chest shot through the limby spruce would mean either a broken handmade cedar arrow fletched with the feathers of my spring wild turkey — or, far more likely and infinitely worse — a poorly hit animal and all the misery for both of us that would entail. If I tried to relax my draw — the only other apparent option — the bull was sure to bolt.

Stuck on the horns of a nontypical dilemma, surely I was.

Ever graceless under pressure, I made the impromptu and radical decision to take one long, quick step to my left, thus opening a narrow shooting lane; with luck, my instinctively aimed and released arrow would prove faster than the bull's instinctive wheel-and-run survival response.

Wrong ... *Crash, thud-thud-thud, crash!* ... gone.

At that moment, standing there staring at the hole in my world where the bull had so recently been, realizing my elk hunting was over for another long year, I could physically *feel* the pain of failure — somewhere between heartburn and nausea. And adding fuel to my already burning frustration was the irksome fact that three days still remained in the season — three days that might provide another chance at that gorgeous freak, or at *any* elk for the freezer. Three days of joyful hunting, at the least. But alas, for me this time it was to be three painful, distracted days dealing with unavoidable "real world" obligations.

And so it was that I found myself slumping homeward through the darkling woods, suffering not just the usual letdown attendant to the end of an unsuccessful hunting season, but a loathsome self-pity and generalized anger as well.

My ego, it seemed, had weaseled onto center stage.

Which, in retrospect, both surprises and disappoints me. I've spent decades believing and telling others that hunting should not be a contest, not even with yourself; that success in hunting doesn't ride on something so simple as merely making a kill every year; any lard-butt road-shooter, given luck or a spotlight, can do that much, proving absolutely nothing. Rather, I've long and firmly believed that the heart of the hunt is not in the kill, but in meeting a challenge as old as humanity itself and doing so with honor, humility, and — yes — *joy*. Come what may. If I feel anything other than joy in hunting, I'm doing something wrong.

These are my convictions. Yet, that last evening of the season I'd gone and got myself drunk on emotions and forgotten most of what I knew. Instead of feeling joy I felt resentment. I felt cheated. I felt that my self-image as a damn good bowhunter and woodsman had been unfairly tarnished; I felt I'd *deserved* that bull. And consequently, walking home that last lonesome night I felt ulcers taking root in my guts.

It was just then, at that lowest of low points, that I heard it a dim distant bugle, followed by a barely audible chuckle, sounding from somewhere far up the mountain I'd just come down. "My" bull, no doubt, enjoying the last horselaugh.

That was all; just that single farewell trumpet. But like the magic it is, it instantly stopped and quieted me, and standing there silently, listening, the evening came to life: I heard the hollow subsonic wing-roar of a stooping nighthawk, an eerie sky-sound that shattered and animated the twilight calm. I saw and heard the dry scratching of a huge fat porcupine clawing its slow way up a ponderosa pine. I heard and watched a tree full of twittering chickadees settling in for the night. And while hearing and seeing these things, I felt myself relaxing, the acidic alien in my guts loosening its murderous grip.

Damn, I thought, *what a privilege it is just to be out here in this enchanted forest at the most magical time of day and year. How could I ever have let myself get so pissed-off in such wondrous circumstances?* I had to shake my head and chuckle.

After all, had I not enjoyed the past three weeks and more of sublime September evenings spent alone (the way I like it best) among the aspens and the elk?

And had not the final three evenings of aching excitement, crowned by an adrenaline-charged stalk and protracted face-off with a singularly magnificent bull, been meat for the most golden of memories?

Would I have chosen *not* to have seen the bull, perhaps not even to have hunted at all, had I known beforehand that a kill wasn't in the cards this time?

Not on your life. Nor even on mine.

Yes, I had "failed," and spectacularly so. But my failure was not out there in the elk woods — it was an internal failure, a lapse of conviction, a situational weakening of character.

The lesson I (re)learned from that experience and the roller-coaster ride of emotions it put me on — and the point I'm staggering so drunkenly toward making here—is simply that it's entirely natural, perhaps even unavoidable, to feel frustration and disappointment when an important goal goes unrequited. And particularly so following an exciting close call — like working a five-pound fish on two-pound line and getting it almost to the net where you can see it in all its grandness and beauty … only to have it slip the hook and sink back into the depths. "Far better," we tend to say, "to not have seen it at all."

And so again I am sternly reminded that the key to consistent hunting success — the key I misplaced that last emotional evening — is to keep in mind, always, *why* it is we hunt, and adjust our expectations accordingly. If my motivation for hunting is narrowed to just killing more and/or bigger animals each year, then — in addition to trading honor for ego gratification, love for lust, the slow subtle pleasures of foreplay for the quick finality of climax — I'm setting myself up for a *lot* of hard falls.

If, on the other hand, the real reason I'm out there is to relax, work hard, watch, listen, learn, and overall to enjoy myself as deeply and broadly as possible — quietly rejoicing in the sights, sounds, scents, and solitude of wild nature—then I'm virtually guaranteed of success. Year after joyful year.

This coming season I will *not* fail, no matter the final score.

Chapter Fourteen

A Winter Vacation

With wapiti season long over and longer yet to come again, it had seemed like a good time for a winter hunting vacation. And if only I'd done my pre-hunt homework before leaving home, maybe I'd have known enough about the crafty little desert Coues deer to appreciate the grand gift I'd just wasted. But Christmas had been distracting and I'd had too little time to get my act together. Or so I told myself at the time. While my hunting buddy, Tom Beck, was an old hand at chasing the diminutive desert whitetail, this was my first try.

From our wall-tent camp in the Bootheel of New Mexico, the Arizona border was only five miles west, and Mexico a day's stroll southward. Ghosts of Geronimo and Pancho Villa actively haunt these rocky moonscape hills, and as I was learning, they love to play little tricks.

My troubles started our first night in camp, when, in celebration of New Year's Eve, I tipped a cup of bourbon. Just one, and normally no problem. But I'd just started taking prostate medication and the two chemicals conspired against me, as I would rudely discover sometime in the wee hours, as freezing rain hissed against the canvas of our tent. Awakened by a pressing concern and dressed only in skivvies, I unzipped from my bag and stepped outside. There I stood, pondering the cold sting of rain on my upturned face when a light flashed behind my eyes. Next thing I knew, I was flat on my back on cold broken rock, regaining consciousness. While I was awake enough to know that if I lay there too long I could go hypothermic, I felt oddly comfortable and was unwilling to try and move. "If death is this easy," I recall thinking ...

Just then, a voice from somewhere above broke the dreamlike spell.

"Are you OK, Dave? Thought I heard a noise, like something hitting the ground."

It wasn't St. Peter calling to me, this time, but my light-sleeping tentmate.

I mumbled an incoherent something in response, rolled over onto my stomach, struggled to my knees like a cow standing up, made it somehow to my feet, staggered into the tent, collapsed on my cot, pulled my bag around my chilled-out bod — and promptly blacked out again.

Which is why, come New Year's morning, I wasn't the sharpest arrow in the quiver. Coyotes yapped as Tom and I chugged strong coffee and made ready for the hunt. As always, we went our separate ways.

The rain had stopped sometime before sunrise and by midmorning the desert sun was almost hot, the previously dry air almost muggy. I had pretty much given up and was thinking more about food than hunting when I dropped into a cool, shady arroyo en route back to camp. I was creeping along the grassy bottom in near silence when a creature the color of cloud stood from behind a clump of manzanita a few feet to my left. The silent, silvery spook stared for a skinny instant, then shot up the far side of the ditch and was gone before I could even think about nocking an arrow.

As the adrenaline subsided, I reflected on the apparition I'd just seen. What impressed me most were the little deer's eerie coloration and perfect whitetail rack in miniature: small by any measure, yet extraordinarily thick and balanced, with deeply convex main beams and several points per side. (I hadn't had time to count.)

Later, over more coffee, sausage, and eggs, I told Tom about my startling encounter and allowed as how I'd have been delighted to take the little buck home, if only I'd spotted him before he busted me. "But no great loss," I concluded. "He was just a shrimp."

"I don't know," said the Coues old-timer. "Sounds like a trophy buck to me."

Often called the Arizona whitetail, this compact cervid's proper name is a bone of proverbial contention. While most hunters say *Coos*, biologists say *Cows*. As a word-nerd, I have trouble with Cows for aesthetic reasons and compromise by rhyming Coues with House, as I suspect the original owner did.

No matter how we (mis)pronounce the name, it's interesting to note that Elliot Coues was a military surgeon attached to a U.S. Cavalry unit whose job was to "pacify" the remaining "renegade" Apaches in the latter 1800s. Out of step with his peers, Coues expressed deep respect for the proud native culture he was helping to destroy. As an astute naturalist, he distracted himself by scientifically describing various "new" desert species, most famously the second-smallest whitetail in North America.

Of seventeen recognized whitetail subspecies, the Florida Key deer is the smallest and lives the farthest south. The slightly larger Coues lives only slightly farther north, on either side of the Mexican border. Going the other way, the largest whitetail variants live the farthest north. This correlation between latitude and body size is no coincidence. As acknowledged in Bergmann's rule, the farther from the equator a warm-blooded animal lives, the larger it tends to grow in adapting to its climate. Simply put, a bigger body is a warmer body, and evolution has this figured.

Noting a parallel phenomenon, Allen's rule states that as warm-blooded species move north, legs, ears, and tails become shorter relative to body size — again, to reduce surface area and heat loss. Conversely, going south, the extremities become larger relative to body size to enhance their radiator effect, as notably personified in jackrabbits and the big-eared, long-tailed Arizona whitetail.

Likewise, the Coues' ghostly pelage is a desert adaptation, obeying yet another biological rule (Gloger's), which links light coloration to aridity. Dryness, not heat, is the critical factor, as evidenced by the dark hair of the semi-tropical Key deer.

As a final distinction, Coues bucks wear the largest antlers of any whitetail variant — relative to body size. Late bloomers, they don't shed velvet until December, and rut into January.

The opportunity to bowhunt such an "exotic" species in moderate weather in midwinter, when no other big game seasons are on, is unique in North America. As a bonus, Coues seasons in both Arizona and New Mexico generally overlap with javelina and quail. And too, there's the postcard beauty and invigorating strangeness of Coues habitat — the geologic, scenic, and historical feel of the borderlands, inhabited by odd creatures, unfamiliar smells, prickly vegetation, eerie light, coyote song, mystery, and deep desert magic.

For example: At the same time I was stumbling into my first Coues buck, a couple of ridges away a local lion hunter was photographing a Mexican jaguar. While anecdotal accounts of the big jungle cats venturing across the border, some of them in the spooky black phase, are common in both Arizona and New Mexico, this was the first one to be documented. And we were (almost) there!

Jaguar. Try *that* in your home deer patch!

If your whitetail experience is limited to tree-standing and making fake scrapes, prepare for a far nobler challenge. Even among the ever-cagey whitetail clan, the Coues is a special problem. First, the animal is neither widespread nor abundant, and can be hard to find. Second, you'll see precious few trees suitable for hanging stands down there in the desert. Third, Coues country is hilly, choppy, and sparsely vegetated, providing ample hiding cover for pint-sized deer but little for upright hunters. Finally, while bits and pieces of Coues habitat offer sandy soil for silent stalking, much is paved with clattering gravel.

Basically, workable options include sitting in a ground blind in the shade, sneak-hunting, spot-and-stalk (very popular), and calling. Coues connoisseurs report that calling can be exceptionally effective. But beware, called-in rutting bucks tend to appear silently, suddenly, and right in your face, daring you to blink or draw.

But more often, shot opportunities at these acutely cautious creatures tend to be at the extreme of accuracy for traditional archers. While I'm a disciple of heavy arrows for heavy game, the featherweight Coues — bucks average less than a hundred pounds, does about seventy — offers an ethical opportunity to launch light, fast arrows at slightly longer ranges.

My own first Coues hunt ended shotless. Yet, as Tom and I packed for the drive home, I was utterly content. Back in Colorado, the snow lay belly deep on an elk and nights were five below. The Bootheel's Peloncillo Mountains and upper Chihuahuan Desert, though cold at night, had provided a welcome break from the harsh mountain winter. In both New Mexico and Arizona, Coues habitat is sparsely peopled, scenic as a John Wayne western, raw-boned and pulsing with promise. Between us, Tom and I had seen five deer, averaging one per hunting day. We were happy campers.

Happy at least, until I got home and opened a book containing photos of trophy Coues racks. After a while I clapped the book shut in self-disgust, chuckling sourly at the memory of Tom's suggestion that the "little" buck I'd almost stepped on might in fact have been a trophy, and my cocky crack that it was "just a shrimp." Now, comparing the photos to what I'd seen that hung-over New Year's Day, I almost blacked out again. The "tiny" buck at which I *might* have gotten a point-blank shot had I not tipped that New Year's drink and thus been hunting better, now looked like a new world record on the hoof.

Beginner's luck, Elkheart style.

David Petersen

Part II

Woodsmanship:
How I Do It
(and how I try not to)

David Petersen

Chapter Fifteen

Privileged Advice

Only in reference to elk hunting have I ever been accused of being a "privileged character," referring to the happy facts that I live year-round in prime elk country, enjoy the friendship of world-class elk biologists, elk guides and veteran hunters, and can usually arrange to be sufficiently underemployed to hunt the full month of archery season each September. I am, as a game warden friend once observed, "a serious predator." What a compliment!

But everything is relative, and to me the privileged characters are those who own horses or mules and can outfit their own wilderness hunts, have access to vast private ranches, and/or can afford to book backcountry hunts with top outfitters. Blessed with none of the above, I'm left to do my elking by foot on public lands. Just like most everyone else. (Road cruisers and ATV addicts are not "hunters" at all, even if they place kills in a record book. In fact, through their rudely disruptive actions and adolescent bully-boy "To hell with everyone and everything else!" attitudes, they are the greatest enemies to traditional hunting extant.)

Consequently, I feel a special bond with other foot-bound public lands elk hounds, especially nonresident traditionalists who plan, finance, and guide their own "hunts of a lifetime" to unfamiliar public lands elk country. Mentally trading places, it's easy to wonder what I would do — which tactics I'd choose to place my limited bets on — if I were in their boots, up against an unfamiliar species in a vast, unfamiliar, and formidable landscape.

The basic tactics for elk, as for other deer, I call the Familiar Four: spot-and-stalk, sneak (a.k.a. "still" hunting), ambush, and calling. Which one or combination is "best" depends on a swirling universe of fast-changing circumstances, including when and where you hunt, game and hunter densities, weather, physical abilities, and personal preferences.

Spot-and-stalk traditionally involves glassing from panoramic vistas in hopes of locating an approachable animal of your liking, then planning and conducting a stalk that takes into account wind, terrain, vegetation, predictable prey behavior and more. Spot-and stalk works best where wapiti are plentiful and at ease, cover is thick, and hunters are few; thus, the earlier in the season, the better. Open terrain facilitates spotting but complicates stalking. And vice-versa.

If you're able to put even a mile (two is better) between you and the nearest road or motorized trail, and if your elk are mellow and behaving normally — feeding in the open during early morning and late evening, retiring to the timber to rest, ruminate, and wallow through midday — stalking can be a thrilling and productive tactic. And remember, when bulls are vocalizing, you "spotting" can be done by ear; even better. While they're no pushovers, elk aren't nearly so jumpy as deer or wild turkeys and will tolerate a limited amount of natural noise and visual disturbance before exploding off the mountain, with "limited" being the operative word. A special challenge with elk is their proclivity, particularly later in the rut, to hang out in big herds. What two elk eyes might miss, sixty elk eyes likely won't. And let a wapiti catch your whiff, and you'll see instantly why the Shawnee called these giant deer "white rump" (as in "running away fast") The nose always knows, and wapiti know it.

Sneaking*:* Hunting as I generally do, in dense mountain forests where visibility is limited and elk are seldom seen at any distance for any length of time, I've come to depend less on spot-and-stalk and more on sneaking around. ("Sneak" hunting is a term I've coined in preference to "still" hunting since the latter is potentially confusing insofar as it suggests sitting quietly in one place, or ambush.) The same blow-down littered, shadowy forest hellhole that works against spot-and-stalk is ideal for weaseling right in amongst 'em, terrain and humidity allowing. The essentials of sneak hunting are no different for elk than for whitetails and most other species: move your eyes a lot more than your feet; keep the wind in (or at least quartering into) your face; avoid sky-lighting, backlighting, or sun-lighting yourself; and dress to blend in, with or without camo, always on the dark side. (Like many other traditionalists today, I've recently come full circle, moving away from commercial camo and back to solid dark trousers and dark plaid shirts and jackets.

For a long time, it was hard to find non-camo clothing with bellows leg pockets and other features that hunters like and need. Happily, makers and shakers of hunting clothing recently have begin to recognize, and are answering to, this happy trend toward non-militaristic individualism in hunting "style" with a greater variety of non-camo hunting clothing available every season.) Midday, when elk are bedded and groggy, is generally most lucrative for sneak hunting, as well as for stalking.

One of my most memorable elk sneaks unfolded on a muggy September afternoon when I infiltrated a bedded herd of two dozen or so cows and calves and ghosted undetected among them for two pulse-pounding hours, searching for a bull that wasn't there. My secret weapons: Unseasonable heat had the animals stupefied, and swarming flies were driving the poor beasts to distraction, jamming their radar and rendering me virtually invisible. In sum, sneaking combines aggressive hunting today, with scouting for tomorrow, while working profitably through the midday doldrums when other tactics fail. (It should be noted that some experienced elk hunters and guides, like my friend Mike Murphy of T Bar M Outfitters in Durango, discourage midday hunting. As Mike puts it: "Far more often than not, you're just going to spook game and ruin the evening hunt. Either bed down somewhere and take a nap, or return to camp for lunch and a nap. Let the game calm down, and give yourself a break."

Which brings us to my own favorite strategy, the one that has consistently (unless I'm playing trophy hunter) put elk steaks in my freezer and antlers on my cabin wall for two decades — is "lowly" ambush.

Ambush, in contrast to being a "low skill technique," as I've heard it arrogantly and misleadingly referred to by "experts" hawking commercial calls, is exacting work, at least if you do it right. It is map poring, preseason terrain scouting, interpreting spoor, and ciphering out such critical and subtle essentials as the direction from which elk are most likely to approach and when, wind patterns at various times of day and in all sorts of weather, consequent stand location(s), best approach and departure routes, and more. Thoughtful ambush, while rarely as exciting as calling, spot-and-stalk, or sneak hunting, nonetheless can be a singularly lucrative archery elk tactic.

Think about it: In good habitat during bow seasons in virtually all elk states and provinces, wapiti chow is abundant. But in much of this same semi-arid western country, water is precious, making waterhole bushwhacking an odds-on enterprise. Ditto for wallows if you're after big bulls, though far less predictably. But patience and faith are absolute essentials, and lots of folks, especially those who didn't come up on whitetail hunting, just can't bring themselves to sit still, generally somewhat uncomfortably, for extended periods. So profoundly do I believe in ambush as the most lucrative bowhunting tactic for elk, I've given it a chapter of its own, to follow.

Which brings us to the final Familiar Four tactic — hyped in more hunting books, articles, and videos than all others combined — the universally acclaimed and purported ultimate in elking (drum roll) ... bugling and cow calling. Frankly, I believe both are irrationally overrated and that for all but deep-wilderness hunts with lots of elk and a scarcity of elk hunters, bugling should be outlawed. (For details and justification of this heretical proclamation, see "The Silence of the Bulls," another chapter to come.) But for now, since all mechanical (non-electronic) forms of calling are legal almost everywhere and this section of the book purports to be how-to, here we go ...

Bugling and cow calling: With calling, it's essential to keep in the fore of your awareness that any animal you call in will have a triangulated ear-lock on your exact location. Consequently, two common called-to elk reactions are circling to get your wind, getting it and spooking; and coming straight in fast, pinning you down so that you can't draw and shoot, giving you a head-on non-shot, or at least pumping you so full of adrenaline that your cool comes radically unglued. Team hunters can overcome these common "too close for comfort" problems by positioning the shooter forward and downwind along the expected approach route and the caller back, a common turkey tactic. When the magic is working, the bull will pass close past the shooter, his attention focused on the caller, providing a close and (relatively) relaxed broadside off shot.

Another common bugling bungler is the bull that bugles back at you, yet refuses to come. So you advance and call again. He retreats an equal distance and answers. And so on, leading predictable to the bull eventually turning off the sound and drifting quietly away. Here again, teaming can sometimes turn the tide, with the caller hanging back to keep the argument going while the shooter runs an end-around stalk, wind and other conditions allowing.

Me, well, unless I'm guiding in remote backcountry, I never bugle any more—just one more privilege of a less-crowded recent past, gone the way of too many inexperienced and/or lazy hunters slouching around the woods, befuddled and bemused by too much commercial hype.

Which brings us, in the end, to "cow" talk, which is something of a misnomer insofar as these catlike mews and birdlike chirps are not "love calls" made only by cows in heat, but social and herding (a.k.a. "coalescence") vocalizations uttered year-round by all elk (though less often by mature bulls), particularly when a herd is moving. Since it hasn't (quite yet) been so abused as bugling and doesn't carry nearly so far, cow calling remains a viable tool that's less likely to spook hunter-shy animals and screw things up for fellow hunters. Got a hung-up bull? If you're a shoot-the-works hunter who likes excitement, win or lose, reassure him with some gentle cow come-ons, and/or mix and match excited cow chirps with aggressive bugling and tree raking, convincing your prey that you're a satellite bull bent on hijacking his girls.

For bowhunters specifically, there's another, largely undebated, use for cow talk. If a bow-shot (or shot-at) elk (cow or bull, and especially calf) hasn't been unduly spooked — hasn't seen, scented, or heard you — cow calling immediately after the shot will often slow, stop, even turn the confused animal back your way, easing both its dying and your blood trailing, and perhaps even granting you a follow-up shot. As told in earlier chapters, it has worked for me on several occasions.

A workable alternative to calling for call-shy bulls is tree raking, colloquially called "horning." Throughout the rut, bull elk, especially the mature models, spend a good deal of time bashing, crashing, and raking the bark and limbs from sapling-size trees. This behavior can be relatively relaxed — such as the slow, bemused raking commonly indulged in by wallowing bulls — or frenzied and violent, as when two rivals are engaged in a bullyboy bluff match.

Many elk hunters know that fake horning — grabbing a dead limb and banging, bashing, and stroking it vigorously against a tree for a few seconds, pause, repeat (precisely as in moose hunting) — can sometimes help to overcome the hesitancy of a hung-up mature bull (it generally scares younger bulls away), fewer are aware that horning can often be an effective stand-alone call. Just as cow talk can sometimes bring in a bugle-shy bull, so can raking pull in even cow-talk-shy animals.

107

David Petersen

And that's it so far as the Elkheart short-course goes — my best "privileged" advice to novice traditional hunters. In reality of course, *all* elk hunters are privileged. Privileged to be alive and healthy enough to follow the chase. Privileged to live in a culture where sport is not reserved for only the rich and powerful. Privileged to be losing sleep, weight, and worry while gaining memories that will cheer us through the remainder of our days, as vivid and stirring as late-night bugles, just beyond the campfire light.

Chapter Sixteen

Eating Humble Pie

Consider, if you will, traditional bowhunting as a metaphor for life. Both experiences are challenging and inherently joyful, energized by hopeful expectations for the future, validated by gratifying memories of the past and, sadly, haunted by bittersweet memories of priceless opportunities lost, squandered, blown.

Which is to say: Like life, it's the nature of bowhunting that no amount of experience and "expertise" is ever enough to guarantee no more screw-ups.

I offer my own repeatedly screwed-up and humbled self as exhibit "A" (as in ass). I'm sixty at this writing, took up archery at eight, and have been actively bowhunting since the age of fourteen, having killed my first deer, as previously noted, only after years of determined effort. In this lifetime of sticks, strings, and wild wary things, I've brought home my share of game — whitetail and mule deer, wapiti, caribou, pronghorn, turkey, and lots of smaller stuff. (I was tempted to haul out the clichéd old hyperbolic "more than I can recall," but that's not really true, since, properly prompted, I can recall like last night's lover every contour of every hill and valley ever hunted and every large animal I've ever killed.) For the past quarter century, I've lived full-time in elk country — and I do mean "in"; during rut, Caroline and I can hear the lusty singing of neighborhood bulls from our bed at night. I'm an ardent student of wapiti biology, ethology (animal behavior) and evolution, and have even been accused of being an elk "expert."

The point being — for all my years of elk study, sustained observation, hunting, and success, I still make mistakes, almost on a daily basis, every year. And the majority can be traced to poor spur-of-the-moment decisions. Or, as Grandma would have it, "Lack of common sense."

109

Bowhunting is a dynamic undertaking, a work in progress that demands constant adaptation to a universe in motion. As bowhunters, we either learn to be flexible, to adapt to changing situations afield literally with every shift in the breeze — or we learn to abide consistent disappointment.

To demonstrate this point, allow me to share in embarrassing confessional detail the causes, consequences, and retrospective cures of a litany of almost back-to-back screw-ups during a month-long hunt that happened blessedly long ago, yet still stings to recall. It was the early 1990s, during the four-year period when I was looking to take a "book quality" bull, as previously told. My opportunities for a conscionable shot at a trophy bull during the entire month of September that year numbered just three — and I muffed 'em *all*. Yet, I still had some fun, and I definitely learned a thing or three while eating my fill of humble pie.

Humbling mistake #1: bungled bugling

All afternoon, a squeaky-voiced spike bull has been wandering about in a thick aspen wood just over the rise and out of sight from my ground hide (hardly a blind), tweeting like a canary with laryngitis. What he hopes to accomplish with these mousy mouthings, I'm not sure. Practicing to be a grown-up, I suppose. Feeling his fresh green oats in this, his first rut, even if only a bystander. I kind of like having him around, livening the woods with his juvenile bravado. Besides, you could hardly ask for better bait for bigger fish.

Sure enough, along toward evening the braggart spike's boasts are answered by a full-throated bugle from somewhere up the mountain. As the bigger bull's voice grows rapidly louder, closer, the yearling's confidence falters; a couple more meek chirps and he wisely zips it up. As the mature bull draws ever nearer, I hear the spike crash off down the mountain, exercising the better part of valor.

When the boss bull finally arrives where the spike just departed — though I can't see the big guy through the underbrush and evergreens, even though he's so close I can almost smell the chlorophyll on his breath — he is greeted by an empty silence. All dressed up with nowhere to go, hot and bothered, he stomps back and forth, bugling so close and loud it's painful to my ears.

110

Then, like a sweet night's dream, he starts to drift away.

Here at last, I reflect, is a chance to bugle and make it work — like back in the good old days before the woods became so crowded with amateurs unable to resist hearing themselves squawk through gizmos they've been led to believe have the magic of a Pied Piper's flute. After years of scaring off more than I've lured in — struggling through the loud-mouthed amateur phase myself — I finally learned to keep my diaphragm in my pocket and leave the grunt tube at home. But this, I dare to hope, is different; all I have to do is jump in where the spike left off, sounding as adolescent as possible, and the big boy, so close and so hot to kick young upstart butt, should run me over charging in.

Now, doesn't that make good, common sense, Grandma?

After checking fit of cedar arrow on linen string, I flick a speck of pocket lint from the neoprene disc, pop it in my mouth, and whine like a puppy begging to be let in on a stormy night.

Silence.

An anxious minute passes. I "bugle" again, and this time the bull answers ... from a quarter-mile away and fading.

In retrospect: Most assuredly, even today, even in crowded roadside public elk woods, rutting bulls can still be bugled-in. And when the magic works, it's hands-down the most exciting hunting experience you'll likely ever know. Certainly the most exciting *I* have ever known. But far more often than not and increasingly ever year, it backfires. The best bugling success is consistently found in truly remote country, miles from the nearest road, trail, and the accompanying game-alarming, mood-shattering mosquito-whine of ATVs. And the earlier in the active rut the better, before the bull hierarchy is established and harems are formed and dominant bulls have little to gain and much to lose by answering a distant challenge.

Leave your bugle at home, or throw the damn thing away, as I eventually did.

Humbling mistake #2: A perfectly good setup, stupidly squandered

The morning has gone from cold to old when suddenly I hear the invigorating knock of a huge hard hoof hitting deadfall. I perk up (under-

statement) and aim all my senses at the sound. Soon enough I'm rewarded by the rhythmic crunching of dry aspen leaves, punctuated by the
occasional sharp snaps of trod-on limbs. Big fellow, coming fast.

I pull up my camo face net, double-check my willowy weapon, take a
deep breath, exhale slowly, and stare arrows at a small opening in the
trees just behind the wallow I am watching.

A few moments more and a dark, antlered head appears. Big antlers.

Pulse throttles up. Hands begin to vibrate. If my mouth weren't
clamped hard-shut, my teeth would be clacking. The pot, she's a'boiling
now and the climax approaches. I am ready!

But the bull is not ready, hanging up at the edge of the clearing.
Suspicious, or merely cautious as befits his kind?

A breeze stirs and the yellow-leafed aspens hum a brittle tune — like
a stepped-on rattler or a Navajo gourd rattle. After looking every which
way in general and my way in particular, seeing nothing, the bull comes
ahead, striding more confidently now. But just before stepping into the
clear, his actions reveal he has cut a compelling scent. I was afraid of
that. A whole herd of wapiti blew through here sometime during the
night, leaving the earth tilled with tracks, littered with scat, and sprin-
kled with urine spots everywhere. His wallowing urge forgotten, huge
black nostrils scouring the ground for that yummy girlie scent, the bull
turns and follows the perfume up the slope — the selfsame slope upon
which I happen to be sitting, sweating proverbial bullets.

When the great beast briefly pauses behind a clump of brush I begin
a slow waist-twist to my left, my bow arm extended and trembling,
thinking this just might work out after all. But while my sitting position
on the slope provides plenty of clearance for a downhill shot toward the
wallow, swinging left into the embankment jams the bottom tip of my
longbow into the ground. No way to draw from this position, and no time
to stand. What I would give for a short recurve!

As the magnificent bull comes up level with the game trail, with only
a couple of spruce limbs left to clear before stepping into the open, he
unexpectedly turns and faces me. He looks me square in the eyes, but my
stillness and camo work their magic and once again he fails to see. Reas-
sured, onward he comes, nostrils sucking hungrily at the cow-scented

earth ... closer, closer, until he's just one step away. One step away and towering high above.

Even as I fear he's about to trample me, the bull goes stiff-legged and jerks up his head, his lance-like antlers looming almost directly over me, one eye cocked suspiciously downward, pre-orbital glands gaping wide with the angst of sudden recognition. He knows.

At the same instant, I realize *why* he knows — last night's elk weren't the only animals to have urinated here, right where the bull now stands.

After a final glance down at the odd figure cowering below him, the bull barks like a foghorn, whirls and crashes away.

Shucks.

In retrospect: Thrice dumb was I. First and worst, I should never have parked my bony butt directly on a game trail. My second error was assuming the only shot I'd be invited to take would be a bull at the wallow, sharply downhill, allowing sufficient bow-tip clearance. My third "expert" goof was to relieve my bladder way too close to my set-up, and on a game trail to boot! I'd had to decide: Was I better off making a commotion crunching up the noisy hill, or taking care of business quietly and conveniently by tiptoeing a few yards off and watering the thirsty dust of the trail?

I reckoned the latter, and I reckoned wrong.

Humbling mistake #3: chemical warfare

Down to the final few days of the season. Evening. The wapiti are coming out to play. I know this because the big lug of a herd bull, who by now has every ripe cow on the mountain in tow, has just started yodeling in his distinctive, gravelly voice. Every bugle is louder, closer. I'm watching the same wallow again, having moved my set-up off the game trail a ways to a big root-crater at the base of a toppled spruce that has since become my favorite hide on the mountain. In this ditch I can sit comfortably, with my butt on a natural bench and only my head above-grade, and from here I can draw and shoot in any direction. And taking a tip from savvy whitetail tree-stand hunters, this time I've brought along a lidded plastic bottle to pee in. Lookin' good.

It takes the indolent, insolent braggart-bull about half an hour to close to within fifty yards. Everything still looks good: The down-slope evening breeze is in my court, I'm calm, well hidden, and no way tempted to bugle; the diaphragm, however, remains close at hand, just in case I want to cow call. Hard to imagine what could go wrong this time.

The question is no sooner thought, than answered. For reasons beyond my limited comprehension, the bull hangs up — just out of sight, twice out of range — from where he bugles for a few minutes more, then falls silent and plods away.

I cow call.

The bull says nothing.

I consider giving slow chase — the bull doesn't seem spooked, really, only suspicious — but twilight is upon us, the animal is moving steadily away, so I opt just to sit and wait. And hope. Who knows: maybe he'll return.

Just before dark a mule deer doe and two leggy fawns come to the wallow-fouled water and drink daintily and briefly. They depart unknowing, undisturbed. A pleasant ending for an exciting, if disappointing, evening spent on stand. I rise and follow the long-gone deer up the game trail to a ponderosa flat, then turn down the mountain toward home and hearth. I haven't quite made it to the cabin when the rain begins.

After dinner (with a big sour slice of humble pie for dessert), I make my usual preparations for the next day's hunt — which, given a nasty turn of weather, includes checking my rain gear. Noticing that the nylon uppers of my rubber-bottomed hunting boots are looking about as waterproof as toilet paper, I step outside and spray 'em down with silicone water repellent.

By morning, the wind is blowing and the storm has settled in like a monsoon. I decide to stay home and catch up on the work I've been neglecting.

By late afternoon the wind has died, the rain slacked to a pissy drizzle, and I'm plumb bonkers with cabin fever. If I hurry, I can make it up the mountain just right for evening prime time.

Arrived at my natural pit-blind, I find the bottom of the root crater a messy muck of mud. What the heck — my boots and pants are waterproof, so I step right in and sit right down.

The rain stops.

I've been on watch for less than an hour when a familiar bugle rings down the mountain from a familiar direction. It's the herd bull again, following more or less the same route and routine as last evening. As the bugling grows nearer, louder, clearer, I'm thrown into paroxysms of indecision. The bull grunts and coughs, stops to beat hell out of some poor defenseless tree. My tactical mind, what there is left of it, grinds into overdrive.

Normally, I'd put my trust in the lure of the wallow. But after this same bull's inexplicable refusal to come in last evening, I just don't know. And too, the storm has left puddles everywhere, rendering the muddy little pool temporarily superfluous, since he can drink or wallow any-where he wants for now. Growing anxious, I think about how quietly I should be able to slip through the dripping wet forest, turning the miser-able wetness to my benefit. Moments later I stand and strike out toward the approaching bugler.

My plan, such as it is, turns on closing fast, quiet, and downwind of the bull. In order to accomplish the latter, I have to loop slightly downhill. As I approach a deeply worn game trail, a family of coyotes erupts in a yap-session somewhere off in the east. I stop ever so briefly to listen: What would the no-longer-so-wild West be without the crazed ancient cries of coyotes? After just a few seconds, predictably, the song dogs fall quiet. I step over the game trail so as not to step into it and possibly leave scent, and resume my stalk.

When the bull bugles again he's much closer but has dodged a ways uphill. I alter course to get back on track for a downwind intercept.

I've covered only a few dozen yards on this fresh tack when I catch a blur of movement ahead, through the bushy aspen understory. I freeze. Thirty yards upslope on the same game trail I just crossed, a long line of cows and calves come parading into view. I count twelve, fourteen, seven-teen animals, then promptly lose interest in numbers when I spot a gigantic rack of antlers swaying above a clump of Gambel's oak.

As carefully as if my life depended on it, I take a dozen baby steps. The bull is just standing there, a little off the trail, watching the cows and calves file past as if tallying his entourage. When the last cow has passed, I know from long experience, he'll fall back in line, walking tail-gun. And

115

when he does, and takes a couple or three more steps along the trail, he'll clear the brush and present me with a bowhunter's bonanza: twenty yards and broadside. Walking, yes, but walking slowly and I'm shooting good this year.

The lead cow disappears from my view up-trail.

Heart chugging loud as a John Deere diesel, knees knocking, hands slightly shaking, I raise my bow and tense my shoulders in preparation to draw. The last cow passes and the bull steps back onto the trail, as predicted. I start my draw ... and the world comes crashing down.

In a mad cacophony of hammering hooves and snapping limbs, the lead cow comes boiling back down the trail, followed close at heel by the whole damn rest of the panicked herd. The bull — standing now within one teasing step of being clear of the brush that continues to obstruct my shot — appears momentarily addled, then whirls and joins the stampede.

Dumbfounded, I can only stand and gawk. What the hell happened up there? I consider trailing the vanished herd, but just as quickly decide against it; don't want to risk spooking them a second time, maybe drive the whole lot plumb off the mountain. Besides, it's getting dark; there are never enough hours in an elk hunting day.

Still shaking, I shamble forlornly up to the freshly churned game run and turn back downhill toward the wallow, looking for evidence as I go. Soon enough I come to the spot where the lead cow's front hooves had post-holed, skidded, and splattered watery mud as she braked hard, spun, and took off back the way she's come. It doesn't take long to figure how this deal went down: This is the exact spot where I crossed the trail and paused while those clever coyotes laughed.

In retrospect, had I stayed put in my muddy hole hide rather than going after the bugler, the herd likely would have come right to me, or at least passed close by, maybe offering a shot at the bull. Or maybe not. (You can't roller-skate in a buffalo herd.) But I didn't stay put, and my stalk almost worked out. What blew it so dramatically was a strong foreign scent on the game trail. And what might have been its source? Wasn't I wearing "scent-proof" rubber-soled hunting boots?

Yes, but ... last night's silicone waterproofing spray. Even *I* can smell that noxious chemical gumbo at a distance; how could I have been so dumb as to think it would dissipate sufficiently overnight that an elk wouldn't notice? Obviously, I didn't think at all.

A couple of uneventful days more, and the season is done for, as am I.

Disappointing episodes? You bet. Still, life has a way of leveling things out. And that's good enough for me. If hunting were a sure thing — if it offered no fresh challenges every time out and could in fact be fully mastered, if it had nothing to teach us about life and death and ourselves through trying and failing and trying again, striving always for unattainable perfection — why bother?

Sour as it tastes at the time, humble pie is among the sourest but most nourishing foods in the trad hunter's pantry. I eat it all the time.

Chapter Seventeen

Bushwhacked!

I'm making like a statue in an aspen grove cathedral when a 6x6 bull big as a Clydesdale comes ghosting out of the woods and stops broadside just thirteen yards in front of me and lowers his head to drink and I draw my recurve and aim instinctively and the arrow sizzles off the string and the lung-hit bull explodes out of there but doesn't get far before falling over dead.

Sounds easy, doesn't it?

Well, it's not. But no complaints, considering I was alone, armed with a simple stickbow, and hunting public land just an hour's hike uphill from a county road. That's what ambush can do for you.

I know hunters who'd rather "walk and talk" and go home meatless than sit in silence and score. I've been there myself and may be again. It's a mood thing, and to each his or her own. After all, we're out there (or should be) to challenge, educate, and enjoy ourselves, and these are keenly personal commodities, never writ in stone. But for meat in the freezer, antlers on the wall, and a bonus of nongame wildlife sightings and experiences, year after year, make mine bushwhack.

For traveling hunters unfamiliar with elk habits, habitats, and hunting tactics, ambush has the additional bonus of familiarity. Rare indeed is the big game hunter who has never had the experience of sitting in a tree stand or ground blind waiting for the elusive whitetail. The techniques are essentially the same, though the terrain and prey are notably different.

Recently, I heard some self-styled hunting video hero refer to ambush as a "low-skill" tactic. I know some Marine Corps infantry and Recon vets who, having been on both ends of hot-lead bushwhacks, will offer a spirited rebuttal! And when it comes to hunting elk, so will I, going so far as to suggest that such opinionated put-downs, when spoken (as they tend to be) by people with toys to sell (in this case, bugles and cow calls), often involve a profit motive. To the contrary, putting together a high-odds ambush involves a lot more than just stumbling into the woods, sitting down, and waiting. It's the antithesis of a low-skill maneuver and in fact takes a lot more woodsmanship, patience, planning, and game-sense than simply strolling through the woods blowing into an overpriced length of vacuum hose.

First and foremost, effective ambush demands that you learn to identify not just elk habitat, but likely prime elk micro-habitats, on paper as well as the ground. Across most mountainous elk range you're looking for thickly timbered, mid- to high-altitude, north-facing mountain slopes with benches of mixed aspen (in regions of the Rockies where they grow) and conifer, well watered and interspersed with secluded grassy parks (because except in winter, elk are primarily grazers). Higher up, forbs-rich avalanche chutes between subalpine spruce-fir stringers just below timberline are morning and evening elk magnets, with day-bed areas predictably nearby, in the fringing timber.

Once "in the ballpark" with a hunting area, locating an effective bushwhack involves scouting out specific potential ambush sites such as secluded wallows, water holes, morning and evening ecotonal browsing areas (transitional edge cover, where forest and meadow meet), midday bedding areas, saddles, and other natural travel corridors, and intersections of well-trafficked game trails.

A lucrative ambush also requires more than a passing knowledge of the daily habits of wapiti, especially during fall, when so much (rut, hunting seasons, seasonal migrations) is going on. It takes miles of scouting and the ability to spot often-subtle spoor, determine its approximate age, and read it for such critical information as what time of day elk are using a certain place, which trails or directions they're approaching from and leaving by, wind patterns, whether you'll be sitting in shade with the sun to your back (yes) or looking into a blinding sun (no) at the time of day you'll be there, and finally — all of this and a whole lot more having been carefully considered — the most profitable location for your setup and how best to come and go without leaving a scent trail loud as a burglar alarm.

Now it's not sounding quite so easy and low-tech, is it? And the worst comes when you find a place that elk are visiting regularly, but because of one or a combination of the above considerations, you just can't make it work for an ambush.

119

In sum, effective bushwhack hunting requires—to trot out an old-fashioned term not much in favor these gadget-ridden, industry-distorted, "get 'er done" days — woodsmanship. Consider ...

Elk must drink. In good habitat in most years, food is readily abundant. But in much of this same semi-arid western country water is predictably precious. Magnify this scarcity by drought (common), and waterhole watching becomes an odds-on favorite during early bow seasons when elk are relatively undisturbed. If you're meat hunting, ambushing a waterhole is especially profitable. While mature bulls, where hunting pressure is high, may drink only at night or along the dimmest edges of day, younger bulls and cows aren't nearly so picky; I've been surrounded by slurping, splashing wapiti at all times of the day.

In the successful ambush flashback I opened this discussion with, the "live action" — from the time the bull appeared to the time he fell over dead — consumed little more than a minute. But the hunt itself was many days in the works. The first two days I spent scouting. On day one I drove national forest roads and glassed a lot of country, settling finally on a convoluted north-facing slope. On day two, having identified a likely "hot spot" from a topo map — a crow's foot of tiny intermittent streams forking from the head of a tight little drainage about nine thousand feet in the Colorado sky, which, I figured, indicated a seep spring — I sneaked in at mid-day (the least likely time for elk to be there) for a look-about.

The spring was there, sure enough, and it was being used. Better yet, there was no human or livestock sign anywhere. Wearing rubber boots to curtail leaving a scent trail, I circumnavigated the spring a hundred yards out, touching nothing while visually examining everything. I noted fresh antler rubs on an aspen and whiffed the distinct barnyard stench of rutting bull in a urine stain in the needle duff. I found droppings and smashed them with a boot to determine freshness and content. I studied game trails and noted whether the freshest tracks in each were coming or going. Finally, aware that cooling breezes come sliding down-mountain each evening (barring a storm), I searched for and found a promising downwind hide — in this case a blow-down aspen for a seat with a bushy young Christmas tree to provide a camo backdrop.

Satisfied with the setup, I left silently and waited impatiently for opening day — then waited another eight evenings there on stand, five back-achy hours at a crack, for my bull to come for his final drink.

When hunting in areas where water is more plentiful, I shift my primary interest to wallows, those shallow, tub-sized mud holes into which rutting bulls urinate then roll like dogs to cake themselves with their own funky pheromones. Frequently, a bull will bugle while wallowing, or as soon as he's done and fixing to leave, helping to guide you in. Approaching a fresh wallow from down-breeze, the stench will alert you a long way out. Considerations for wallow setups are identical to those for waterholes other "game-attraction feature" hides.

After years of experimentation, I've come to prefer watching wallows in midday, waterholes in the evenings, and sneaking around of a morning. By preparing several ambush setups in several areas, you can rotate and avoid polluting any one place with your frequent presence and cumulative scent.

Across all my years of serious elking — hunting hard and long, studying elk in books as well as in the backcountry, experimenting with every legal, ethical, and tenable tactic — I and the hunters I've guided have taken more and better elk via ground ambush than by all other means combined.

Tree stands can work. But elk aren't nearly so spooky as whitetails, rendering an elevated hide unnecessary. Moreover, once you're lashed into a tree, you lose the ability, which an informal ground blind grants, to quickly change locations or go chasing after passing game or a bull hung up just over the rise. Why lug around what amounts to a sea anchor or albatross when you don't need it? Although some outfitters will place elk archers in tree stands as a way of handling more clients with fewer guides, most often it's do-it-yourselfers who, having grown up on whitetails and tree stands, know no other way to hunt. And elk do get killed from trees. But bottom line for me, as a veteran of several years of jockeying choppers for the Marines, I like the down-to-earth feel of boots on old friend earth, especially when the only trees I generally have around me are tall skinny aspens that wave spookily in the slightest breeze. And too, it's darned hard to arrange a double-lung shot angle on an elk close below you, and with animals this big and tough, nothing less than a solid double-lung shot angle is ethical or even practical. Consequently, I spend my ambush hours sitting on a stump or a fallen log, or just plain dirt (I always carry a small foam butt pad), back scrunched into a bush or leaned against a tree, as unmoving as I can manage and ready, I hope, for anything.

Even on days when no elk show, sitting in ambush provides a privileged peek into the myriad very private lives of an undisturbed forest family life — a fortune in sights, sounds, smells, and feelings that mobile hunters rarely enjoy. Pine squirrels squabble and tail-chase and hurry here and there while hoarding winter food, blissfully unaware of the hungry-eyed pine marten slinking ever closer. Little birds flit in to drink and bathe, then fan their wings dry and flit away. Bigger birds — our brother and sister hunters — glide past low and slow on silent wings and the woods fall so quiet you can hear the blood pulse in your ears. An hour before dark a bemused bear comes shuffling by, clueless of your presence, yet so very close that the measured tap-tapping of your pulse becomes a tom-tom boom.

Half an hour more and suddenly he is there, quiet as a ghost and taller than your tallest dreams, a 6x6 big as a Clydesdale. You are ready. He lowers his head to drink ...

Chapter Eighteen

Blood and Guts Made Easy

My first elk was a five-hundred-pound spike bull that fell to a Model 94 Winchester at thirty yards. While I'd grown up bowhunting whitetails in central Oklahoma — I killed my first deer there, at age eighteen, with a forty-three-pound Ben Pearson Bobcat recurve — I'd rarely seen wild elk and had never hunted them before moving to Colorado in 1980. In our first years here, Caroline and I were very poor. And so it was at least in part from necessity that we lived a semi-subsistence lifestyle and truly needed wild meat. In fact we still are (poor by all "official" economic standards) and still do (need wild meat). That need, combined with my total ignorance regarding elk, led me from a lifetime of trad bowhunting, temporarily to the slam-dunk efficiency of a rifle. After approaching that first spike and assuring that he was thoroughly dead, I remember thinking — suddenly dripping with sweat on a twenty-degree October morning — "*Now* what do we do, Dave?"

It was four steep miles down to my bivouac camp (where I subsequently built the little cabin we live in still today), and I was all alone.

What I did, of course, was what had to be done. I gutted and quartered the pony-sized deer, just as I'd done with hundred-pound Oklahoma whitetails years before. In my day pack I carried two sheath knifes and a Swiss Army folder. All were top-quality stainless and sharp as I could get them. I also had an Arkansas stone for touch-up. Working under perfect conditions of light and weather, it took me nearly four hours to get the innards out, the head off, and the carcass divided into five huge parts, hide still on — four quarters with bones still in, and the neck — plus twenty pounds or so of precious backstraps and tenderloins and another ten pounds of meat strips sliced from between the ribs. Before I was done, I'd dulled all three knives beyond resharpening with the Arkansas, and fairly wrecked my young (I was thirty-five), strong body horsing the monster around. In the following days, through the pack-out and butchering chores, my inexperience in working with mountains of freshly dead meat led to yet more complications, wasted effort, wasted meat, and needless exhaustion. In short, that first wapiti was a crash-course education in post-kill reality.

My second elk, the following October, was also a spike, again killed from thirty yards with the same little carbine. This time the field dressing, packing, and butchering went ... well, no faster or easier at all, really.

After that, having gained a bit of experience and confidence in hunting and field-dressing elk, I sold the Winchester (which I'd bought only after we arrived here), and used the money to buy an elk-weight (sixty-four-pound) factory recurve. With that bow and a series of other recurves and longbows (in recent years I've made my own), I've taken, on average, a wapiti a year, providing all the "beef" my petite wife and I can eat. And more often than not, due to my preference for evening ambush hunting, the field-dressing chores have played out in the dark. I've also dabbled in professional guiding, for both traditional archers and riflemen, leading to yet more practice in daylight and dark. Gradually, across these years of practice converting elk to elk meat, I evolved my own time- and labor-saving technique for handling very large animals alone, and without needing an arsenal of knives. Nor am I the only one. Like other obviously good ideas, "my" technique, or something very near it, becomes self-evident with experience and consequently has occurred to other hunters, guides, and outfitters who get to do it often, and often do it alone.

My personal best time for field-dressing an elk — a five-point bull weighing about six hundred pounds — is ninety minutes, from whole animal to bagged quarters, hide off but bones still in. Normally, I need two hours or so, working alone on animals I've shot just before dark, and which often seem to make it to the bottom of some brush-clogged gully to die in the most awkward possible position with rain beginning immediately after and flashlight batteries going prematurely dead. Unless I'm guiding for money, I never pull a cape, which doubles the field-dressing time. Boning out the meat requires another hour, but I generally leave that chore for the following morning, after the meat has firmed-up a bit. The immediate concern is getting the meat as cool as possible as soon as possible, keeping it clean, and protecting it from flies and bears.

But first, you need an elk. You'll also need three or four big, heavy-duty, breathable cloth game bags, like those marketed by T. Mike Murphy Outdoor Products. (They're expensive compared to lesser bags, such as those available at WalMart, but are much larger and better made, and will endure endless rough treatment and last for many years.) I've gradually evolved to "making" my sheath knives by putting my own antler or wood handles on Norwegian-made Helle blades. But no matter the brand, the important thing is a blade that's not too big or thick — for maximum leverage and control, the handle should be larger than the blade — holds and edge well, and is easy to resharpen. It's also important to stop working every few minutes and retouch the blade (I pack a diamond bar and a little scissor-type sharpener that employs crossed carbide sharpening blades) *before* it gets dull (at which point you'll need to retouch it with a broadhead file). For backup, I pack a smaller Helle, finding the slender little tool superior for certain precision chores. Another useful accessory is an inexpensive Gerber folding saw with interchangeable bone- and wood-cutting blades, worth its weight many times over in time and effort saved, though hardly essential to an experienced blade-wielder.

To begin, with the animal lying on either side (the way they tend to die), amputate the two top leg ends, front and rear — separating the knee joints with a sturdy knife, or cutting above the joints with a bone saw. Unless you're pulling a cape or want a skull mount, there's no need to remove the head.

At mid-chest, directly over the breastbone, slit the hide, insert your blade cutting-edge up and unzip all the way down the belly, taking care not to puncture the gut-bag, working around the "proof of sex" region to just above the anus. Now slit the hide up the bottom of the neck, from chest to chin, if you want the marginal neck meat. (While I'm among the last to waste the flesh of any animal, elk neck meat is so intensely layered with fascia and otherwise marginal that Colorado law no longer requires hunters to retrieve it, and few do. Ditto rib meat.)

Next, slit the hide up the insides of the two up-side quarters, working from knees to centerline cut, taking care to leave a flap of skin with proof of sex (mammary, one testicle, or penis) attached to a hind quarter if the state you're hunting requires. Now you're set to skin the top (up-side) half of the hide off in one big sheet, from legs and belly to spine and a bit beyond.

That done, it's time to carefully puncture the naked carcass just below the bottom rib (behind the diaphragm), to vent the abdominal cavity and prevent internal gases from accumulating and causing a "gut explosion." While I work fast, generally in cool weather, and have never experienced a blow-up, it has happened to others and the result is rough on both meat and hunter.

With the freed top half of the hide stretched out behind the animal to serve as a ground cloth on which to place chunks of meat, remove the exposed (up-side) backstrap by slicing vertically down the length of the spine, then making a second incision parallel with the ribs, to meet the first line of cut. With a few deft blade strokes, the front quarter/shoulder, attached to the body only by muscle, comes right off. The ham is another story and often quite a struggle, requiring both brute strength, a bit of acrobatics, and surgical precision to avoid nicking the bladder or intestinal pouch, both of which may bulge and protrude right where your blade is slicing. (Orienting the carcass so that the head is downhill at this stage, if possible, helps to relieve the gravitational stress.) Probe gently with fingers and blade for the big hip ball joint, cutting the attaching tissue all the way around until the ham twists free.

With one backstrap, one shoulder, and one ham removed (plus up-side neck and rib meat, if you want or are required to take it) — essentially, the entire top half of the animal — stash the ham in a game bag of its own. Loose cuts and shoulder can share a second bag. Cinch the drawstrings to keep out flies, and place the bags in the shade, preferably leaned against a tree trunk to maximize air circulation and speed cooling.

Now roll the remaining half of your elk (or moose) over onto the stretched-out hide—this is easily managed alone by using the lower legs as handles — and repeat the process exactly, so that all that's left is a legless, hideless, backstrapless torso. If you want to save the hide, there she lies, all in one big (very bulky and heavy) piece.

Only now, and only in order to retrieve the tenderloins and any preferred organs, is it necessary to reorient the carcass so that the belly faces downhill and slice into the body cavity, spilling the messy beans behind the diaphragm. An alternative method that sidesteps gutting altogether, and which I much prefer, is to saw through a few ribs near their connections to the spine and pry them away from the body sufficiently to facilitate reaching in and liberating the tenderloins, which run along either side of the inner spine.

If you'll be packing the meat out on your back, at some point — right now if you have the daylight left and the flies aren't bad, or first thing in the cool of morning — you'll want to debone the four quarters. Using the inside of the hide or a game bag as a ground cloth, slice up the inside of each quarter from bottom to top, plumb to the bone. With a small blade (here's where the little scalpel-like Helle comes in handy), remove the bone by cutting carefully around until you can work it free. Most often, you'll wind up with several muscle-bundle hunks of meat. Boned, your average quarter-ton cow or young bull elk will reduce to less than two hundred pounds of pure clean meat. If you have access to horses or mules, you may want to leave the bones in for the pack-out, as they provide rigidity, sturdy lashing points and a more stable ride in panniers. And that, by George, is *that*.

Except, of course, for the butchering and wrapping at home.

With practice, the only part that *never* gets easier and never should, is the first bit — finding a cooperative elk.

Chapter Nineteen

Confessions of a Jerky Junkie

I magine, if you will, the likely beginnings of a culinary legend ...

You're a Stone Age hunter-gatherer roaming the pristine expanses of the icy Eurasian Pleistocene, a very long time ago. You and the dozen other adult males in your clan hunt almost every day and take it as seriously as life itself. Still, you're not always successful. When you do make a kill, if it's small enough to be cut up with a sharp-edged stone and carried over your shoulders, you lug it back to camp. But when a really big one goes down — a woolly mammoth or rhino, a giant bison or aurox — it's easier to move your camp of three dozen souls to the kill site and eat the monster where it fell, packing down as much raw meat as you can manage before it rots, as your people have not yet learned to create fire, in fact have never even seen fire before, so have no way of cooking or preserving meat.

Or almost no way. Sometimes, in summer, while you and the boys are out chasing dinner with spears, clubs, and rocks, your women cut scraps of fresh meat into long thin strips which they drape over wicker-works of willow to slow-dry under the sun. Meat prepared this way keeps for a while, but not always long enough to see you through periods of no game. And it's bland. Moreover, the flies are often so horrific as to make sun-curing impossible.

This is how it is, how it's always been, and so far as you can see into the future, the way it will remain. When the hunting's slow, you and yours go meatless, subsisting on seeds, roots, and greens while dreaming of bloody fresh red flesh. And when you have it, you eat way too much.

Then one chilly day, just after the wildest, most brilliant and terrifying thunderstorm you've ever experienced, you spot a strange, vertical blue-gray cloud rising from a distant valley and stalk it to a burning pine snag. Being clever fellows, you recognize immediately that fire is warm — painfully warm if you get too close, but just right at a small distance. You also notice that fire eats wood, so before it dies out you feed it more branches to keep it fat and happy. After a while, unable to separate yourselves from this hypnotic new magic, your group sends its two youngest hunters to fetch the rest of the clan.

As the days and nights pass, you gradually get a handle on this strange new business. It hurts like the blazes when you stick a finger in it, but is pleasantly warm at arm's length. It brings light into darkness, allowing you to move about camp at night without tripping over your sleeping children. And it frightens animals, keeping nocturnal predators at bay. Great stuff! Truly a gift from the gods. After a few failed experiments, you even learn to coax flames from an almost-dead ember by gently blowing and feeding it dry grass and, consequently, can now transport fire from one campsite to another.

Quite by accident, you've also discovered that fresh meat dropped onto a bed of coals soon darkens and starts oozing fat and smells and tastes better than anything you've ever imagined. And you can eat a lot more of it without getting a bellyache. In another lucky stroke, your wife placed her meat drying rack in the stream of a fire's wind-driven smoke in a ploy to keep the flies away, and stumbled onto yet another new and wonderful discovery. The smoked meat not only is free of fly eggs and tastes a whole lot better than its sun-cured predecessor, it's also far more sturdy — looks like it might keep for months. By smoking quantities of meat strips and wrapping them in rawhide bundles, you'll never starve for flesh again.

Happy days!

Or something rather like that. However it may have been discovered or invented, as it was independently and repeatedly worldwide, today we North Americans know smoke-cured meat as "jerky," an Anglicization of the Spanish *charqui*.

Scholar Richard E. McCabe, writing in *Elk of North America*, reckons that the average American Indian in "primitive" (pre-agricultural) times consumed from two to four pounds of fresh meat per day, every day he and she could get it. The rub was, they couldn't get it every day. That's where jerky and its more colorful cousin pemmican — from the Cree for "put-up fat," or, more literally, "manufactured grease" — proved themselves to be winter lifesavers. No matter how prepared, the flesh of choice for Plains tribes was bison. Plains people also enjoyed pronghorn and bighorn, when they could manage to bag these far less numerous and far more spooky prey. In the eastern forests, America's native hunters concentrated on whitetails and, to a lesser extent, black bears.

Throughout their extensive range, wapiti were hunted by American Indians, but not so much for their meat as for their thick skins (especially the neck), which yielded an exceptionally tough rawhide preferred for the making of moccasin soles and the covers of war shields. Elk were hunted as well for their decorative canine "ivories" and their singularly magnificent antlers. Oddly, most Indians considered elk meat to be inferior in taste to other game, and it spoiled relatively fast, even when jerked.

No matter the game used, jerky was most often further processed into pemmican, a concentrated, tasty, and nutritionally balanced survival food. To make a batch of pemmican the family chef would pound a suitable quantity of dry jerky into a powdery paste. Next, she would stir in a more or less equal amount of bone marrow, bear fat, or some other animal grease, together with a smaller quantity of dried, pulverized berries, pits and all; chokecherries were widely favored where available. Thus, in pemmican you had high quality protein, carbohydrates, and a vitamin/mineral "supplement" all in one convenient, tasty food.

This colorful concoction was next formed into sheets or small loaves, which were packed tightly into tough rawhide containers called *parfleches*. When serious long-term storage was the goal — as when putting up a winter's rations — the native cook would seal each parfleche of pemmican (or jerky) by pouring a layer of melted fat over the top of the contents before securing the lid flap — much as modern canners use paraffin. A parfleche of bison jerky or pemmican so prepared and carefully stored (often buried) might keep for decades. In fact, one still-edible stash, determined to be at least 150 years old, was unearthed in Montana some years ago.

Jerky and pemmican served American Indians not only as winter rations, but were also preferred traveling foods for war and hunting parties. Neither required cooking before eating, and both were denser and lighter than fresh meat — pemmican weighing about a third to half as much as its raw equivalent; jerky a mere one-sixth.

When European hunters, trappers, and explorers invaded the Americas, they were quick to adapt to native foods. Lewis and Clark and their merry band, to cite thirty-one examples, relied heavily on jerked elk to stave off starvation during their prolonged wanderings in the Far West. Wrote Meriwether Lewis on wintry January 20, 1806: "On the morning of the eighteenth we issued 6 lbs. of jirked Elk pr. man, this evening the Sergt. reported that it was all exhausted; the six lbs. have therefore lasted two days and a half only. At this rate our seven Elk will last us only 3 days longer."

A voracious bunch of carnivores that pack must have been, given that six pounds of jerky is the dehydrated derivative of roughly thirty-six pounds of fresh meat, which ciphers out to some twelve pounds of wapiti per man per day.

Still today, jerky remains a favored food among hunters, hikers, and others outdoors folk who travel light and by foot. (Your average modern ATV sport, of course, can haul in not only his favorite fatty foods, but cases of cheap beer, whose containers he feels obliged to carelessly toss about.) But to get the best flavor and avoid the nasty carcinogenic hazards of chemical preservatives and smoke flavorings using in most commercial "snack" jerky today, you have to make your own. I've been doing it for decades, and across those years, through experimentation and failure and more experimentation, have come up with a recipe that even the most critical jerky junkies I've tested it on hail as "*damn* good!" If you'll keep it to yourself, I'll share my secret recipe with you here and now.

If hunting was slow last fall, keep in mind that this concoction works its magic equally well with almost any sort of meat — from industrial beef through all big game meats to fish, wild turkey, and even geese. While it's traditional to use inferior cuts of meat for jerky, I approach my jerkery as an art form to which it's worth tithing a portion of the best — tenderloin, backstrap, top rump — of every animal I kill, relegating the lesser cuts to the chili pot.

For a smoker, I make do with an old two-rack commercial electric job discarded by a friend after the heating element burned out. I replaced the element and have used the simple rig to jerk countless pounds of elk, mule deer, moose, pronghorn, turkey, trout, and salmon. If you shop around, you can purchase, brand new, an almost identical unit for under $40; or a large-capacity jumbo model for about $60, or an even larger, propane-fueled smoker for a hundred or so. If you want to get fancy, design and build your own (on my list for this summer, as it has been for years). You'll also need some wood chips or shavings. Favored commercial offerings include hickory, mesquite, alder, and various fruit woods. I've tried them all and prefer that good old hickory wood. Here in the Rocky Mountain West, where we have no hickory, Gambel's ("scrub") oak closely mimics hickory in the flavor of its smoke and is readily available, assuming you have access to a chipper.

Of course, the most important component for traditional jerkery is also the most difficult to come by — wild meat. When I'm tenacious and lucky enough to bag an elusive wapiti (the most plentiful big game species in my high-country neck of the woods and my personal favorite meat, no matter the Indians' lowly opinion of it), I select jerky fodder as I'm butchering, carefully trimming away all fat, ligament, and fascia (the surface film that covers and separates muscle bundles), then double-wrapping the meat in waxed freezer paper in two-pound packages (the capacity of my smoker).

Come jerking time, I retrieve a package of meat from the freezer and place it in the refrigerator the night before. Usually, the meat will be about half thawed come morning, stiff and easy to slice into thin strips, cutting cross-grain. I try for strips or slabs as thin as possible, and never thicker than one-eighth inch; width doesn't matter so much. Thicker slices take a lot longer to smoke and tend to come out a bit too rare and rubbery for my tastes. If you can't get your slices down to an eighth-inch, beat them into submission with a meat hammer or the lip of a cast-iron frying pan. That done, here's my "secret" marinade recipe:

1 cup beer
1 T. lemon juice (fresh-squeezed, if possible)
1 T. soy sauce
1 T. Worchestershire sauce
1/2 to 1 t. salt, as dictated by your blood pressure and tastes
1/2 to 1 t. coarse-ground black pepper
1 clove fresh minced garlic, or (if you must) 1/2 t. garlic powder

Hand-blend all this good spicy stuff in a big bowl then drop in the jerky strips. Marinate for at least an hour at room temperature, stirring occasionally, until the meat is fully thawed.

While the meat is marinating, fetch in the wire racks from your smoker, make sure they're clean, and place them side-by-side on a counter or table top with newspaper beneath to catch the drips. Dump the meat strips from the marinade into a wire-screen strainer to drain for several minutes, then arrange them on the smoker racks with a little space between so the smoke can rise between. With the racks full, use paper towels to gently blot the tops of the strips (too much moisture on the meat will slow and confound curing), and they're ready for a smoke.

Or almost. Some like it hot, and if you're among this number, as I am, now's the time to lightly sprinkle the racked-up strips with crushed red pepper: New Mexico chili powder is best, if you can find it; otherwise, cayenne flakes, like they give you at the local pizza parlor, will serve.

After placing the loaded racks in the smoker and closing the door or lid, fill the smoker pan with chips or shavings of your chosen wood, place the pan on the heating element, plug the unit in — and start waiting.

Check the unit every hour or so. When smoke quits rising from the top vent, refill the burner pan with more wood chips. After a couple of hours, rotate the racks top to bottom to balance the curing process. My old smoker generally needs about four hours to get the job done, depending on the outside air temperature. Others may be faster or slower. Be patient. Hold out for medium-dry, moderately brittle jerky, but stop well short of crispy.

After unplugging the smoker, remove the racks and place them on newspaper for an hour or so, until the meat is completely cooled. Now peel the jerky strips from the racks and you're done. That two pounds of raw meat we started with is now a double handful, a mere few ounces, of gourmet-quality jerky that your friends will try to steal and strangers will offer their wives and daughters for.

For long-term storage, stash your jerky in an airtight jar and keep it in a freezer or refrigerator. A more traditional and portable jerky safe is a cotton or muslin bag hung in a cool, dry place. Do not store jerky in a plastic bag unless you savor the flavor of mold.

For a day's hunt or hike, grab a big handful of your homemade *charqui*, seal it in a plastic bag (a day or two won't hurt), and keep it handy in pack or jacket pocket; nibble away as the urge strikes. Come evening, to beef-up a camp soup or stew, cut or tear a few pieces of jerky into inch-long shards, drop them in the boiling pot and watch them fatten up. Jerky bits also enliven scrambled eggs, omelets, and sandwiches. As a fan of ultra-light backpack hunts, I've subsisted happily for as long as five days on nothing but water, jerked elk, trail mix, chocolate-covered coffee beans, and a flask of George Dickel.

Like anything worth the doing — say, traditional archery and bowhunting — becoming an expert jerky junkie takes practice, experimentation, and patience. And like traditional bowhunting, much of the satisfaction of eating homemade jerky arises from the effort itself.

The trip, *amigos y amigas*, is the destination.

Chew on that for a while.

Chapter Twenty

Going Squirrelly

"It's easy, Sarge. I just walk into the woods, sit down on a log in the shade with a tree to my back, and stay put. Hour after hour, evening after evening, for as many hours and evenings as it takes. And I love every minute of it; never get bored; there's always *something* going on, always something to learn."

That was my reply, over a dinner of grilled elk backstraps, to a nonhunting friend and fellow recovering Marine when he asked how I manage to bow-kill an elk at less than fifteen yards almost every year.

"I'd go squirrelly with boredom," observed Sarge, chuckling. "And then I'd fall asleep."

Of *course* he would — because he's not a hunter. As bowyer and longbowman Aldo Leopold noted with a knowing grin in his American classic, *A Sand County Almanac*: "When the deer hunter sits down, he sits where he can see ahead, and with his back to something. The duck hunter sits where he can see overhead, and behind something. The nonhunter sits where he is comfortable."

But why, Mr. Leopold, does the nonhunter, comfortable or not, so easily become bored in the woods?

Because, says Aldo, "The deer hunter habitually watches the next bend; the duck hunter watches the skyline; the bird hunter watches the dog; the nonhunter does not watch."

And thanks to this comfortable inattention, he soon goes squirrelly from boredom and nods off to sleep … or scurries back to car, camp, or cabin, where he, or she, feels more at home thanks to technological distractions.

In fairness to Sarge, and in truth, I too go squirrelly during long stretches of inaction while waiting in ambush for elk. Yet I never get bored and I never nod off. For one thing, the logs I prefer for seats are anything but comfortable, pressing hard and lumpy against my bony

butt. And too, my brand of "going squirrelly" is of a wholly different sort
than the nonhunter's.

Across the years, I've whiled away hundreds of ambush hours sitting
and watching and listening and pondering the finer points of *Sciuridae*
language and behavior. Might as well, since the little boogers are everywhere I go. Certainly, you can hunt elk where there are no trees, thus no
tree squirrels. But as traditional archers, whether stalking or sitting, we
need dense cover in order to get killing close to our prey. Toward that end
I avoid big meadows, sage flats, and other vast openings in favor of the
densest aspen and conifer woods I can find. And in such lush places, there
always are squirrels.

While we have several varieties of nut-brains here in the southern
Rockies, by far the most common, and commonly the most annoying, is
the mouthy little red. Also called pine squirrel and chickaree, the red
squirrel (*Tamiasciurus hudsonicus* is the predictable "nature" writer's
"ain't I smart?" scientific nomenclature, available in any good wildlife
guidebook) is abundant in conifer-forested areas throughout the Rocky
Mountain states and New England, ranging north well into Canada and
Alaska. And wherever it lives, it loves to harass hunters — or to entertain
and occasionally even aid us, depending on our mindset, mood, and
attention to its vocalizations and body language. While my observations
and interpretations are hardly scientific, the various calls and the meanings I've surmised for them are amazingly consistent from year to year,
squirrel to squirrel ... at least hereabouts during frantic September,
when the squirrels, like the elk and their human predators, are in a state
of constant arousal.

The most common red squirrel vocalization is the ratchety, long-
drawn *Churrrrr*, generally followed by a rapid-fire string of high-pitched
barks that sound uncannily like the post-bugle chuckles of some mega-
dwarf bull elk. This all-purpose call is voiced from the nest tree at first
light and last, every time a cone is chewed off and tossed to the ground
and, it seems, whenever and for whatever occasion a tree-rat so pleases. I
interpret this churr-bark call as a combination "All's well" and self-
confident territorial declaration.

More mysterious is a quieter call, more contemplative than aroused,
for which I have no name, no logical explanation, nor even a comprehend-
ible description other than to say that it reminds me of some senile old

man high on helium, muttering incoherently to himself. Since it's generally sounded from the ground, in relaxed situations where the omnivorous rodent is searching out and sampling various foods (reds dine not only on nuts, but mushrooms, the fruits and seeds of brushy plants, carrion, ground-nesting birds' eggs and chicks, baby bunnies, infant gray squirrels, bones, antlers, and more), I take it as bemused culinary commentary.

But as a hunter, of greatest interest and frustration are the pine squirrel's two distinct alarm cries. First is the hyper-excited, rapid-fire, exquisitely annoying bark-fest that so often defeats the best efforts of predators, human and otherwise, as we attempt to weasel anonymously through the woods. If you're merely lollygagging along, taking no pains to be quiet, they'll generally leave you alone. But if you're obviously sneaking, acting predatory, the scurridaen wrath is unrestrained. I've had particularly tenacious squirrels follow me hundreds of yards, leaping like tiny Tarzans from tree to tree, until finally, together, we reach the invisible edge of the tormentor's territory and he or she hands me off to the squirrelly neighbor down the line and so on. Tag-team hunter harassment; there ought to be a law! (Ah so, but, as we've learned so tragically with today's lawless OHV abuse, laws are only as good as their enforcement.) At its worst, tree-rat harassment can be enough to drive a gentle man to vengeful violence. Sadly, I know.

Once and long ago, when I was still relatively young (forty-ish) and impatient, and did most of my hunting by sneaking around rather than sitting and waiting, the above-decried tag-team red-squirrel alarm phenomenon went on just a little too long one day, a little too loudly, until finally I lost my cool, nocked an expendable grouse blunt, drew my sixty-four-pound recurve, and took harmful aim at the little red bastard perched on a limb screaming at me from twenty yards away … and let fly.

It's hard to describe the sinking feeling in my guts when that long-shot "warning" arrow actually hit its mouthy little mark, whom I'd only meant to scare away and silence. Well, I silenced him all right. Skewered through the middle, the surprised little beast tumbled to the ground, twitched once or twice then lay unmoving, to scold no more forever. Overcome with unplanned guilt, I hurried over and picked it up and apologized and skinned and gutted it and built a small fire on the spot — a funeral pyre of sorts —and scorched its stringy little bod and forced myself to eat it, without benefit of salt or hunger. If you've ever tried to eat a pine squirrel, you know what a gruesome undertaking it is: bloody and stringy and very strong tasting; nothing like its tasty eastern and Midwestern hardwoods cousins.

Anyhow, after forcing that one down, I never wanted to taste another. Nor, thus, to kill another. This connection has since become for me a personal taste test for ethical hunting: If I kill it, I *eat* it. If I don't want to eat it, how can I morally justify killing it? I can't. And if I can't or don't even try to make my killing a moral act, I become a curse to respectable hunters and the always-struggling-toward decency of humanity. And an abomination to the caring nonhunting public, who are always watching.

In other words, in my humble but long-studied worldview, to kill without eating is to become the most influential of all anti-hunters. Simply and self-evident as this seems, it's way over the heads of too many among us.

Uh ... sorry.

O.K.

The second, and more intriguing, of the two pine-squirrel alarm calls I've learned through attentiveness to differentiate is a loud, slow, metered and modulated *chit ... chit ... chit ... chit*. Sometimes it's brief, but often it continues for minutes at a stretch, depending on how long it takes for the perceived danger to pass. I once considered this call to be purely an air-defense alarm, having repeatedly heard it sounded just prior to the sudden silent shadowy appearance of a winged hunter: most often a great-horned owl or Cooper's hawk, both of which are expert at jetting alone beneath a thick forest canopy to snatch inattentive rodents from limb or ground. Reds also sound the *chit ... chit* alarm every time a human-variety jet approaches, beginning several seconds before standard-issue human ears can hear the distant rumbling growl. But in recent years, I've noted that this same metered, richly nervous alarm may also announce the approach of a pine marten — a big, catlike weasel that's pure lightning on the ground and almost as agile at tree-climbing as the squirrels (among other small mammals) upon which it preys. But confusing the issue, and just often enough to make it promising, the slow *chit ... chit* can also alert us to the approach of a lone cautious elk. In my experience (again, all I have to go on with my squirrelly prognostications), reds *almost* never (never say "never!") bark at a *group* of moving elk, which — what with all their mewing and chirping and bugling and limb-busting, generally make one hell of a racket — yet may become alarmed by the tiny sounds made by moving singles. (Ravens, on the other hand, as hinted at in previous recountings, frequently follow and scream at elk *herds* on the move, but only during rut — a story of another feather.)

The latter phenomenon — reds sounding the alarm at approaching elk — accounts for my original interest in squirrel talk, and my placing it into the "how to" category of hunting yarns. When I hear the *chit ... chit* bit, I seriously perk up and stay that way until the intruder reveals itself or the caller relaxes and quiets down. In one memorable instance, with black-powder hunter Bruce Woods sitting nearby as witness, the distant and persistent *chit ... chit* of a pine squirrel forewarned the approach of a lone 6x6 bull.

Even though red-squirrel alarm calls most often signal something other than the approach of game, and often seem to signal nothing at all, any bowhunter who ignores the voices of the forest is a flaming fool. Or at least he or she is overlooking one of the biggest pleasures and most essential skills of true hunting. To become a good hunter, one must become a good *animal*. In foregone slower times, we called it woodsmanship. These lazy, disconnected, "make it quick and easy as possible at any price" days, the hunter's quiet attention to natural detail too often is drowned out by the roar and whine of off-road engines, our own (shame!), or someone else's. Ought to be a law agin' it! With kick-ass enforcement to match! As poet-hunter Jim Harrison succinctly understates the growing, growling problem: "Engine noise is an effective way to dispel the spirit world."

Of course, the trouble with trying to use squirrels as approaching-game alarms is that they, like some spouses — uh, I mean people — we all know, tend to comment on *everything*. Including, as noted, would-be sneaky bowhunters. Happily, once you stop moving and get settled on stand, most *Sciuridae* will quickly accept you as a benign part of the scene and return to business as usual. Many times (including just moments before the silent appearance of the first elk I ever killed, back in '81), I've had unaware pine squirrels scurry up and stare at me from a foot or two away — head cocked sideways, one shiny brown nut of an eye glistening with curiosity and mischief. Occasionally, they've even bounded up a camouflaged pant leg and bounced across my lap, paying my bony carcass no more heed than if it were a fallen tree. Just this past September, my hunting buddy/biologist Tom Beck had a red squirrel leap onto his head and knock his camo hat off while he sat in evening ambush over an active elk wallow. In my books, having a squirrel mistake you for a tree is the best of omens, signifying that you've successfully blended into your surroundings and have utterly disappeared. If a squirrel doesn't know you're there, neither will (upwind) the next world record elk.

Of course, there's always the rare paranoid sociopathic militia-mentality troublemaker red who just doesn't know when to shut up and mind his (or her) own business. The only thing for it then, short of shooting and eating the annoying beast and spoiling your hunt in the process, is to get up and go sit elsewhere.

Even so, even for all their noise and bother, just as Rachel Carson warned of the horrors of a DDT-created "silent spring" devoid of birds or birdsong, I can't imagine an autumn elk hunt without pine squirrels animating and enlivening the scene — helping to keep me awake, entertained, and alert across all those anything-but-boring hours sitting on stand. I only wish they tasted better.

Chapter Twenty-One

Turkey Tactics for Wapiti (and vice-versa)

The recently deceased tom lay in regal repose among spring-green grass and dandelions, its iridescent copper breast feathers glowing softly under a late-day April sun. Nearby, my pal Ken was working on one of his own, scratching out a familiar tune on a well-worn slate.

Earlier on this second day of Colorado's April/May spring tom turkey season, Ken had called in the gobbler that was now destined to be guest of honor at my dinner table. An arrogant strutter, the lustful bird stopped and displayed at under twenty yards — faced full away, tail fanned wide, blocking his vision behind — presenting me with nature's own bull's eye. At my shot the bird responded with an uncoordinated leaping and thrashing of wings that took him nowhere fast.

Now, half a mile farther along the same ridge, it was Ken's turn. A master caller and veteran turkey hunter, my friend was working a vociferous tom who had hung himself up in a brushy patch of Gambel's oak just fifty yards downhill. For more than twenty minutes the bird answered Ken's pleading slate yelps tit for tat, yet stubbornly (and wisely) refused to come. Obviously, his macho pride wanted the flirty hen to come to him, the way it's supposed to be. (If only such were true with human birds as well, my youth would have been far less frustrating!) If and when the gobbler finally weakened his resolve and began his final approach, I'd take over the calling while Ken prepared to take the shot.

At least, that was the plan.

But turkey hunting being turkey hunting, the tom had other ideas and suddenly fell quiet. When another ten minutes of provocative yelping and purring failed to bring further reply, we knew we'd been beaten. If there'd been a bit more daylight left, we'd have circled wide to get on the opposite side of the gobbler, set up again and given the wise old boy another try. But sunset and roosting time were approaching, so we decided to save this particular challenge for another, younger day.

We stood from our makeshift hides in the shade of adjacent ponderosa pines and exchanged a few quiet words. When, in preparation to move along, I hoisted my tom to my back with a grunt, a horse-big 5x5 bull elk (his last-year's antlers due to drop any day) rose from his brush-hidden bed only fifteen yards away and crashed off down the hill and through the woods, toward where Ken's tom had been. The bull had been there all along, through all of our calling, talking, and shuffling around. To him, I guess, we were just a couple more turkeys.

Encountering the bull was a thrill — it always is — but it came as no great surprise. The landscape we were hunting that day is representative of preferred winter/spring habitat for both wild turkeys and wapiti (and mule deer, and blue grouse, and mountain lions, and bears, and ...) here in the southern Rockies — mature ponderosa pine forest with a rich understory of Gambel's oak broken with frequent small, grassy clearings. This combo provides multiple species with two of the Big Three of wildlife habitat: food (fresh acorns in autumn, acorn mast and twig browse in winter, tender new branches and buds in early spring, over-wintered acorn mast in spring) and cover (thermal and hiding). The third ingredient, of course, is water, abundant in the mountains in winter in the form of snow, and in spring as snowmelt. As a bonus benefit, the mature ponderosa forest ecology provides prime spring "rutting" grounds for Merriam's birds wherever they occur throughout the Rocky Mountain West.

But mountain turkeys share more with elk than overlapping habitat preferences. They also overlap in breeding and defensive behaviors, making hunting the two radically distinct species surprisingly similar. Consequently and happily, if you've never hunted elk in rut but are an experienced turkey chaser, you're way ahead of the game. And versa-vice. Consider ...

Tom turks, like bull elk, are highly vocal during their breeding season. This makes calling an effective hunting method for both, and hands-down the most fun. No other sporting experience has ever thrilled me like bugling for autumn bulls (which, as I keep bemoaning, is largely a lost cause today due to marketplace excesses and hunter abuse, my own included), and yelping for spring longbeards, and having either answer. Even if you never see your prey, you've made verbal contact and raised your pulse for a while. If you've mastered calling either one, you can easily adapt to calling the other.

Turkeys, like elk and more so, are supremely wary and possessed of keen senses, through turkeys have no sense of smell. However, what a gobbler lacks in the nose department, he more than makes up for with wrap-around vision, uncanny hearing, fear of everything that moves, and hair-trigger instincts. And so it is that turkey hunting, like elk hunting, requires full-body camo or other blend-in clothing, plus silent stealth while moving through the woods, setting up and, especially, when the heat is on. If you've acquired sneaky clothing and perfected your sneaking skills on turkeys, you can apply them directly to elk.

Cow elk, like hen turkeys, love to spoil the fun. Ask any elkoholic trad archer what single factor has most often blown his stalks and sneak-hunts, and he or she is likely to respond "sentry cows."

No one I know except me stalks spring turkeys, but hens nonetheless can be major obstacles to bagging toms. I recall the first day of a recent season when I had to pass up a close shot at a Tominator gobbler display-ing arrogantly in a small clearing two dozen yards to my front. Problem was, a hen was stuck like pine pitch to the me-side of my potential target and staring arrows in my direction. I couldn't make the small shift neces-sary to get into shooting position, much less draw my longbow, even when the tom was looking away, for fear of spooking the suspicious hen. Moreover, even should the hen show me her hind end for a moment, thanks to her position I couldn't shoot at the tom for fear of hitting the hen. Before long, the close-knit couple wandered back into the oak brush and were gone — the clueless tom led away by the increasingly suspi-cious hen.

Lesson: Even as we must take constant care against tipping our hat to an alert hen while calling in and drawing-down on a tom, so must we scan constantly and carefully for sentry cows when stalking a bull ... notwithstanding the term "sentry" isn't nearly so militaristic as it sounds. In fact, any relaxed, feeding or bedded herd is going to be more or less scattered, sometimes over a fairly large area, just so long as they're close enough to maintain visual and/or vocal cohesion in the event of trouble. Since a typical rutting-season herd contains several cows and calves and only one bull, chances of first encountering an outlying cow or calf rather than the lone bull are high. Given this scenario, and adding in the fact that most stalks on rutting bulls are vocal rather than visual — you are working in on an unseen bugler and have all your senses focused on the origin location of the sound — it's dangerously easy to overlook elk bedded or feeding amongst cover between you and the target bull.

But before you can close the deal, win or lose, fall elk hunting, just like spring turkey hunting, often involves lots of tippy-toe walking and cautious calling. Serious elk hunters may walk several miles a day, often following ridges, stopping now and again to bugle or cow chirp down into dark canyons in hopes of locating a talkative bull. Once a responsive animal is pinpointed, you clam up and try to calculate a high-odds stalk. If the bull (or bird) indicates his willingness to come to you, briefly stop calling, move in to a hundred yards or closer, depending on terrain and wind conditions — on windy days you can often risk getting closer — and set up before resuming your vocals.

Similarly, just as experienced turkey callers let the frequency and tone of a tom's gobbles determine the frequency and tone of their replies — tit for tat is the rule of thumb — it's best to let an approaching bull set the pace and intensity for all close-in conversation, whether you're bugling or cow calling. If he's excited and talkative (bull or bird), answer him call for call, reflecting an equal amount of excitement. If he goes quiet, you go quiet too. If he sounds an alarm bark (or putt), you do the same.

When the calling action gets eyeballing close, two elk hunters — working just like two tom hunters — can be a deadly team. A rutting bull homing in on a bugle or cow chirp will focus his attention on the source of the sound, giving the shooter — who is set up between caller and game on the downwind side — a close, relatively relaxed, high-percentage shot opportunity.

In sum, by being aware and taking advantage of the many habitat, behavioral, and strategic/defensive similarities between spring turkey and fall elk, the hunter adept at either can translate those skills to the other with remarkable ease and success.

Chapter Twenty-Two

Bunny-Bashing Basics

Autumn through winter in most parts of America is rabbit season. And to me, "rabbit" means cottontail. While I've known a few apparently sane folk who say they enjoy eating jackrabbit, I've 'et jack, way back in the Boy Scouts — an experience I found sufficiently satisfying to last a lifetime. But, my cap is off, way off, to anyone who can consistently kill them with a stickbow, given their skittishness and bounding speed. Howard Hill did, I know, but that was Howard Hill, and even He burned a lot of arrows in the process.

While the snowshoe hare is a lot bigger and meatier than the cottontail, and in some ways easier to hunt, its habitat is restricted and high, making it a regional rather than universal offering, and quite the physical challenge. And to me, the snowshoe's flavor, while agreeable, doesn't match that of the cottontail.

Just last week, between Christmas and New Years, wanting to wring a last bit of value from our 2006 small game tags, Milt Beens and I drove a hundred miles to a cottontail hotspot. Here in the mountains this time of year, the snow is deep and bunnies are hard to find, spending most of every day down in some relatively warm hole, coming out at night to feed, party, and leave enticing tracks everywhere. A half-day walk might produce a blurred sighting or two, at best. But out there on the sagebrush/rabbitbrush/beanfield flats of western Colorado, "bugs" (*a la* Bugs Bunny) are thick as the fleas they carry, and unlike their mountain cousins, rarely go to ground.

In a meaty example of how the primary motivation and joy of trad bowhunting reside in the act of doing it, the process, rather than the

145

product, in six hours of hard hunting, Milt and I took dozens of fun shots — fifty yards, running, whatever, in the process losing two arrows each, breaking two cedar shafts each (as usual, just behind the heads), and generally had ourselves an action-packed blast. Our bag for all this effort was a single 'tail that Milt nailed cleanly in the head. And then we switched to shotguns. Having committed to drive two hundred miles round-trip this day, and gas prices what they are, we came prepared to bring home the bacon, as it were, one weapon or another. And that we did! In a final two hours of hunting, we bagged nineteen more bugs, thus attaining our daily limit of ten each. And I'd be lying to claim it wasn't fun.

But still, as I admitted to Milt during the drive home, I'd have traded all ten of my lead-shot-sprinkled bunnies for the one he bagged with a longbow.

When we do it next, a week from today if the snow slacks off enough to allow it, having got my freezer well-stocked with rabbit, I'm taking only the bow … and a whole lot of arrows!

In my openly biased opinion, the cottontail should be designated America's official Favorite Game Animal. Consider its qualifications: With the exception of squirrels in some areas, no other animal has introduced more young people to hunting than the cottontail. It's plentiful almost everywhere. While it can be extremely challenging to bowhunt (depending on season, subspecies, habitat, and other particulars), its abundance makes the 'tail a readily attainable first kill for youngsters and other beginners, given appropriate time and effort. Seasons and bag limits are generous, no expensive equipment or extensive experience is required and, bottom line, it's delicious on the table. (In a twist on the old "Tastes just like chicken" joke, to me, cottontail tastes just like turkey, only better.)

Thank the gods of bowhunting for the all-American cottontail rabbit … or is it a hare?

Granted, it's a hare-splitting distinction — rabbit vs. hare — leading to widespread confusion in common and regional usage: The jack "rabbit" is really a hare, while the domestic Belgian "hare" is actually a rabbit, and the snowshoe "rabbit" is a hare. But the most famous misnomer of all involves the infamous Easter Bunny, a.k.a. Peter Cottontail, who in fact began his mythical career as a European hare of Celtic vintage, when and where there were no cottontails. And so on.

Name-calling aside, both species, rabbits and hares, belong to the order Lagomorpha (literally, "hare-shaped"). While lagomorphs likely first appeared in Asia (like so many other familiar "North American" species), they've been resident here for the past 50 million years or so. The order Lagomorpha includes two families: the alpine-dwelling Ochotonidae, better known as the pika or coney; and, of far greater interest to hunters, Leporidae, the rabbits and hares. All lagomorphs have cleft upper lips (giving rise to the unfortunate expression *harelip*) and long, rodent-like incisors that grow constantly to compensate for wear. But contrary to popular misconception, lagomorphs are not rodents.

Most hares are larger than most rabbits and have bigger ears in proportion to body size. Additionally, most hares have black-tipped ears while most rabbits don't. Rabbit kittens (yes, cutesy as it sounds, that's the proper term) are born helpless in nursery nests, often shallow ground dens, constructed especially for the occasion by the expectant doe. Hare kits, meanwhile, are birthed in the open, wherever the doe happens to be at the time, and enter the world with vision, a warm coat of fur and, within just a few minutes of birth, the ability to run like … rabbits.

The familiar American cottontail, genus *Sylvilagus*, comprises fourteen species, including eastern, western, New England, mountain, marsh, and desert varieties. As its regional names suggest, the cottontail is common across America, ranging from East Coast to West, and from southern Canada as far south as Argentina and Paraguay. Most widespread and plentiful of the fourteen species is the eastern variety, present in all forty-eight contiguous states and beyond.

When you consider that virtually every North American predator — from the tiny least weasel to the great grizzly bear, plus most winged hunters, you and certainly I — consider the cottontail to be one of the most delectable items on nature's menu, the abundance and tenacious prosperity of the little mammal is downright amazing. Certainly, Peter is adept at running (up to twenty miles per hour), burrowing, and otherwise hiding from those of us who would invite him for dinner. Yet the real secret of the cottontails' survival and success is its fondness for sex. Fact is, nature has endowed cottontails with a horniness rivaling even that of human teenagers. Moreover, cottontails attain sexual maturity fast; depending on species, does can be ready to breed within just eighty days after birth. A gestation period of less than a month allows for the production of from two to six litters during the annual half-year breeding season (roughly February through August, peaking in May). Finally, litter size is large, with three to six kittens common and up to eight not unusual. And if that's not enough to keep their numbers up, cottontail does can become re-impregnated immediately after giving birth and some species, in a remarkable survival adaptation called *superfetation*, can take on a second litter even before offloading the first, thus achieving overlapping pregnancies.

In sum, a single cottontail doe has the potential to produce as many as fifty young per year — more than even *I* could eat.

To further ensure their long-term survival, cottontails have the potential to live ten years. Of course, few animals die of old age in the wild, and predation, disease, and harsh weather combine to reduce the average cottontail lifespan to fifteen months for adults. Among healthy cottontail populations, human hunting is believed to have minimal impact on overall death rate and population maintenance — which is to say, if we don't kill and eat them, something else will. As in all wild species, heaviest mortality is among the young, with some **90** percent of infant cottontails perishing before reaching maturity.

And little wonder death is so common among cottontail young. They begin life weighing only an ounce or two and are blind, without fur, and utterly helpless, looking and sounding (*squeak-squeak*) like naked mice. But after just a week of guzzling their mother's nutritious milk, cottontail infants are well-furred, bright-eyed, and squirming about in the nest. Another week and they'll have tripled their birth weight and are ready to venture out on short treks. Within a month of birth, young Peters are weaned and on their own, win or lose.

Adult cottontails are eating machines, devouring a salad bar of wild greens, nuts, berries, and seeds, plus cultivated crops, my wife's garden and, on rare occasion, insects. And to get the most from it all, they eat everything twice. In a phenomenon known as *refection*, most of what is swallowed by lagomorphs is recycled — defecated as soft pellets, re-swallowed, and run through the digestive system a second time. (Rather like chewing cud backwards.) This unusual survival strategy is particularly important in winter, since cottontails neither hibernate nor hoard food for the lean months, and must make the most of whatever they can find.

Growing up in central Oklahoma, I became so infatuated with rabbit hunting as a high school student, I kept beagles specifically to facilitate the chase. But a *chase* it generally was, with the hounded bunny predictably breaking from cover and running in a wide circle in order to keep within its familiar territory. With a shotgun in hand, the caper was to stand on a stump or other elevated spot and wait for the runner to return. Then point, lead and ... *Ka-blam!*

For archers, unless you don't mind losing a lot of arrows, cottontail hunting is not a rowdy chase but a sneak. "Walk slowly and quietly, carefully searching the brush and woodpiles for a shiny black eye," advised my first bowhunting mentor when I was only eight. As I would soon learn and have proven countless times since on countless bunny bowhunts, he knew what he was talking about. My favorite rabbit days are cold mornings just after a snowfall, when the cottontail's distinctive tripod tracks lead directly to its daytime hideout. The standard tactic for gunners is to kick or hop onto every brush- or woodpile in hopes of spooking the quarry out. But with a bow, once again and as always, a quieter approach is in order. Circle the hiding cover slowly, looking long and hard for a bit of brown fur or that shiny black eye or a tremor of movement. Often, your persistence will make the hider nervous enough to move around a bit within its cover, thus revealing itself. Two bowhunters, working opposite sides of the same cover, or a well-trained dog, can make this technique quite productive.

While the Judo point is favored by many archers for all small game, it tends to get snagged when shooting into dense brush, leading to unnecessary misses and broken shafts. My favorite bunny point is a plain steel blunt. Milt prefers damaged broadheads — his favorite is the venerable Bodkin — with their tips broken off just in front of the ferule and filed flat. If you're lucky, the ground or other proximate backstop will halt the shaft as it emerges from the soft-bodied prey, keeping it from passing entirely through and preventing a wounded animal from escaping (though bunnies rarely go far after being hit anywhere with an arrow). Big, bright-colored flu-flu fletching is a bonus, especially in the snow. As much as I hate it during rifles big game seasons, I paint my rabbit shafts day-glo orange.

Of course, as with most game, the "best" hunting methods and equipment depend on local conditions and personal choice, as do recipes for cooking your kill. My own favorite, which my wife calls "chicken-fried rabbit," is fast and easy to prepare, delicious and even healthy (a very rarity with fried meats), like so ...

Caroline's chicken-fried rabbit:

Cut one or more cottontails (smaller, younger bunnies are the most tender and tasty of course) into pieces and soak for an hour in cold salted water (to draw out any remaining blood). Rinse and blot dry.

Dust pieces in white flour, seasoned to taste with salt and pepper.

Dip dusted pieces in a batter of one cup milk and one whole egg, whipped (egg white will suffice).

Roll battered pieces in flour again.

Fry in a medium-hot skillet without lid, using just enough olive oil — a couple of tablespoons max — to generously coat the bottom. When the pieces are golden-brown on their down-sides, gently turn once with a spatula, and brown the other side.

After removing Peter from the pan, use the remaining oil, with its bunny juice and crunchy fryings, to make country gravy. Serve with mashed potatoes, biscuits or cornbread, and your favorite veggie ...

Hot damn!

Part III

Campfire Philosophies

David Petersen

Chapter Twenty-Three

Do Animals Have Feelings That Hunters Can Hurt?

A Meaty Conversation with Valerius Geist

A while back, I was privileged to spend a week at the rural Vancouver Island home of Dr. Valerius Geist and his vivacious wife Renate. Aside from his celebrated careers as wildlife biologist, scholarly and popular writer, and university professor, "Val" Geist is also an enthusiastic student of Pleistocene megafauna (large animal) evolution and an avid campfire philosopher. Motivated by the assumption that you too sometimes struggle with the harder questions of hunting — trying to honestly and intelligently explain hunting to your own satisfaction so that you can honestly and intelligently explain it to others — I offer the following fireside discussion with Val Geist exploring the emotional depth of the creatures we hunt … and thus, their capacity to experience physical and emotional suffering.

Dave: As an ethologist, evolutionary biologist, wildlife ethicist, and hunter, to what extent do you believe our fellow animals know humanlike emotions: fear, joy, sorrow, elation, love, mental and physical suffering, and all the rest?

David Petersen

Val: As I scientist, I can speak authoritatively only about what can be scientifically proven or disproven — that is the nature of science. Therefore, I cannot speak authoritatively about animal emotions, or even about emotions in my fellow humans. Although various external and behavioral *symptoms* of emotion — smiling, crying, laughing, fright, flight, fight, and more — are clearly visible, the *emotions themselves* are hidden inside the individual, beyond the reach of scientific verification, quantification, or denial. Thus, as a scientist, I can only *infer* the existence of suffering in my fellow animals. Even so, while I cannot scientifically measure suffering, I *can* scientifically measure damage. If an animal has been structurally damaged—say, scarring or bone breakage from an old hunting wound — then I can say, "Yes, there is almost certainly suffering involved here."

Where this gets really difficult is in deciding where to draw the line, if at all, between which animals are capable of experiencing suffering and other emotions, and which are not. Given that emotions cannot be quantified but only inferred, how, or even should, such a scientifically arbitrary distinction determine the way we treat different animals? A common approach is to draw a line between sentient and insentient. On the sentient side are creatures, such as people and other apes, that possess highly developed central nervous systems, who clearly have an awareness of themselves and their world, and who evidence a high degree of self-determination, even spontaneity, in how they act and react in various situations. Insentient creatures, those lacking well-developed central nervous systems, presumably know or feel little if anything. Now, if you ask if I, as a scientist and a hunter, believe that elk are sentient — capable of experiencing mental as well as physical suffering — yes, I do. Do elk have self-determined intellect, the ability to weigh options and act spontaneously? Yes, they do. They, like us, can *think*.

Yet, animal thinking clearly is not based on a coded language, as is human thinking. And that — a coded, or symbolic language, where a certain arrangement of sounds comes to stand for very subtle and specific intellectual concepts — is what makes people special among animals. While I cannot climb inside you to feel what you are feeling, by utilizing our shared language you can describe your feelings to me in great detail, employing words that symbolize your feelings. Thus, by relating and comparing your descriptions to my own past feelings, I can achieve a very high degree of empathy with you. While many other species have highly evolved body languages and mutually understood vocalizations, only humans enjoy coded — symbolic, metaphorical, even poetical — language.

The root problem in trying to determine the degree of suffering of various living beings and treating, or mistreating, them accordingly, is that the common distinction between sentient and insentient is based on a false dichotomy. What science demonstrates is that no such division exists. All life originates from and depends upon DNA coding. And all life, *all* of life, no exception, attempts to protect itself from damage. Consider the lowly potato. Cut it open and what happens? Soon, the damaged and exposed surface begins to weep, then it crusts over and turns brown, in effect building a wall to protect the remaining undamaged tissue. So I ask you: how does the insentient potato *know* it is injured and how to protect itself from further damage?

Dave: Via photochemical reactions resulting from sudden exposure to oxygen and/or sunlight.

Val: Of course! Which tells us that even the potato must be sensitive to messages saying that its exterior has been damaged. In the same way, *all* living organisms are aware of damage and will attempt to protect themselves. Therefore, the distinction between sentient and insentient is invalid, since no living thing is truly insentient: unable to sense injury. Furthermore, this universal sensation that damage has occurred must be described as pain or at least as discomfort, as when you suffer an itch that simply *must* be scratched. You don't need a central nervous system in order to experience such sensations and react to them — to protect, repair, and attempt to become whole again.

Dave: It strikes me that the standard response to what you are saying would be that while all living things may in fact *feel*, there is certainly a hierarchy of feelings.

Val: No! You try and prove that scientifically! It can't be done!

Dave: Granted. Yet, our inability to prove a thing doesn't necessarily negate its existence, and vice versa.

155

Val: At this point you're proceeding on a false assumption, on *faith* — blind belief in something that cannot be proven one way or another. The great tragedy that drives such debates of sentience and suffering — and it is a tragedy — is that you and I, all human beings, all animals, can only live by degrading other life into our own body structures. There is no escape from this fact. Life can *only* live by killing and eating other life. The only reason we choose to eat salad is because the salad ingredients are *alive*, thus fresh, delicious, and nutritious. Our teeth are shearing through living protoplasm with every bite! Or pick up a granola bar. The granola bar contains the raw or roasted "children" of plants. You, or whoever made that granola bar in your behalf, have killed the beginnings of new life — seeds, nuts, and grains — in order that your own life may be sustained.

What this means is that if you value your own life, you must value all the other life that makes your life possible. And what that feeling translates to is a certain reverence for *all* life. And the very notion of reverence for life does not accept divisions. Consequently, the vegan/animal rights ethical stance, being based on the false assumption of the sentience vs. insentience distinction and the idea that we can do anything we want to insentient life forms without guilt but nothing at all to the sentient, has no verifiable or scientific basis. Therefore, it has no philosophical or ethical basis either. It is only faith: an arbitrary conglomeration of assumptions. Once you make such assumptions, you can build all sorts of air-castles atop them, but there is no objective foundation to any of it. Consequently, the only logical response is to have reverence for *all* life.

Dave: It seems to me that misinterpretation of the term "reverence for life," as proselytized most famously by Dr. Albert Schweitzer and echoed by today's animal rights champions, is a common problem for both views. At one extreme, the most unrepentant carnivores — including not only the most thoughtless hunters among us, but also people involved in the caged-meat industry, including of course the millions of Americans who consume industrial meat products — collectively, this anthropocentric mindset either gives the value of nonhuman life no consideration at all, or consciously devalues nonhuman life to the point of feeling it deserves no concern. At the other extreme — as epitomized by the Jainists and emulated by vegans and some vegetarians — "reverence for life" is misconstrued as an absolute rejection of death as an essential part of life.

Val: I love gardening, gathering, fishing, and hunting. Each of these activities involves me in the great drama of life and reminds me, with every step and breath I take, that life comes from and takes away other life, and therefore *all life is precious*. I also gratefully acknowledge that we human animals owe our very existence to our fellow mammals. Across the several million years of our evolution from *Australopithecine* to *Homo*, hunting and being hunted worked to shape us — physically, intellectually, socially, even spiritually — and made us what we are today. For example, we loudly hail the ability to read as a great achievement of our species ... but just try tracking, upon which reading historically is based. As experienced outdoorsmen and naturalists, you and I can both attest that learning to track is a lot more difficult than learning to read. For reasons far beyond food, we owe our very existence as humans to the nonhuman others.

Dave: Indeed, animal tracks, as perceived by human hunters, were the first "written" language if you will; that is to say the first metaphors, nature's crude rudiments of a coded language wherein one thing represents, or allows us to envision, a whole universe of other things. To begin, in order to be an effective tracker, you have to recognize which track represents which animal. Beyond that, you must be able to "read" from the track/symbol such essential information as how old the track is, what the animal was doing when it made the track or tracks — walking, feeding, standing, running, alone or in a group — from which information, further extrapolating, the animal's gender, health, and emotional state can be substantially intuited: Was it stalking, feeding, limping, relaxed, nervous, frightened? From there, combined with extensive knowledge of the prey and terrain, the expert tracker can go on to make educated guesses about where the animal may now be, what it may be doing, and even its state of alertness.

Val: Precisely! And this ability — to literally *read* all sorts of useful information symbolically contained in animal tracks, thus removing much of the element of uncertainty from the hunt — allowed our early ancestors to become highly successful stalkers. And stalking, at least early in human development, was our primary approach to hunting, providing the meat-derived proteins and fats essential to rapid brain development, and so on, spiraling up and up.

Dave: And in parallel with hunting, the gathering of edible, medicinal, and psychotropic or shamanistic plants likely facilitated the evolution or development of classification, naming, and oral language.

Val: Thank you! And so it is, in ways far beyond nutritional sustenance, that we owe our very existence as humans to the nonhuman others, both animal and vegetable, with whom we synergistically evolved. As humans and especially as thoughtful hunters, how can we *not* love and respect them?

Chapter Twenty-Four

A Trip to the Meat Market

At the meat market recently, my attention and sympathy were drawn to an aquarium tank containing a dozen or so semi-live lobsters. Their claws were bound with thick rubber bands, their world reduced to a few gallons of stale gray water — waiting to be purchased and tossed (some say screaming, though lobsters have no vocal cords) into the boiling pot. From the lobster tank, my darkening thoughts wandered to the meat case with its endless neat rows of pink "product" neatly arranged on white plastic trays, and from there, thinking back along the ladder of production, to the gruesome slaughterhouse, the putrid poultry and egg factory, the immobilizing veal pen, the inhumane caged-pig production-line "farm" and the many other grisly and environmentally hurtful commercial operations that provide the human world with the animal flesh and protein our omnivorous species instinctively craves.

By comparison, I was reminded once again, hunting for the meat we eat is a wholly natural, healthy, and moral proposition — beneficial not only to the hunter, but, I will argue, to the hunted as well.

Of course, as the vegans — those hard-nosed vegetarians who shun not only meat but all animal-derived products including eggs, cheese, and leather — are quick to point out and evangelical in their pointing, the human body does not *require* meat in order to survive and even prosper.

And they are right. In fact, for a couple of years long ago, when I was young and strong and living on the West Coast — where I could not hunt without driving all day and being among a crowd — for reasons of practicality and personal disgust with the commercial flesh industry in America, I became a half-assed vegetarian myself. And enjoyed athletic vigor all the while. In fact, my veggie, cheese, and egg period in California (occasionally augmented by fish I caught or speared) was the fittest and most active time of my life. I walked at least three fast miles a day bare-foot on the beach, ran at least four more, swam regularly in the cold Pacific, pumped tons of iron, chased the girls and caught a few (including a lifetime keeper named Caroline), and all with energy left to spare. But in order to make even half-assed vegetarianism perform this well you really have to work at it; you have to study nutrition, know what you're doing and, frankly, eat a lot of brilliantly boring stuff.

Yet and still, come dinner time each evening, something vital — some ancient gnawing *something* — clearly was missing.

Then one evening shortly after moving from urban coastal California to rural Montana, I was offered meat at the home of a friend. It was wild meat — the cleanest, leanest, most healthful food there is. My friend had caught me in just the right mood: hungry and broke. I accepted gra-ciously and ate voraciously a delicious road-killed whitetail stew. Next thing I knew I was enjoying meat regularly again. And as often as possi-ble it was, and remains today, meat earned the good old-fashioned hard way — by hunting North America's richly abundant deer, elk, pronghorn, wild turkey, grouse, rabbit, and more, with a bit of wild-caught fish for variety.

It's only a slight digression from here to note that when thinking and talking about the rights and wrongs of modern hunting (there are plenty of both), it's essential to remember that we can hunt in America today only because wildlife is so abundant. And wildlife is so abundant today only because of the ten-unpopular actions of an enlightened handful of yesterday's hunters — specifically, Theodore Roosevelt and a hundred or so fellow sportsmen/conservationists who had the moral will and political weight to introduce protective wildlife legislation and get it enacted and enforced.

By the late 1800s, due to habitat conversion to farms and rangelands by settlers and the ongoing unregulated slaughter of wildlife by market shooters (these guys had no self-imposed rules of fair play and thus were not hunters as we use the term today), North America's cervid (deer family) populations had been reduced to an all-time low with many species being shoved hard against extinction and some subspecies (Mer-riam's and Eastern elk, for two sad examples) shot to oblivion. It was no "animal rights" group, no "hunters' rights" extremists, but conscientious hunter/*conservationists* who sounded the last-minute alarm, calling for the enactment of protective laws, vigorous enforcement of those laws, and the levying of special taxes on hunting and hunting-related hardware — taxes earmarked for funding wildlife protection, restoration, and management, along with habitat acquisition, restoration, and improvement programs.

In this forceful way, America's dwindling wildlife treasure, together with a goodly measure of our national pride, were snatched back from the brink. Today, North America supports the highest numbers of elk, deer, black bear, and other big game species anyone living since the mid-1800s has known.

But hunting is killing. What of the killing? In the minds of many critics, what hunters do for "pleasure" cannot be reconciled by pragmatics alone. Killing is primarily a moral issue.

One such concern commonly expressed by animal rights advocates has nothing directly to do with protecting animals, but rather is motivated by the belief that hunting and killing for "pleasure" morally degrades those who do it, especially the impressionable young.

I respond: "You are mistaken." I have never seen the implied negative transition from gentle to cruel acted out in another hunter. And for myself, after a lifetime of hunting I have not found killing animals in order to eat them, no matter the "pleasure" I may take in the challenge, to have desensitized me to death and suffering, much less to have instilled a wantonness for blood and violence. *Exactly the opposite!* It was fair-chase hunting and fishing that first brought me into alignment with wild nature and coached me, gradually but surely, to become a naturalist, a conservationist, and an unabashed spokesman for animal welfare (which is *not* the same as animal "rights").

They say it takes one to know one, and being one myself I like to believe I understand the collective psyche of hunters better than do the antis and nonhunting public, and I have come to believe this: If a hunter is a drunken, bloodthirsty slob, which some regrettably are, he or she was so *a priori*, before and independently of hunting, rather than as a result of it. Lord knows today's hunting ranks are fat with slobs — but what corner of modern life is not in our "Me first!" culture? And exceptions never make the rule.

But what of the prey, the "victims" of the hunt, the true bloody meat of the moral matter?

I have witnessed the nightmare of the slaughterhouse, held my nose while touring a poultry operation, watched claw-bound lobsters stupefied in a ten-gallon purgatory ... even as my hands have turned crimson with the still-warm blood of wild creatures I have killed. Having experienced all of this, were I forced into the choice by some wicked witch, rather than being transmogrified into a pig in a small wire cage or a steer (don't forget, steerdom begins with castration) fattening in a fetid feedlot for slaughter, I would beg to be made a deer or elk or *anything* wild — born free, living as instinct demands, and eventually dying swiftly by well-placed arrow or bullet launched by one who cares about me and my world and isn't merely killing for money, and in the end my flesh gratefully, respectfully, and knowingly consumed. If getting shot or stuck with an arrow doesn't sound all that appealing, consider wildlife's other most likely options for departing this beautiful world — starving, freezing, being ripped apart by fang and claw, the slow torture of internal para-sites and disease (often as not introduced by domestic livestock), a messy midnight rendezvous with a speeding semi delivering fresh "harmless" veggies to the local supermarket.

Nobody rides for free.

Nothing gets out alive.

Moreover, were wild animals magically given voice in the matter, I venture that even they would endorse predation ethical human hunting, since without hunting and the financial, political, management, and research support it provides, only a relative few wild animals would likely be here today or will be here tomorrow, period. And most of those few would be in private, for-profit ownership — the very worst sort of "factory farm" — not running free on public lands for all to enjoy.

If it ain't broke, Grandpa wisely advised, don't try to fix it.

Hunting ain't broke, but that's not to say it doesn't have some low tires, grinding gears, a sputtering engine and lots of loose spokes. So what can we who truly care — hunters, nonhunters, and antis alike — do to tune up the morality of modern hunting?

Plenty.

Hunters can start by examining our true personal motives for walk-ing about with bows and guns, looking to kill. We can and must police our own ranks — our relatives, friends, and selves especially included, hard

A Man Made of Elk

as it may be — saving the salvageable while vigorously disenfranchising the slob-hunter cancer that taints, weakens, and threatens to take *all* hunting down with it.

And who, exactly, is this often-derided but largely faceless "slob hunter"? He or she is variously a cruise-around road shooter, an ATV addict, an armed drunk, a slovenly purveyor of litter, a poacher, a flagrant trespasser, a liar and a cheat — in short, an amoral moron who predictably performs similarly in nonhunting endeavors as well ... parking in the handicapped zone, cutting in line at the theater or market check-out, running stop signs, letting his well-fed house cats roam loose to prey on songbirds, cheating, cheating on his or her spouse, lying at every opportunity, and otherwise acting the jerk. You get the picture: He or she is not just a slob *hunter*, but an all-around flake and loser.

Nor can we separate slob *hunters* from the media and marketplace forces that encourage and abet for profit the objectification of wildlife, cheating via technology, trophy gluttony, and generally obnoxious hunter behavior.

Caring hunters must support mandatory hunter ethics and essential skills education and help to make it increasingly effective. We must lobby for a more eco-centric wildlife management paradigm along with more strenuous game law enforcement, swifter justice, and stiffer penalties for violators. (Too many judges refuse to take wildlife crimes seriously, failing to see that crimes against nature are likewise crimes against man.) And hunters must strive to shape strongly positive examples for today's young people, who may become tomorrow's hunters ... or not.

Nonhunters, meanwhile — accounting for more than 80 percent of North Americans — can strive for open minds, demand the proof of claims and counterclaims made by all sides, and try to understand that slob hunters, in all their perverted and highly visible forms, neither speak nor act for the majority of hunters. Nor, for that matter, do such high-visibility, industry-sponsored lobbying groups as the U.S. Sportsman's Alliance (formerly Wildlife Legislative Fund of America), the bombastic pro-ATV lobbying group Blue Ribbon Coalition, and NRA (which recently killed an otherwise sure-thing wilderness designation in prime big game habitat here in Colorado — Brown's Canyon, on the Arkansas River — because it would have closed an old wagon trail being illegally used by a few local motorheads) ... none such self-proclaimed sportsmen's organizations in fact represent the minds, morals, or best interests of true hunters. Likewise, sleazy "Whack 'em and stack 'em" publications, videos, and television programs — the latter epitomized by the staggeringly stupid and annoying *Outdoor Channel* — appeal only to the perverse, deluded, young, or otherwise mentally disadvantaged "sportsmen." *Nobody* hates such despicable "horn porn" as deeply as do traditional ethical hunters.

Yet fault is universal and the nonhunting public must also beware that True Believer anti-hunters, like the worst of preachers, politicians, and "hunter's rights" crazies, often are dissemblers waging dirty fights.

Animal rights folk, if their true interest is in fact the long-term well being of wild creatures, rather than wanting to impose *their* moral code, right or wrong, on others, can try to set their emotional disdain for *all* hunting and *all* hunters aside, in favor of joining with ethical hunters and the concerned nonhunting public to fix what's broke with hunting today — that is, attacking and disabling the bad and applauding and encouraging the good—to benefit both wildlife and humanity in the long run. By all means, attack what is wrong with hunting — including baiting, contest hunting, high-fenced canned killing operations, OHV abuse, excessive hi-tech advantage, general lawlessness, and plenty more.

Done right, hunting and killing your own meat is as natural and moral as making love (another unpopular activity in some puritanical circles). Because the dying is visible and the blood is literally on the consumer's hands, hunting implies and entails an infinitely greater connection to the reality of our food than does the thoughtless of the commonplace trip to the meat market, where the flesh of once-sentient life has been disguised by off-camera professionals and objectified by commerce as neatly wrapped product.

"Daddy," a friend's young son recently asked, "Where did this chicken we're eating come from?"

"Uh ... a farmer," my bushwhacked friend heard himself stutter, though he knew it was a cop-out. "As soon as he's old enough to understand," he assured me, "I'll set the boy straight."

Let's hope that's not too late. When I was in grade school, back mid-century, a normal part of public education was a field trip to the local slaughterhouse. Today, few parents want that, while the "meat industry" has learned better than to invite it.

Of all our institutionalized cruelties to fellow animals, none is more gargantuan, horrendous — and made purposely invisible — than the commercial livestock industry. I choose to hunt elk rather than buy beef. I get my pork in the form of half a free-range grass-fed pig each fall from 4H farm youngster (an endangered species). Eggs, chicken, and cheese come from a specialty market that deals with a cooperative comprising certified organic and cage-free suppliers. Others who are bothered by the cruelties and health dangers of factory farming choose vegetarianism. While all life feeds on death, we always have choices.

Which brings us down to this bottom line: In order to stay on moral solid ground, what do we *owe* to the animals we eat, if anything? The majority of Americans, voting with their purchases, might as well be shouting "Nothing!" At the opposite minority extreme, vegan animal rights champions say "Leave them entirely alone; they are exactly like us!"

To me, we owe the animals we eat two things at the least:

First, we owe them the freedom to exercise their bodies and to express at least their most basic instincts. Pigs *need* to root in dirt and mud. Chickens and turkeys *need* to peck and scratch for bugs in the dust and flap their wings at will. Cattle *need* to walk and graze freely. Elk and deer on game farms *need* to be freed, as they have not been domesticated into robotic creatures and therefore suffer unduly in captivity.

Second, we owe the animals we eat fast, painless, "never knew what hit 'em" deaths.

In both of these essential measures of moral obligation — the physical freedom to move about in a habitat that allows the expression of basic instincts, and a fast and humane death — fair-chase hunting, undertaken as it should and morally *must* be, is simply unsurpassed.

Chapter Twenty-Five

The Sacred Game

And another hunting season approaches, renewing the ancient bloody passions — for as well as against the chase.

As distinctly opposed to egomaniacal executioners of petting farm captives, techno-weenies, and motorized morons, true hunters are quietly thoughtful predators playing a proper, exacting, and important role in the natural scheme of things. It is, after all, predators, human and otherwise, who sculpted the incredible defensive tactics of prey species. Predator and prey: a quintessentially symbiotic relationship and the engine that powers upward-spiraling intellectual evolution among all creatures great and small — as Darwin was among the first to recognize, and no open-minded thinking person denies today. To wit:

Those animals (and plants, for that matter) that are born with or somehow acquire through genetic "happy accidents" even minor physical features or behavioral traits that provide them with an advantage over others of their kind, tend to live longer, breed more often, and procreate and pass on their genes more successfully than those less well adapted to their environments. In the face of this fiercely selective competition, those individuals and species less fit are gradually squeezed out, while those better adapted to their life niches prosper and grow ever stronger.

Through this never-resting, imperceptibly slow winnowing process have evolved the most masterful self-defense organisms in the mammalian world, the deer, or cervid family. To get within striking range of any species of deer, predators must defeat a truly remarkable eye-ear-nose-nerve defense strategy. This is the challenge that excites the serious, no-shortcuts, no-BS bowhunter.

Consider vision. Deer see differently than we do. The eyes of all mammalian predators, yours and mine included, are set side-by at the front of the head, a.k.a. face, a few inches apart, so that each eye views an object from a slightly different angle, providing binocular vision, which, in turn, facilitates precise depth perception. Whether you're a mountain lion about to leap from a ledge onto the back of a passing deer, or an archer aiming a bow instinctively, it's essential to have an accurate sense of the distance to your target. The trade-off is severely limited peripheral vision among predators, far less important in the wild than in high-speed commuter traffic.

On the flipside of the visual scenario, since a major threat to prey species is the possibility of predators sneaking in from the sides or rear, natural selection has positioned prey eyes on opposite sides of the head, providing extensive peripheral vision. The losses are binocular vision and fine-tuned depth perception. But no great matter. For prey, visually determining the exact distance to something suspicious isn't nearly as important as knowing if, when, and how that threat moves. And prey eyes are attuned to detect the slightest rapid movement.

Working in conjunction with cervid eyes are big, top-set ears that swivel independently, like scanning radar, which capture sounds in stereo, much as predatory eyes receive images. If something within the deer's extremely wide field of vision moves, the animal, always alert, will spot it. And if the mover makes any sound, the deer's ears will provide an instant fix, confirming direction and distance. Between the two, far more often than not, the hopeful hunter goes hungry.

Even so, the most remarkable of the deer's defenses is its nose — virtually undefeatable unless the wind is constantly in the predator's favor, which situation deer strive diligently to prevent by employing such clever tactics as circling suspicious forest features downwind — say, a camouflaged bowhunter on stand — and bedding facing downwind in order to watch to the front while the nose guards the rear.

As to being subjected to what some critics phrase the "terror" of the hunt — deer evolved as pure prey, marvelously nervous by nature and necessity. What human observers may interpret as terror, to them is both routine and felicitous to their species makeup and survival. In this regard, if hunting were banned or unwisely restricted, rather than gains in the welfare of wildlife, as hunting's critics envision, we would see rapid increases in overpopulation and its horrific upshots — increased collisions with automobiles, contagious diseases, genetic decline, overgrazing, mass starvation, a loss of respect by humans, and general misery all around.

No matter what one thinks of hunting, to condemn and attack it broadside and indiscriminately is to threaten the lifeblood of evolution

167

and the primary tool of modern wildlife management — thereby imperiling wildlife itself. The essence of wildlife is wildness. And the engine of wildness is predation.

Chapter Twenty-Six

Meditations on Poaching

On a chill Colorado evening awhile back, with big game bowhunting season done for another year, I tagged along with a pack of local biologists and game warden friends to help trap and ear-tag mule deer for a habitat-utilization study. It wasn't hunting, but it was fun — and unsettling in an unexpected way.

As we shuffled cold feet and waited in hiding for enough muleys to gather over the alfalfa bait to justify popping the blasting cap that would drop the big rope net, one of the wardens told a story about a vile and unrepentant trophy poacher he'd recently arrested. That got the others to telling their own poachers-from-hell stories, one after another, to the point that I was relieved when the boom sounded, the net fell and all conversation abruptly stopped. Frankly, I found it easier to physically wrestle frightened netted deer to the ground than to mentally wrestle with the troubling implications of the wardens' stories, some of which involved bowhunters.

Since that evening, I've been thinking a lot about how our image with the nonhunting public — including antihunting activists — is continually damaged from within, not only by blatant wildlife crimes, but also by plain dumb screw-ups that honest hunters often make and which can be misinterpreted by an innocent and uninformed public as poaching.

What follows is a lifelong traditional bowhunter's meditations on purposeful poaching — and on the plain dumb screw-ups we all inevitably make. Thinking way back, to the very roots of humanity ...

As previously stated (excuse my redundancy in this, but it's the basis of my personal philosophy), until more or less ten thousand years ago, every human who ever lived, anywhere on Earth, made his or her living wholly by hunting (including fishing), scavenging, and gathering, together termed foraging. Throughout the 6 million years of our slow evolution to full humanity, this was how it was.

As a neo-animist, I view the Garden of Eden as a metaphor for the free-wandering lifestyle of our foraging ancestors. Likewise, I read Eve's bite from the apple — the fruit of forbidden knowledge and a symbol of horticulture — as representing humanity's fall from the grace of wildness, into the servitude of crop-growing and tending. Thus did our sinful meddling with the dead-end knowledge of horticulture — the manipulation and domestication of wild nature — get us booted out of a forager's Garden of Eden. This same transition, from foraging to farming, bartered away humanity's ancient interaction and synergy with the rest of wild nature (before civilization, we too were wild), in exchange for utter dependency on the unending *production* of food — hard-won product — rather than gathering, which was nature's gift to Man.

Worse yet, we've not only cast ourselves from the Garden of Eden, these me-first days we are clear-cutting the Garden behind us.

Along with humanity's adoption of a sedentary (as opposed to a game-following, seasonally nomadic) horticultural lifestyle, with its increased productivity, security, regimentation, and boredom, came a wrath of attendant ills: overpopulation, epidemic disease, professional soldiers, criminals and clergy, the concept of private property (including women and slaves), landlords and serfs, and a rigidly hierarchical class system at the top of which squatted a parasitic and generally malevolent aristocracy who enacted and enforced repressive laws designed expressly to protect and enrich themselves at the expense of everyone else. (Sounds familiar, don't it?)

And in time, one of the greatest losses that came with this land ownership-based social stratification in the Old World was hunting, which was taken away from the working folk and reserved as "king's sport." For an independent, prideful, hungry, and inherently anarchic peasantry, poaching the king's venison thus became — not just a source of protein, but also a gratifying means of striking out against aristocracy, privilege, and social injustice. In England, Robin Hood, mythical or real, was the patron saint of this gutsy class of bow-toting Haydukes.

Of course, the penalties for poaching royal wild meat were draconian. For first offenders, lopping off the fingers or hand that drew the bowstring was a favorite punishment in Jolly Olde. If the miscreant persisted, he might well lose his head. On balance, it's hard not to side with the poachers … except that, if left unsupervised, they would and in fact did promptly exterminate everything edible in sight. Poachers and poor folk are rarely far-sighted people.

But that's all history now, and not even American history. In America today, we enjoy millions of acres of game-rich public lands, and anyone with the simplest of weapons, the price of a hunting license, and the means to get out of the city for a weekend, can hunt a variety of challenging and delicious species of wildlife. Legally and honorably.

So why, then, do we have so much wildlife crime? Why do some wildlife managers estimate that one game animal or bird is killed illegally for every one taken legally?

For many modern game thieves, I suspect, poaching still embodies a satisfying element of anarchism — a symbolic reclaiming of a little of what the aristocracy is perceived to have stolen from the people, thus providing an exciting, freezer-filling way of getting even with an unfair world. The bow and arrow, of course, is the near-perfect weapon for this sort of work, being both silent and deadly. It doesn't help that there aren't nearly enough game wardens to go around — a fact not lost on savvy wildlife miscreants. And even when caught, the hands of poachers no longer are chopped off, but generally only lightly slapped by a soft, urbane judiciary that too often perceives crimes against wildlife as far less serious than crimes against people and property — forgetting that crimes against our public wealth of wildlife *are* crimes against people and property.

It strikes me as ironic that "the hunting philosopher," Jose Ortega y Gasset — the celebrated author of *Meditations on Hunting*, an eloquent and insightful little book quoted perhaps more often in explication and defense of hunting than any other single source—professes a left-handed respect for the skilled poacher. The superb woodcraft of the "professional" poacher, Gasset proposes, writing in the early 1900s, qualifies him as the only "true hunter" left in the civilized world — a reviver of long-lost predatory instincts who lives closer to nature because of it.

"The poacher," the thoughtful Spaniard muses, "is, in distant likeness, a Paleolithic man — the municipal Paleolithic man, the eternal troglodyte domiciled in modern villages. His greater frequenting of the mountain solitudes has re-educated a little the instincts that have only a residual nature in urban man. [He has] the superiority of the professional, of the man who has dedicated his entire life to the matter, while the amateur can only dedicate a few weeks of the year to it."

Some poachers, no doubt, view themselves in this flattering "Paleolithic man" light. But let's remember that *Senor* Gasset was privileged European through-and-through. And in Europe still today most game and game lands are reserved to the rich and privileged, granting the modern European poacher a residual anarchistic Robin Hood flair.

I think as well that Ortega romanticized the poacher overly much, neglecting to take into account the always-negative results of unbridled personal action in an increasingly overcrowded world. Gasset was, after all, a philosopher — by definition, one who prefers the heady wine of ideas to the sobering tonic of reality. The rest of us — legitimate hunters, wildlife managers, and an increasingly observant and critical nonhunting public — view modern wildlife outlaws, those who kill illegally not for food but for ego gratification and/or profit, in the flat gray light of exactly what they are: common thieves, liars, cowards, cheats, and threats to the future of everything wild we care about.

No glory there, José, not a speck, no matter how "professional," woods-wise, and skillful a given crook may be. (Increasingly in fact, like too many so-called legitimate hunters, poachers use cheater technology as a replacement for skill and effort.)

And the worst of the lot, both morally and ecologically, are the ego- and/or profit-driven headhunters. I am left to wonder how killing an animal, often including endangered species — illegally, unemotionally — for just its antlers, horns, skull, or hide, then lying and cheating to get undeserved record-book "recognition" for the illicit take, can be rationalized by those who do it, those who aid and abet it for profit, and those who know of it and fail to take action. Worst of all are the impotent, deeppocketed, moral nonentities with weak egos and minds who buy their "trophies" from professional poachers.

It *can't* be justified, of course — not by any sane standard of sportsmanship, fair chase, honor, decency, or (since most of this sorry lot are male) ... manliness.

In my view of things, the buyers and self-proclaiming "harvesters" of poached "trophies" are the penultimate limp-wicks, equalled in shame only by the slaughterers of game-farm pets.

Cultural influences contributing to wildlife (and other) crimes in America today include the negative examples of sleazy industrial politics, mercenary professional athletics, for-profit religious evangelism, the "Me first!" Wall Street mindset — in short, we derive much of the motivation, justification, and drive to poach and lie and cheat from the childish sense of competition and craving for personal recognition and fame that append themselves, like grinning leaches, to the frenzied and impersonal nature of modern, cutthroat, for-profit civilization.

Even so, with all of that said and notwithstanding, the relative minority of willful criminals who go afield *intending* to use hook and crook to plunder America's wildlife riches — whether for meat, money, or personally perceived glory — as troublesome and reproachful as they are, aren't the primary problem.

Statistically, the majority of illegal hunting acts—those cracks in the armor of our collective honor through which our critics love to jab their media and legal lances—are not committed by intentional criminals, but by regular Joes and JoAnns, gunners and archers alike, traditionalists and pulley-pullers, beginners and experts; hunters who go afield with every good intention of playing a straight game, but who, in the face of sudden tempting illegal or unethical opportunity, weaken and release that illegitimate arrow or touch that felonious trigger.

The point I'm meandering so drunkenly toward here is simply that in hunting, no one is safe from occasionally being tempted, not even those of us who hunt only with traditional or even primitive equipment and attitudes.

Of course, temptation itself is not a crime. Temptation afield is merely a close encounter with what the great American hunter and conservationist Aldo Leopold (who hunted not only with shotguns, but in his younger years with wood bows and arrows he crafted himself) identified more than half a century ago as one of the simultaneously most enjoyable and troubling aspects of hunting — the fact that most often, no one is out there watching us. We're operating either on individual honor, or on the collective honor of a small group of friends. What separates the spontaneous wildlife criminal from the ethical sportsman, then, isn't merely being *tempted*, but *giving in* to temptation.

Temptation can hardly be premeditated; it just happens. Thus, it can never be utterly avoided. Even Jesus knew temptation. And always, the outcome rides on a single critical decision: to act or not to act. In short —

as another dead European philosopher, the famous French existentialist Jean-Paul Sartre, would have it—as free men and women, *we are the products of our own decisions*, day by day moment by moment, decision by decision. The way we approach hunting — the self-restraint and honor we do or don't bring to it —can be viewed as a metaphor for how we approach life itself; for *character*. In hunting, as in life, it's not the words, grand or humble, but the *actions* that truly define the person.

In the end and absolutely, we need more, and more stringent, wildlife law enforcement. We need more and better ethics education conducted via every possible venue. We need stiffer anti-poaching laws nationwide — such as Colorado's widely supported Samson Law, which elevates the poaching of any trophy-class game animal to a jail-time felony. And we need less lenient court judgments and sentencing for convicted wildlife criminals (who often as not are not the starving poor, but small-town bigshots with heavy local connections).

Certainly, we must defend ourselves against unfair attacks from myopic animal rights zealots. But we can't let our focus on the vastly overblown antihunter threat blind us to the less obvious but no less critical skirmishes within ... within the hunting ranks ... within *ourselves*.

Life isn't simple. The hunting vs. anti-hunting argument isn't cleanly black and white. An easy majority of hunting's critics are not antis per se — not radical animal rightists philosophically dead-set against all hunting and dedicated to its total demise, as the self-serving U.S. Sportsmen's Alliance would have us believe. Most, a huge majority of our critics, are simply nonhunting Americans who don't like a lot of what they see and hear from hunters.

If we can win the quiet skirmishes within ourselves and within the hunting community — doing what we can, together and individually, to cut down on both intentional and spontaneous wildlife crimes — we will have won a major battle, perhaps *the* battle, against the enemies without. We will have deprived our critics of their most powerful weapons against us ... the skeletons rattling so loudly from our very own closets.

Chapter Twenty-Seven

The Silence of the Bulls

Too much of a good thing ceases to be so good. And that's the case today with bugling for rutting bulls.

There are just too many of our prolific carnivorous species every-where anymore, especially, it seems to me, in the autumn elk woods. And too many of we too many have taken to spending too much time tromping around with grunt tubes protruding from our faces like life-support systems and the self-pleasing screams of our own faux bugles echoing in our ears — and everyone else's ears as well, wherein lies the rub. The result across most if not all of elk country's easily accessible public lands has been to shut the real bulls up. And when that happens there are *no* winners. Hunters who bugle where too many others have bugled before, might as well be yelling through a bullhorn: *Here we come! Elk beware!* Bugle pollution also works against other, quieter hunters. And by shutting down the real bulls through too much calling of our own, we're disturbing the rut itself, thus threatening the future of elk and elk hunting. No only here in my home state of Colorado, but anywhere that allows elk hunting during the rut.

As restated far more succinctly by preeminent outdoor and trad bow writer Don Thomas: "During the Montana archery elk season, the principal function of elk calls has become to confirm the location of novice hunters to more experienced hunters and elk alike."

Don uses the plural "calls" to include cow calling, which is fast heading the way of bugling, for precisely the same reasons. But one squeaky wheel at a time, and the loudest gets greased first.

Skilled bugling for rutting bulls, in the right circumstances, can be among the most exciting and effective techniques available to early season hunters, as a few of my own stories, mostly from the good old days, attempt to reflect. But bugling has been so over-marketed and

175

consequently overused that today it rarely works in the road- and motorized-trail accessible front-country areas where most of us are forced to congregate. More often, front-country bugling backfires like an out-of-tune ATV. That's why experienced hunters rarely bugle any more at all, leaving those who never *stop* bugling to flag themselves as greenhorns who've spent more time indoors watching the *Outhouse Channel* and BS bugling videos than outdoors studying elk and learning, among other things, that wapiti are hardly slaves to instinct who can't help but respond to every call we make.

Well, in point of fact elk *do* respond to all of our calls. But increasingly those responses — clamming up, running away, going nocturnal, and lying low through the daylight hours in some blow-down hellhole safe from harm's way — work hard against both caller and called. Were bugling not important to elk during the rut, it would never have become an integral aspect of their reproductive strategy, much less the rut's annual anthem.

As we've seen, the wapiti rut opens in mid-August, when a surge in testosterone production causes new antlers to harden, velvet to shed, testicles to swell, and comrades to become combatants. By mid-October most eligible cows have been bred, bull testosterone levels plummet, testicles shrink, and the mountains fall silent again. Or almost so. According to studies in Oregon and Colorado, actual copulative breeding is concentrated into a roughly three-week period in late September and early October, peaking around September 26, though bugling may continue or revive as long as even one cow remains in heat.

Among the primary functions of bugling are advertising and stress reduction. As Olaus Murie observed half a century ago in *Elk of North America:* "During the rut, the bulls are in a turmoil of unrest. The physiological development at this period has produced a swollen neck and other sexual changes. The tremendous sexual urge and intense emotional state of the animal require definite expression. The elk cows are very evasive. The bulls are under terrific strain, and the bugling appears to be but a partial outlet for the pent-up feelings."

Other "partial outlets" for bullish testosterone poisoning include wallowing, tree and brush rubbing ("horning"), sparring, and outright battle. Of course, the *ultimate* outlet for a rutted-up bull's "tremendous sexual urge and intense emotional state" — the point of the whole elaborate ceremony — is to breed serially with a congeries of ovulating cows. And here too, bugling plays an essential role. As preeminent wild ungulate biologist Valerius Geist summarizes in his lovely book *Elk Country*:

"A bull's aim, clearly, must be to breed as many females as possible. The earlier he begins advertising, the more females he can 'convince' of his ability to provide effective shelter from harassment from young bulls, while teaching the cows that they are 'in control.' The more he advertises, the fewer females are likely to leave him, attracted and made curious about other actively bugling bulls. Consequently, the frequency of bugling coincides with the greatest amount of female activity. Also, it is in the bull's interest to out-advertise other bulls or to shut them up if it is in his power to do so."

Consequently, when a herd bull "bugles back" to another bull, or to a hunter's calls, his response is not intended so much to put fear in the challenger, as it is to reassure his cows. As Geist explains in his chapter "Adaptive Behavioral Strategies" in the scholarly classic *North American Elk: Ecology and Management*: "To retain a loyal harem, a bull must differentiate his behavior from that of his rivals. His advertisements should condition the female positively to his presence. This makes bugling an integral part of the courtship sequence."

"Condition the female positively to his presence" begs a further bit of explanation, to wit: The mature bull has learned, through multiple ruts, the advantages of patience and gentle behavior in courting pre-estrous cows (unless they should try to desert him). In contrast, younger bulls are awkward and pushy in their frenzy to mate without getting caught and butt-kicked. By bugling frequently while treating the ladies gently, thus reassuring his cows *they* are in charge, the herd bull positively imprints his distinct voice on his harem, making them *want* to stay with him, and helping the herd reunite should it be separated.

The first inexpensive, realistic-sounding, mass-produced bugling devices — the marketing breakthrough that precipitated the rage for bugle hunting — came to my attention sometime in the 1980s, in the form of neoprene disks, or diaphragms. The great advantage of the mouth-held diaphragm over other call designs is that it can be employed hands-off, freeing the hunting archer to draw and shoot while actively calling. For long-distance work, the diaphragm can be amplified with a grunt tube.

Like most bowhunters, when I first learned of this "revolutionary new way to hunt bull elk in rut," I hurried to town to buy a pocketful of the little half-moon magic bullets. For a grunt tube, I salvaged a two-foot length of discarded vacuum-cleaner hose. To the growing annoyance of my wife and dogs, I practiced daily for weeks. Come September, I abandoned my traditional tactics of sneak hunting and ambush, in favor of galloping over the mountains to scream, growl, and chuckle my fool head off, hoping to provoke a response. Which I often did. But a response is not necessarily a bow-range bull, and even back then — with far fewer early season hunters and far fewer among us calling to far less sophisticated bulls — occasionally it worked but mostly it didn't.

To combat this frequent and depressing silence of the bulls, and being blissfully ignorant of the social dynamics of the rut, we greenhorn true- believers simply trumpeted all the longer and louder, pioneering the tradition of go-for-broke blowhard insanity that rages unabated in some circles still today. "Well," we excused ourselves, "at least we're *doing something*."

Yes, we were "doing something."

We were screwing things up royally.

In a recent e-mail exchange, I asked Professor Geist: "How might rutting bulls in a bugle-polluted environment compensate for the loss of the long-range, vocal, social communications provided by bugling?"

"I suspect," he replied, "that heavily hunted and called-at bulls sleep it off in dense cover during the day and conduct their breeding business at night, when they probably roam about more. (Not good!) And mature bulls probably breed a few less females per estrus cycle. (Not good!)"

"Not good!" indeed. Herd bulls already suffer an increased risk of winterkill due to physical exhaustion, stress, weight loss, and battle injuries accrued across the weeks-long rut. Any added "roaming about" in attempted compensation for being robbed of their freedom to vocally advertise, translates to even more calories burned, greatly increased stress and, bottom line, a more vulnerable animal when the snow starts to fly and the mercury bottoms out.

Likewise, cows not bred by silenced mature bulls are more likely to be bred by adolescents, confounding the whole evolutionary purpose of a hierarchical breeding scheme, which is to allow only the fittest bulls, the time-tested survivors and proven habitat maximizers — the alpha males as it were — to sire the next generation. Additionally, cows that fail to hook up with silenced herd bulls and are corralled by younger males are exposed to more stress throughout the rut. Perhaps you too have seen a slobbering raghorn or even a precocious spike harassing a frantic cow or two during the opening days and weeks of the rut — until the big boys start to sing and the girls all flock to Papa's protection.

Or *would* sing, if we'd just shut up and let them do their thing.

Even the troublesome younger bulls suffer from a silenced rut, being motivated to do more "roaming about" of their own in search of stray cows, and more fighting among themselves to try and keep them. No member of elk society, it seems, escapes the penalties of intense bugle pollution. Not even unborn calves, since, with inexperienced bulls as sires, there's an increased chance of delayed fertilization. Elk cows ovulate on a three-week cycle, remaining fertile and receptive to breeding for only six to ten hours per cycle. Miss that brief window of opportunity, and it slams shut for another three weeks. If you roam elk country year-round as I do, you've seen the tremendous size difference between on-time and late-born calves such a delayed rut can bring.

Certainly, inexperienced sires aren't the only cause of delayed fertilization. Studies indicate at least three major factors affecting the timing of ungulate reproduction. First is *female nutritional status* — if a cow is undernourished, she will not ovulate. Second is *age of sires*. Third is *disturbance of the rut*. As Colorado traditional bowman and emeritus research biologist Tom Beck points out: "All three are important, but relative importance tends to be localized and site specific, varying from place to place and from year to year. For instance, in parts of Montana, Idaho, and Washington, female malnourishment is often the heavy hitter. But where nutrition is adequate, as it tends to be in southwest Colorado, bull age and rut disturbance often assume greater influence on reproductive timing."

The classic studies of these three variables — sire age, nutritional status of pre-estrous cows, and rut disturbance — as they affect the timing of cow elk impregnation, were undertaken by James Noyes of the Oregon Department of Fish and Wildlife, and others, across two five-year trials conducted at the Starkey USFS experimental station in northeast Oregon. Consider these excerpts from those studies, as summarized in the *Journal of Wildlife Management*:

179

"The 90ᵗʰ percentile pregnant female was bred on 5 October by 5-year-old males and 21 October by yearling males. ... The largest differences in mean adjusted conception dates pooled by age of males were between yearlings (4 Oct) and 5-year-olds (21 Sep). ... Results from the second trial confirm the effect of male age on conception dates observed in the first trial. As male age increased, conception dates became earlier. ... Although we observed a similar relationship in general, females were in better nutritional condition during years with yearling male sires, yet conception dates were significantly later than during years when older males were the primary sires. ... Optimum conditions for early conception and subsequent calf survival in elk populations likely consist of high female nutritional condition and mature male sires operating together. ... *If an early and synchronous rut and birthing period are desired, mature males are required. In addition to affecting an early rut, providing older males is consistent with the social structure that elk evolved under and may satisfy aesthetic values of hunters and the general public.*" (Italics added.)

Independent studies conducted by the Colorado Division of Wildlife (D. J. Freddy, *et al.)* largely concur.

Of course, two or even all three factors can and often do work together negatively, as when disturbance not only molests the natural expression of bugling, but also disrupts the feeding and rest schedules of pre-estrous cows. And the greatest, often the *only* disturbance to elk during the rut is early season hunting, most notably during muzzle-loading seasons. Summarizing the results of his own field studies and those from Starkey as published in the *Journal of Wildlife Management*, biologist Dave Freddy, elk researcher for the Colorado Division of Wildlife, reports that "major movements of elk could be stimulated by the timing of early hunting seasons, somewhat independently of the number of hunters in the field. In fact, these major movements could be induced almost any time during early fall simply by altering opening dates, and appeared to be independent of any natural migratory urge or biological cues — *they were human induced during the critical breeding season.*"

The closer we look, the worser it gets. What to do?

"In case of doubt about the impact of excessive calling and other hunter disturbances on the biological and social welfare of elk," advises Geist, "the wisest policy would be to postpone all elk hunting seasons until the rut is done!"

Indeed, *all* concerns about early season hunter harassment of elk and fellow hunters are but symptoms of allowing hunting when perhaps we should not.

However, until research irrefutably establishes the precise chain of impacts resulting from hunting elk while they're trying to mate, a biological argument for relief is politically untenable. Nor should it be required. Given the increasingly sorry quality of early elk seasons across so much of elk country today, observably resulting from too many motorized and bugle-blowing hunters causing too much disturbance, the desire for a quieter, more natural and satisfying hunting experience should be lever enough to prompt voluntary restraint among hunters—practicing enlightened self-interest — even as most state game agencies continue stubbornly to deny any need for change.

Hunter-biologist Beck agrees, having had too many of his own September bowhunts (some of which I've shared with him) ruined and cut short by bugle pollution, massive motorized invasion, and general hunter overcrowding. "And by far the worst of it," he complains, echoing what I have seen myself, "is during muzzle-loading season."

I live to bowhunt September elk. As the season nears each year I almost tremble in anticipation of the forthcoming symphony of genuine bugling and the heady incense of pheromone-perfumed wallows. I'm frankly addicted to it all — and to being an active *part* of it all. But when playing my part not only becomes undeniably disruptive to both hunter and hunted, and hurtful to my own success in particular, it's clearly time to show some restraint. Just because we love to hunt in a certain way at a certain time of year, and have been doing so long enough to consider it tradition, or even a "right" (among the most arrogant and abused words in America today), doesn't in fact *make* it right.

Given the exploding numbers of nimrods who have come rumbling into elk country in recent years to hunt the rut, armed with increasingly lethal and far-reaching compound bows and muzzle-loading rifles and equipped with a staggering array of such hi-tech aids as infrared game-monitoring cameras, scent-proof camo clothing, no-brainer game calls, GPS topo mapping, optical range finders, "genuine cow-in-heat elk urine" (a filthy game ranching product), and so much more, all of it morally suspect no matter its legality — perhaps the day is not so far off when the necessary science *will* get done to prompt sluggish, combat-shy wildlife agencies to address the obvious fact that too many bull tags are being doled out to too many hunters packing too much firepower and causing too much disturbance during what are intended to be *primitive* weapons seasons set in the delicate heart of the rut.

Hi-tech, flat-shooting, long-range, sight-equipped compound bows are *not* primitive weapons. They are single-shot and somewhat muscle-powered, but precisely the antithesis of primitive.

Modern muzzle-loading rifles that can be quickly reloaded and consistently kill at 100 yards and beyond are *not* primitive weapons.

And as soon as you hit the starter on a dirt bike or ATV, no matter what weapon you carry, all notion of primitiveness goes up in a noxious cloud of exhaust smoke.

While there are many options short of stopping all hunting during the rut, all require the cooperation of hunters. Such halfway possibilities include moving and/or shortening all September seasons to preclude hunting during the active breeding interval, about the last ten days of September through the first ten days of October ... significantly limiting the number of early season bull tags ... updating the definition of "primitive" weapons to honestly reflect current technological reality ... predicating privilege on a graduated scale of technological sophistication; those who choose to employ more hi-tech advantage should expect to receive less "primitive weapons" advantage, and vice versa ... and, absolutely most important of all possibilities, outlawing the use of all motorized vehicles off designated roads.

On an individual level, concerned early season hunters can voluntarily abandon bugling and moderate our cow calling as well. Nonresident archers whose hunts are generally limited to a week or two on public lands can come earlier rather than later in September. And we can leave the motors turned off, or better yet, back on the ranch where they belong.

Compared to more regulation, such voluntary measures are relatively painless and clearly the right thing to do. *If* we want to curtail early season overcrowding, bugle pollution, and motorized disturbance of the rut in order to restore a *quality* hunting and outdoor experience today and assure it for tomorrow ... *if* we want to vouchsafe healthy, behaviorally natural populations of wapiti for all time (while immature bulls, age three years and younger, are currently performing sufficiently to keep herd numbers high in most areas, short-term reproductive quantity does *not* assure long-term genetic health and herd quality) ... *if* we want to continue boasting that hunters were not only the first wildlife and wild-lands conservationists, but *remain* among the most concerned, informed, and effective forces working for wildlife and habitat today and tomorrow … *something*, someday soon, is going to have to change regarding early season elk hunting.

And any way we slice it, that something must be us.

David Petersen

Chapter Twenty-Eight

Modern Hunting, Ancient Philosophy

The out-of-doors is our true ancestral estate. For a mere few thousand years we have grubbed in the soil and laid brick upon brick to build the cities; but for millions of years before that we lived the leisurely, free and adventurous life of hunters and gatherers. How can we pluck that deep root of feeling from the racial consciousness? Impossible!

—Edward Abbey

Why do we hunt?

More precisely: Why do so many among us *want* to hunt, and why does it feel so deeply satisfying when we do it well? Digging as deeply into our hearts and minds as we can manage and bear, what might be the ultimate *source* of our shared need to hunt, the prime mover underlying all other, more visible and measurable motivations? What hidden engine powers the more obvious drives — those things we so often name as "reasons" for hunting but which in fact are merely among its more easily identifiable *rewards* — including meat, trophies, challenge, companionship, and the far-flung pleasures of being outdoors?

Assuming that such a prime mover can be identified, we then must ask if it provides a suitable foundation upon which to base a revitalized hunting philosophy today. If not, we may well be in trouble. But I say yes, and yes. There *is* a universal, bottom-line reason we hunt, and it *does* provide a rock-solid base for rethinking and revitalizing our current hunting philosophy, which is horribly crippled.

A Man Made of Elk

As often as possible in mid-August, just before elk season opens, I visit the San Luis Valley, in south-central Colorado, to camp and bowhunt the wily pronghorn. As described in an early chapter, it's a vast, eerily beautiful place, wrapped around by blue-green mountains, with the big beige crotch of Great Sand Dunes National Park anchoring the north-east corner. The area I hunt is heavily vulcanized, sparsely vegetated, dramatically lonely-looking, and holds a special attraction in that it, like the Alaskan tundra, makes me feel that I've time-traveled back to the Pleistocene. And in fact, the San Luis Valley is rich in deep-time archeo-logical sites.

At the wild tail end of that great icy epoch, ten to twelve thousand years ago, the human denizens of the San Luis Valley were semi-nomadic spear and (probably) atlatl hunters known today as the Clovis and Fol-som cultures. Perhaps, as has long been accepted, they were the recent descendants of adventurous Asian hunters who migrated to America via the Bering land bridge and then spread their population like wildfire throughout the continent — somehow reaching the East Coast long before they were thought to have arrived on the West Coast, even as they miraculously left abundant evidence of occupying South America thou-sands of years before they were believed to have arrived in North Amer-ica.

That's the old, apparently flawed yet tenacious official view, and while still popular in some True Believer scientific circles, an increasingly accepted and far more engaging hypothesis asserts that the Clovis cul-ture, thought to be America's first people, may not have been descended from Mongolian emigrants at all, but rather from caucasoids (bearing Caucasian facial features but not necessarily white) who arrived much earlier than the Asians — eighteen to twenty-five thousand years ago, perhaps, traveling by land, sea, and ice from southern Europe's Iberian Peninsula. Or maybe from the Sea of Japan. Opinions vary and no one claims to know for sure. Nor does it matter much to this discussion. What matters is that these prehistoric Americans — whoever they were, when-ever they came here and from where — were full-time foragers who earned good honest livings following and hunting mammoths and other Pleistocene megafauna.

But the Clovis paradise was short-lived, since coincident with the retreat and disappearance of the continental ice sheets, the stodgy old mammoth, overspecialized, suffered a meltdown of its own, unable to adapt to rapid climate and habitat changes and slow to reproduce. While human hunters, Neandertals in Europe and Clovis hunters here in the Americas, doubtless facilitated the finale, it was most likely climate and habitat change, not hunting, that most significantly doomed the big pachyderms to extinction. And with the end of their traditional prey species, the Clovis culture (and Neandertals elsewhere) faded out. Or so it seems fair to speculate.

With the great tuskers gone, the Folsom folk, who seem to have immediately replaced their Clovis predecessors in the San Luis Valley and elsewhere, focused their predatory attention on giant wide-horned bison, which they ambushed at glacier-gouged potholes throughout the valley. The stone rings containing these ancient hunters' campfires — Folsom and Clovis — even the very coals from those fires, along with artful stone tools and the tool-scarred bones of butchered prey, continue to be unearthed throughout the San Luis in exciting abundance.

It follows, naturally, that each time I visit this magical place with its ancient hunting history and preternatural Pleistocene ambiance, my thoughts run to one of the primary influences in developing my hunting and life philosophy. I'm referring to Dr. Paul Shepard: Pleistocene prophet, deep-time philosopher, and father of the vital new science of human ecology — the study of humanity's evolution in cooperation with wild creatures in shared wild settings.

In Shepard's vision — in fact a radical revisioning of the standard take on our so-called savage ancestry — our human hunting heritage leaps to lively, meaningful life, reconfirming our convictions, yours and mine, that the hunter's life is the good life, today as it was for time immemorial, until the advent of domestication and agriculture ... but only if we do it right.

And "right" in hunting means hard work, wrap-around respect, and no guarantees.

Among my favorite Shepard quotes is this: "In defiance of mass culture, tribalism constantly resurfaces." True hunters, past and present, no matter our differences in geography, culture, gender, and experience, are kindred spirits, a scattered tribe united by our shared love for what Shepard, employing clever double meaning, calls the Sacred Game — that is, the *elk* is the sacred game, just as the elk *hunt* is the sacred game.

Nor, Shepard counsels, does humanity's built-in, eons-evolved attraction to wild nature and wild animals reveal itself through hunting alone.

Why, for instance, do young children, across all cultures, respond more enthusiastically to animals, real and toy, than to any other category of objects?

Why are the names of animals and the sounds animals make among the first words uttered by most children worldwide?

Why is the color green so commonly perceived as restful and reassuring, while red excites and agitates?

Because all of these natural-born affiliations with nature in general and animals in particular — collectively called biophilia (love of nature) — arise from a common source: our long evolution, not merely among, but *as* wild animals.

Even as a pre-teen I was already wondering why I felt such a gut-churning drive to hunt, fish, camp, hike, explore, and be outdoors. It has never been something I take for granted; no mere "recreation" or "sport," but a heart-pounding *requisite* to personal contentment, satisfaction, and sanity. Why did I become a passionate hunter from the age of eight? It wasn't just for the meat, though almost from the start I ate everything I killed. It wasn't just for fun, though the best of fun it was. It was rarely (just once in fact) for trophies, and never in a competitive record-book sense.

Certainly, companionship played an early role, insofar as the best of my friends and their fathers — our chauffeurs, guides, and teachers — all were avid outdoorsmen. Yet, from the day I could legally drive, I've hunted mostly alone, and mostly with a bow. For me, hunting has never been so much a social as a solo passion, like a bird's urge to fly, a fish's fervor to swim … like instinct.

The "why" behind all this was always fun to think about, though definitive answers remained beyond my grasp … until I met Paul Shepard, who explained my life to me; in fact, he explains all life on Earth to anyone who's willing to listen, with hunting at its heart.

In overlapping careers as scientist, scholar, philosopher, teacher, and writer, Paul Shepard, who died in 1996, spent an active life examining the skin-tight fit between human nature and wild nature, leading to his widely celebrated proposal that millions of years of evolution, under the live-or-die tutelage of hunting and gathering (together termed foraging), made us human.

As a hunter, of course, this strikes me as very cool.

But far cooler — far more important to hunting today and tomorrow — is Shepard's revelation that while the last ten thousand years, ever since foraging was replaced by herding and farming — have radically altered the way we live, they haven't changed the way evolution *shaped* us to live ... which is in small, mutually-supportive clans and larger tribes linked heart-and-gut with wild nature via hunting and gathering. In our cores, Shepard proclaims, we remain Pleistocene foragers.

This radical retake on the traditional Big Three questions of philosophy — Where do we come from? Why are we here? How should we live? — has led human ecology to be dubbed "the subversive science," by disciples and critics alike, because it shakes the very foundations of civilized culture: economics, politics, religion, gender roles, health, diet, child-rearing, education ... *everything* we have been led to believe now comes into question.

Biologically, as a species, we've not had sufficient time in just ten thousand years of agriculture, and only half that of civilization (defined by literacy and city living), to have evolved any meaningful change (that is, adaptation) in our collective DNA wiring diagram (the ten-cent word here is genome), which was shaped across millions of years of evolution and alters, on average (says scientific consensus), no more than 1 or 2 percent per hundred-thousand years in the human animal. Just as the American and Asian wapiti, likewise separated for only ten thousand years, remain one and the same species in every way, so do we remain essentially unchanged across those same ten millennia.

Genetically — mentally and physically — we *are* the Clovis folk who roamed the San Luis Valley and its surrounding mountains some twelve thousand years ago — Ice Age-adapted predatory omnivores. And compared to contemporary life, it strikes me that life back then was far richer in quality, if far leaner in quantity. As described by Pleistocene evolutionary biologist Valerius Geist: "The picture that inevitably emerges of our distant ancestors as shaggy brutes is absolutely false." Rather, "they were apparently fun-loving, brave if not a little reckless, altruistic, intelligent, and deeply emotional — in short, a magnificent people. The advent of agriculture ... was indeed a 'fall from grace.'"

Why do we hunt? In some apparently significant part, we hunt because we are biologically and psychologically predisposed to do so. Hunting, fair to say, is a central thread of our genetic fabric, part of our generic heritage, its roots as deep as our species' tenure here on good green Earth. DNA evidence suggests that humanity's prime ancestor split with a common ancestor to us and the chimps and began the long evolutionary trip to sapience more or less 6 million years ago. By 4.5 million years ago, prehumans had achieved upright posture and moved out of the shadowy jungles to become creatures of the ecotones, those rich "edge cover" habitat seams where forest meets savanna and the richest of both wild worlds overlap.

Skipping forward through another 2 million years of stop-and-go evolution, the earliest hominid, or manlike creature, thought to have possessed the uniquely human abilities of fashioning stone tools and using them to butcher large animals was *Australopithecus garhi*. He and she would not have been professional predators quite yet, but active scavengers and opportunistic hunters who roamed the Ethiopian savanna edges 2.5 million years ago in search of fruits, vegetables, seeds, nuts, roots, and easy meat in the form of insects, sluggish reptiles and amphibians, bird's eggs and infant, injured, or disadvantaged (say, trapped in a mud bog) birds and mammals, plus the remains of larger animals killed by predators or accident.

Since a specific need for specialized slicing, chopping, and crushing tools, logically, would have pre-existed and provoked their invention, our ancestors' carnivory can logically be said to have precipitated the invention of tools designed to help satisfy that meaty appetite. The gathering of fruits, nuts, and seeds requires nothing more than fingers. And root-digging technology need progress no farther than the tip of a sturdy stick. But to peel off a hide and slice meat from bone, to carve out the tongue and get to brains inside a skull or the marrow inside a femur, specialized tools become a priority. While you can do it all with the crudest sharp shard of dense rock, you can do it all *better* with better, more specialized tools. And evolution is all about getting better.

This point — that meat eating facilitated proto-human inventiveness, pointing the gradual way to sapience — was well put long ago by Canadian bio-philosopher C. H. D. Clarke, who proclaimed that "man evolved as a [meat eater]. In South Africa, there were at one time [2 or 3 million years ago] two types of pre-men. One was a great shuffling hulk with a dentition that shows he was a vegetarian [*Australopithecus robustus, et al.*]. The other [*A. africanus*] was small and active, and fed on flesh as well as vegetable matter. This is the one that can be identified as having a place in the human pedigree. Vegetable gathering produced no tools, no forethought or planning, no tradition, no social organization. Pre-man the hunter, in developing and using all of these for the chase, became man."

That view belongs to the adaptive, or "behavioral" school of human evolution. The complimentary trophic, or nutritional approach tells us that the brain is a high-metabolism organ and can evolve — gradually attaining greater size and complexity — only on a diet rich in the exact blend of fats, calories, and other nutrients found in wild red meat, which, though low in cholesterol, contains five times the essential fatty acids of modern "bad fat" domestic red meat, plus high concentrations of iron and other minerals, vitamins and proteins imperative to brain development. Had our deep-time ancestors in fact been strict vegetarians — as some vegan extremists wish to believe — we would not be human today.

In two direct and providential ways, then — by promoting the development and refinement of manufactured tool technology (stone, of course, but also bone, antler, and wood), and by providing the right nutritional stuff for dynamic brain growth—did meat eating facilitate our progress toward humanity *even before we became true hunters.* The stage was now set for the third crucial contribution of carnivory to human evolution: systematic, organized group hunting with its mandates for upward-spiraling intelligence, cooperation, communication, food sharing and bartering, altruism, family and social bonding and lifetime cohesion, forethought, and planning. While many animal species demonstrate some of these characteristics in various degrees, only humans embody them all to the nth degree.

And so it transpired that by the opening of the icy Pleistocene, about 1.6 million years ago, that our forebears had already been scavenging and hunting opportunistically, catch-as-catch-could, for thousands of generations (much as chimps do still today), having progressed from gregarious bipedal brush apes to our immediate ancestor and arguably the first dedicated professional hunter, *Homo erectus* — who, at least toward the end of his long tenure, had mastered fire, good clothing, and sturdy shelter, a sophisticated tool kit, the beginnings of art and, most students accept, both complex spoken language and a rich spiritual life — just one short evolutionary step from whole-hog humanity as we know, love, and bemoan it today.

By the close of the Pleistocene, ten thousand years ago at its most recent, we were a done deal, exactly as we are today in every little detail and had been for a hundred-thousand years at least.

And what got us there, what got us *here* for better and worse today, was our daily give and take not only with one another, but with the natural wildness that housed, fed, and shaped us, carving and honing us across untold generations of hunting and being hunted by large wild beasts. Certainly, hunting wasn't the only evolutionary force at work. But as Shepard sums it up, organized hunting was primary and indispensable: "The dynamic of escape and pursuit is the great sculptor of brains. Hunter and hunted are engaged in an upward, reciprocal spiral of consciousness with its constituents of stratagem and insight ... a progressive refining of mind by cycles of predator and prey whose dances [through time and natural selection toward optimal adaptive survival] became less and less random, more and more choreographed."

And so the human urge to hunt, which *feels* so much like instinct, almost certainly *is* instinct, springing from the deepest primitive core of our racial memory. And the flip-side of this same coin — something that few modern people seem to grasp — is that a complementary instinctive "need" *to be hunted* is built into such dedicated prey species as elk, deer, and antelope. Without the continuation of the precise sort of physical and intellectual exercise provided by predation and evasion, our spectacular prey species, so beautifully sculpted by the artful knife of natural selection, would soon devolve into mere meager shadows of themselves, as pampered park and suburban deer are even now becoming in many parts of North America.

Predation and evasion *is* a sacred game, without which nothing in nature would be the same — without which nothing would even *be*. In a world with no predation—where no living organism feeds on other living organisms — there would be no food, no adaptive evolution, no quality control via culling of the easiest to catch and, absolutely, no intelligent life on Earth. (Not that there is much anyhow, at least in the exclusively human realms of culture, religion, and politics.)

Certainly, we are the most intelligent animal this world has ever known. And the greater an animal's intellect, the less its actions are dictated by instinct. Consequently—as a particularly hypocritical segment of hunting's critics howl — instead of killing our own meat, we could join the civilized majority in ignoring our predatory instincts to become full-time supermarket carnivores, rejecting our evolutionary roots as so-called bloody savages even as we hire professional killers and cutters to do our dirty work for us, politely off-camera, while in the process contributing to what social critic Gerry Mander rightly calls "the commodification of the sacred."

That is, to true hunters present and past, hunted meat is sacred meat.

Industrial meat is soulless product.

But there's more to this story than nutrition. A whole lot more. For countless millennia, hunting not only facilitated our physical survival, it was the wellspring of the world's first and only universal spiritual worldview, or religion — flowering repeatedly, spontaneously, without any missionary effort, everywhere unspoiled hunters lived or continue to live today. This ancient, universal hunter's philosophy is animism, a word whose root meanings include "soul" and "breath." To an animist, every aspect of the natural world — from mammoths to monsoons to mountains — has self-awareness, a sense of dignity, indignity, and reciprocity, and possesses intrinsic worth independent of its utilitarian value to man. Through the so-called superstitious workings of animism, primal hunters are guided to maintain high ethical standards while practicing sustainable conservation via enlightened self-interest.

Another way of stating the animistic view is that what we call "luck" in hunting is controlled by a cosmic karma or Golden Rule of reciprocity: Respect the animals we hunt and the habitat that sustains them, and they will look kindly on our needs as hunters. No more mythical than any other religion, all of which is supernatural, I like this idea a lot, as it facilitates individual dignity, order, and justice in an otherwise chaotic universe.

For a contemporary example of animism in action, anthropologist, writer (*The Island Within*), and hunter Dr. Richard Nelson reports that among the traditional Koyukon Indian subsistence hunters of northern interior Alaska, to disrespect an animal — by boasting of your hunting skills, using taboo hunting techniques or technology, speaking disrespectfully of the animal or mishandling and wasting meat — will spoil your entire tribe's luck when hunting the offended species, until and unless tradition-prescribed ceremonial amends are made.

With a belief system like that, it's easy to imagine that the peer pressure to hunt, speak, and think ethically regarding prey animals is tremendous, and tremendously effective — which is exactly the sort of self-restraint and self-policing that "recreational" hunting needs today. In short, modern hunting needs a *conscience*, and the animistic viewpoint, better than any other spiritual guidon, provides it.

A modern manifestation of animism is the biology-based philosophy of deep ecology, whose academic terminology camouflages the spiritual elements of animism, yet its premise is identical: *Everything in creation has intrinsic value and deserves fair treatment and respect*. By any name, this ancient hunter's philosophy is a winner, promoting personal humility while viewing egoism, waste, greed, and cheating as taboo, counterproductive, and utterly unthinkable, and celebrating life and biological diversity, bonding humans spiritually as well as physically to the rest of creation, and providing the truest and most defendable basis for morally and ecologically sound wildlife ethics.

Yet, in blatant opposition to our animistic hunting roots, the modern techno-hunting culture embodies what biologist and hunting ethicist Tom Beck poetically dubs "a failure of the spirit," leading to the parallel erosion of hunter ethics and the public disrespect we suffer today. Simply put: You can't defend acts and attitudes that are morally indefensible according to the value system of a majority of your culture or tribe. As Shepard says, modern "hunting is an easy target ... the commercialization and perversion of the hunt — the game hogs, the drunks, the shooters of cows, the facades of camaraderie — make the war against the hunt both easy and facile."

The handwriting is on the wall, writ large by Shepard, Aldo Leopold, Tom Beck, Val Geist, and a growing number of awakening others — yet precious few hunters and even fewer hunters' organizations, the outdoor industry, the outdoor media, or wildlife management agencies have taken note, preferring to dig ever-deeper bunkers of denial while chanting that tired old losers' mantra:

"We won't give an inch!"

Such heads-in-the-sand refusal to think and welcome change where necessary is an arrow to the heart of hunting, as evidenced by the current — and, I must say, often justified, popularity of wildlife ballot initiatives. If we don't start striving more seriously to clean up at least our most obviously flawed attitudes and behaviors — those words, practices, and tools that blatantly disregard the dignity of wildlife, wild places, and "fair chase" — if we don't move soon to clean up our own act, an increasingly concerned cultural/tribal voting majority will do it *for* us, occasionally misled by the false claims of the antis and occasionally making big mistakes, yet voting honestly from their own true sense of moral right and wrong.

My message in all of this is that the shortest and surest path to hunting's salvation is to be found by looking into our pre-agricultural past for ways of living and thinking that evolved, were continually tested, refined, and proven to work through more than 99 percent of human history, but which increasingly are ignored today — lessons that remain wholly valid and can help us to cope with this ecologically simplified, technologically complex, and culturally confused world we've made for ourselves and which so negatively influences hunting (and so much else) today.

No one is talking about "going back" to living in caves or tipis and hunting with spears and atlatls, or even exclusively with stickbows. Nor are we talking about rejecting all the many positive aspects of modern life — such as, for example, George Dickel, blues music, and Victoria's scintillating secrets. Rather, we're talking about *looking* back, *listening* back. and learning anew the lessons accrued through millions of years of acquired experience in hunting and living honorably, sustainably, and therefore wisely and well.

The ancient lessons to which we should be listening all confirm that humans are not separate from and the intended cruel rulers of the rest of creation, but an equal and inseparable piece in the grand mosaic of life and death in this hands-on heaven we call Earth. The animistic philosophy demands that we give something back — not material offerings or sacrifices, but love, respect, protection and, when necessary, a willingness to forego a tithed portion of our personal desires — in return for all we take away.

As Abbey advises: "We are kindred all of us, killer and victim, predator and prey."

Coming at this same argument with different words, the poet e.e. cummings cautions that "A world of made is not a world of born." Too much of modern hunting, with its industry, media, and ego mania for gadgetry, shortcuts, celebrity, convenience, and selective-species management, belongs to the morally and materially unsustainable world of made.

Meanwhile, true hard hunting reunites us with, celebrates, and strengthens the world of the naturally born.

Going beyond these general comments regarding the philosophic value of the animistic worldview to modern hunting, I'll suggest a few specifics that can help us shape stronger and more meaningful hunting ethics, both personally and as exemplars to the next generation of hunters, if there is to be one.

1. *Mentoring.* All primal peoples place strong emphasis on the structured guidance of youngsters in proper ways of living and hunting. Mentoring takes two primary forms: teaching and example. By praising the benefits of ethical hunting in our hunter education classes, we are positively mentoring novice hunters. Yet personal, one-on-one guidance remains essential to the successful evolution of a positive personal hunting ethic. Recognizing this need, even I, a selfish old hermit of a hunter, have in recent years emerged from my cave to give mentoring a go—and the rewards have been munificent. If personal mentoring doesn't fit into your life or personality, at least explain and encourage it among your hunting tribe.

2. *Rites of passage* were and remain integral to primal hunting cultures. Among the most universal, for males at least, was the "vision quest," wherein a young man, after receiving proper spiritual instruction, was sent alone into the wilds, under stressful yet controlled circum-

stances calculated to induce personal, life-changing bonding with wild nature. When the initiate returned, he or she was considered to be and expected to act like an adult. While perpetual immaturity is a curse of all civilized cultures, which have no formal rites of trial and passage, child-ish adults are nearly nonexistent in primal foraging societies. Although the ancient hunter's tradition of the vision quest has recently been co-opted and bastardized by New Age muffin-heads and goo-roo profiteers, it remains quite valuable when practically applied and should be incorpo-rated into the mentoring of all young hunters. With a bit of imagination and creativity, the possibilities are endless and can easily be tailored to individual needs.

3. *Personal and tribal rituals of respect for slain animals* are univer-sal among primal hunters. Nothing sappy or soppy is required — merely a few moments of quiet admiration for the animal, combined with some form of thanks: stroking the animal's body, perhaps an apology or assur-ance of respect and appreciation voiced aloud, followed through by ongo-ing respect and dignity in the way the animal is handled, photographed, spoken of, prepared for the table, consumed, and recounted in stories of the hunt. (At this juncture I'm tempted to digress into a rancid rant against the blatant disrespect so often shown for the prey by modern hunters, particularly in sloppy, tongue-bulging, blood-drenched photos appearing in hook-and-bullet magazines and ads for hunting services and products ... but I won't, because it only makes me angry.)

4. *Gender equality among hunters.* While we've gotten a good start on this one in recent years, we must continue openly and honestly to accept women among the ranks of true hunters. All unadulterated hunter/gatherer cultures, so far as anthropology can determine, were far more egalitarian than any civilization has ever been. (With sedentary agriculture came the concepts of proprietary ownership and the innate superiority of men as defenders of the homeland, which, in turn, led to the rise of patriarchy, or male dominance, and even the concept of women as property.) In nomadic hunting cultures, while men and women played different social roles and performed different physical tasks according to biological dictates and physical capabilities, neither sex overtly ruled the roost. Not only were primal foragers apparently far more socially egali-tarian than we are today, their women likely played far more active roles in hunting than most moderns realize. According to recent research,

women (and children) served as game scouts, set and checked snares, nets, and other traps, assisted in game drives and, in some cases, joined the men in actively hunting big game.

Certainly, fewer women than men *want* to hunt, and should never be pushed into it by overly eager male partners. But should you know a woman — wife, daughter, or friend — who wants to give hunting a try, you'll do well to help her out.

Across millions of years, our ancestors evolved to live the natural, healthy, comparatively relaxed (working just enough to feed, clothe, and shelter themselves), spiritually sane and ecologically sustainable lives of foragers — predatory omnivores. With the advent of agriculture about ten thousand years ago — which scholars are coming to view not as an eager "revolution" toward which our species innately aspired, but as a survival adaptation necessitated by a growing human population stressed by post-glacial climate changes and overhunting leading to decreased prey populations. As clearly demonstrated by archaeology and other careful investigations, agriculture was adapted at first by only a relative and regionally circumscribed few cultures, then gradually forced upon the rest, as it continues to be today.

In sum, over thousands of years, as we gradually traded hunting for herding and gathering for growing, we came increasingly to view our fellow animals less as sacramental flesh and more as mere property. More recently, we've relegated even the tasks of farming and herding to professionals, giving rise to a sheltered culture of de-natured supermarket foragers, vegetarian and omnivore alike.

In happy contrast, ethical hunters are active participants in the essential Sacred Game. As such, we cannot deny that life feeds on death, nor do we even want to. Paul Shepard's Sacred Game is a game that all wild creatures simply must play, predator and prey alike. To quote Sitting Bull: "If we do not hunt, we will die of heartbreak." And, I say again: so will the antelope, the elk, and the deer. In order to stay wild, healthy, and free, they need us, even as we need them. That's the way life's meant to be, as designed and clearly demonstrated by the ongoing process of selective evolution. That's the way life *is*. Anything less is a dangerous attempt to squeeze a universal morality from post-agricultural metaphysical dogma and personalized "perfect world" preferences.

Shepard says: "Wildness is what I kill and eat, because I too am wild."

Certainly, we hunt for meat, for challenge, for trophies, for companionship, and for the visceral joy inherent to the whole glorious process. But again I must ask — one last time — *why* do we find wild meat, big antlers, personal challenge, campfire companionship, crisp September sunrises and stinky elk wallows so uniquely and viscerally *joyful* ... even when the price we have to pay to experience these joys includes the deaths of fellow creatures, blood and guts on our hands, and the wrath of those who don't understand?

To rephrase that question less charitably, as our harshest critics are wont to do: How can hunters claim to love the same lovely creatures we take so much pleasure in killing?

Because — one last time — hunting is "what we are meant to do," insofar as it is a major part of what, until the most recent moment of human times, we have always done. When done right, hunting is in fact an expression of our instinctive (biophilic) love for the animals we hunt.

No child is *born* a Catholic or Jew or Muslim or doctor or lawyer or Republican or Democrat or priest — we must be *made* into these things by culture and personal experience. Rather, every child is born an animist, with a natural affinity for animals and the outdoors and freedom, with a body and mind perfectly adapted to a life of nomadic foraging. To prevent these born instincts from flowering, they must be subverted from the beginning by a censorial culture, as they so successfully and tragically are today. Through this cultural brainwashing process, depending on our circumstances and experiences, many among us become utterly denatured, while a lucky few, you and I, retain our natural traditional wildness.

In the end, culturally invented moral values, especially as applied to our relationships with wild nature, are fickle and unreliable: they are *made*. Wild nature, as embodied in our genes — that is, in our biological souls — provides *the only absolute and unchanging truth regarding life and death on Earth*: past, present, and forever ... and thus offers the only reliable basis for sustainable hunting ethics and felicitous life philosophies.

Onward then, out of the shadows of our formative past, through the flickering firelight of this terribly confusing life, back into the great unknown.

Chapter Twenty-Nine

Control

From childhood on, we are taught and encouraged to seek control — over our bodies, minds, and behavior; over our environments, futures, and fates; over our personal and professional lives and, via the metaphysical belief system of one's choice, we even try to control what happens to us after we die. Most of us, most of the time, struggle through life seeking control as a matter of course, without even thinking about it.

Regrettably, in the hunting arena as well, where the greater parts of our pleasures derive from purposely testing ourselves against things we historically have not bee able to control — wild animals, wild weather, wild country, our own limitations, luck — many among us doggedly continue to try. Up to a point, this is good and even necessary. But beyond the ambiguous boundaries of "good and necessary," inappropriate attempts to control the hunt can side-trail us onto ethically shaky terrain while eroding our hunting pleasures, satisfactions, growth, and pride of personal accomplishment ... and deflate our wallets to boot.

Consequently, I come to the campfire council today to propose that the less *stuff* we clutter our hunts with in pointless pursuit of control, the happier hunters we will be.

What do we really *need* (as opposed to merely want) in order to successfully challenge wild country and wild animals, and to hunt, kill, field dress, and transport meat in relative comfort and safety? Look at photos of the early icons of traditional bowhunting. Visibly, they carry stickbows and wood arrows. They wear rugged, individualized clothing, often wool pants and plaid shirts, the only truly "traditional" camouflage. And they carry gear to fit the season, terrain, and game, including a belt knife and a frame pack suitable at once for hunting, subsisting, and hauling meat and horns. A pair of binoculars may dangle from the archetypal traditional bowhunter's neck, and tucked away in pockets, pre-dictably, are compass and map.

A few more essentials — you know what as well as I do — and that's all she wrote.

In order to hunt safely, comfortably, with dignity and success, we *don't* need an $8,000 ATV perched on a $3,000 trailer pulled by a $40,000 SUV to get us there and home. We *don't* need "scent-proof" designer camo clothing, electronic trail-timers and infrared cameras, automatic game "feeders" (in fact, hi-tech bait stations), optical range-finders, cell phones, night vision scopes, a pharmacopoeia of chemical scents and scent-killers, Taj Mahal portable ground blinds and tree stands, and on and on *el barfo.* Perusing the ads in most bowhunting magazines and outdoor gear cata-logs today is enough to make loyal traditionalists laugh out loud ... and then break down and weep for what our sport has lost.

Certainly, I don't condemn *all* of the stuff enumerated above, though I sure hate *some* of it. Nor am I saying it's all useless junk. I am saying that none such is *necessary* for a good and successful hunt, and that often such stuff serves primarily to encumber us, slow us down, steal our traveling money, and generally interfere with achieving happy and satisfying hunting ends.

A hunter is rich in relation to the amount of *stuff* he or she can afford to hunt without.

The root problem with contemporary hunting is that too few among the hunting ranks today are old-style *outdoorsmen* and women — hardy folk who take pride and find joy in expanding "just hunting" into an ever-richer outdoor experience, an ever-growing personal adventure. Most nimrods today are mere dabblers and pretenders, uncommitted to fair chase and frantic to make a kill with the least effort and time invested, and then scurry home to a warm den with "trophies" on the walls, cold beer in the frig, and outdoor pabulum on TV. Why work to develop a woodsman's skill and patience, strive to know the game and its big wild world, endure prolonged discomfort and resist applying maximum pur-chasable control over the hunt ... when it's so very easy and socially acceptable to "challenge nature" with a fortune in *stuff,* rather than with spine, grit, dignity, and respect?

Why, indeed?

David Petersen

Notable exceptions noted, more than any other persuasion of hunters, I believe that traditionalists know the answers to all such whys,
having discovered the ancient, essential secrets of simplicity, clarity of
intent ... and *self*-control.

Chapter Thirty

The Mule Deer Wars

Are coyotes eating into deer hunting opportunities in the West?

"The Mule Deer Wars." That's what some came to call a recent and recurring western "range war" controversy.

The trouble began in the 1990s, when wildlife managers started reporting lower muley populations and decreased fawn-to-doe ratios throughout the West. Today, the numbers are rebounding in most areas, following a historical pattern of natural population swings, with some help from modern scientific wildlife management.

So then, if the problem is in decline, where's the rub?

No rub, really … until the next time around.

Rather than a lingering rub, there's a lesson here to be learned, and remembered.

What the rub was, was that a splinter faction of tunnel-vision hunters grew tired of waiting for nature and professional wildlife management to "bring the muley back." In Colorado, Utah, Idaho, and elsewhere, these fear-mongers fingered coyotes as the Big Bad Wolf and set up a paranoid howl about the "predation threat" leading to the end of all hunting in the West if harsh measures weren't taken soon. In sum, they demanded a war on predators in general, and song dogs in particular.

In response to this statistically insignificant but loud minority, in 1999 the Colorado and Idaho wildlife departments launched long-term investigations into the causes of the perceived muley decline. Both studies soon enough reported, in line with previous similar research throughout the West, that coyotes *are* capable of keeping an already *isolated and critically low* deer population from recovering — a rare phenomenon known as a "predator pit." Yet, as study after study has shown, predation does not limit deer populations in the big picture and long run, so long as habitat is healthy.

Of course, if your favorite muley hotspot happens to tumble into such a pit, and you're the impatient type, the "big picture and long run" don't count for much.

Here in Colorado, it went to senior Division of Wildlife (DOW) biologist Tom Pojar to undertake the mule deer "decline" study. He began by exploring prenatal realities. Using ultrasound technology on net-captured, post-rut does, Pojar compared current and historical pregnancy rates. Having determined that "breeding and fetus production were not the cause of low fawn-to-doe ratios," Pojar moved on to investigate rut timing, which, if delayed, can depress fawn production and survival. Again, no problem.

Logically, if a normal number of fawns are being conceived each fall and born each June, yet their numbers are below normal, something is killing them *after* they hit the ground.

In pursuit of the mysterious killer or killers, Pojar undertook the three-year Uncompahgre Plateau fawn mortality study, near Montrose in western Colorado, a heavily hunted, overgrazed, and OHV-infested area. From spring 1999 through winter 2001, Pojar and his field team captured, radio-collared, released, and monitored a total of 230 fawns. Of those, 102 died, most soon after birth: 38 succumbed to sickness and/or starvation, 28 to coyotes, 9 to bears, 7 to felines (bobcats and/or mountain lions) and 20 to "other" causes, most notably roadkill.

In the end, Pojar reported: "My data strongly suggest that coyote predation on newborn fawns is not the cause for low recruitment in this mule deer population," accounting for only 12 percent of fawn mortality, a ratio consistent with studies elsewhere, past and present, and widely considered normal and natural.

Which is to say: While coyotes and other predators definitely eat deer, they don't appear to be eating any more today than yesterday.

And too, the number of fawns reported in this and other studies as being killed by predators is almost certainly high. For instance, says Pojar: "A sick fawn leaving a scent trail of diarrhea is predisposed to predation and likely would have died anyhow" (of its illness, whether a predator found it or not). Similarly, inadequate cover due to livestock overgrazing, clear-cutting, or oil/gas development leaves fawns more vulnerable to both predators (insufficient hiding cover) and weather (insufficient thermal cover) — as does malnourishment, which in turn often results from human activities and/or weather.

Additionally, noted DOW large carnivore research biologist Tom Beck: "Given what little evidence we usually have to go on — often just a few bits of bone and a greasy spot in the grass — an unknown percentage of what we flag as predator kills doubtless are fawns that died of other causes and were merely scavenged."

Indeed, nature operates in sublimely subtle circles of cause and effect, rendering all simplistic "obvious" causes suspect. Up in Alberta, for example, researcher Susan Lingle determined that: "The more rugged and difficult the terrain, the less effective coyotes are at killing mule deer. *Roads or other developments that eliminate or diminish rugged terrain, or prevent mule deer from moving to that terrain, will increase the risk of predation.*"

Meanwhile, the Idaho study yielded results reinforcing those obtained in Colorado and elsewhere. According to researchers Mark Hurley and James Unsworth: "Quality habitat is the most significant factor determining the size and health of mule deer populations. All other factors, such as weather, predators, and human-caused mortality, are mitigated for or exacerbated by quality of habitat."

Taking a more active and controversial approach than Colorado, the Idaho study included an attempted extermination of coyotes in four of eight study areas. Across its first four years, the Idaho coyote study "managed" (killed) almost a thousand coyotes (at an average cost of $167 each!) — resulting in negligible gains in deer "production." As Hurley puts it: "Killing coyotes costs about $1,000 for each buck that survives its first year and about $6,000 per 4.5-year-old trophy buck.... You would have to remove 70 percent of the coyotes each year to have an effect, and no one in the world is going to get 70 percent."

Nor is any state wildlife department able or willing to indefinitely foot such an astronomical bill for such meager returns. "And the voting public," added Tom Beck, "would never stand for it."

Yet, a tiny contingent of hunters, whom the normally soft-spoken Tom Pojar calls "predator-phobics," remained doggedly convinced that coyotes were ravaging mule deer herds and should be permanently "controlled," no matter the financial and political costs. Not to mention the ecological costs.

CDOW biologist Tom Beck, meanwhile, concluded that the whole "disappearing deer" issue had been "blown out of proportion and taken out of context by the complainers. In most parts of the West, the muley decline has been minimal — around 10 percent. In the worst isolated instances, numbers dropped about 40 percent. We saw a similar slump in the 1970s. That one, like this one, spawned predator phobia and a political push for research. In the 1980s, the herds rebounded without our help, just as they seem to be doing now."

In addition to predation, a related concern for some was, and remains, that competing ungulate species — livestock and elk — are displacing mule deer.

"Certainly," observed Beck, "a range can support only so many ungulates. Bring in more livestock or elk — and elk numbers have exploded throughout their western range in recent years — and *something* has to give. That something is mule deer. But livestock numbers are not likely to decrease in the current political climate, and few hunters are willing to sacrifice their newfound riches of elk for more mule deer. Our only choice is to maximize the potential of existing habitat."

And, I would add, work to stifle the continued permitting of too many cattle and sheep on public lands, leading to too much overgrazed and effectively lost wildlife habitat.

Another concern for some was, and remains, that in parts of Montana, Alberta, and elsewhere, whitetails are encroaching onto mule deer habitat. Under favorable circumstances, whitetail bucks will out-compete muley bucks to mate with mule deer does. Should this go too far, some logically worry, the whiteys might genetically squeeze out the muleys in their overlapping habitats. But here, in some areas at least, there may be a workable stopgap. As Tom Beck has noted, putting more hunting pressure on whitetails while protecting mule deer offers at least "a quick fix in the short run."

Yet the most dangerous long-term enemy of mule deer populations and hunting throughout the West — according to Beck, Pojar, and a clear majority of other biologists out in the trenches of the Mule Deer Wars — was and is not the whitetail, not livestock, or elk, or coyotes, not even over-hunting, but a growing and increasingly consumptive and nature-ignorant human population, prompting habitat loss and splintering.

"Subdividing," cautions Beck, "fractures and consumes critical, low-lying winter wildlife habitat. Also, most subdivision residents have dogs, and few of them are properly controlled. If we were to conduct a fawn mortality study near any rural subdivision, my bet is that the primary predator would be Homer the family hound."

Tom Pojar agrees.

More subdividing also means more motorized traffic, more fences, and more roads, further fracturing habitat, increasing roadkill, and blocking wildlife migration routes — upon which, unlike whitetails, mule deer (and elk) utterly depend.

Meanwhile, the Chicken Little hunter faction that esteemed *Rocky Mountain News* outdoor columnist and longbow hunter Ed Dentry dubbed "the coyote posse," stuck stubbornly by their guns and compound arrow-launching devices.

Few gave the Mule Deer Wars more thorough and objective thought than the Mule Deer Foundation, a national hunter-conservation organization based in Reno, Nevada. In a published statement, Executive Director Bill Morill, together with Utah State University Professor of Wildlife Conflict Management Terry Messmer, an MDF board member, summarized the group's position thusly:

"MDF recognizes that predator management is a legitimate conservation tool.... Controls may be appropriate when a population is below habitat carrying capacity and it has been concluded that predators are the factor keeping the population suppressed. It is in such a situation that MDF may support predator control during a critical period of a year (such as fawning) or a limited period (say for two years) for a certain area until the population recovers to an acceptable level. However, the use of these tools should be prescribed as part of larger deer herd unit management plans [incorporating] habitat and harvest management."

About the same time, former *Mule Deer* magazine editor, MDF board member, and syndicated outdoor columnist Scott Stouder asked: "What's wrong with mule deer populations in the West today? It certainly isn't coyotes. Maybe we should expend our limited resources in areas that will make *real* differences — like wide-scale habitat preservation and restoration of the West's public lands. Mule deer are not generalists in forage and habitat selection, as are elk. Nor can they thrive in our backyards like whitetails. Muleys are the terrestrial equivalent of salmon; quintessential ecosystem health indicators. *If mule deer herds are in poor health, the land is in poor health."*

Across much of North America today, wildlife habitat is so fragmented into small private holdings that an "ecosystem management plan," as many experts have long called for, would seem untenable. Happily, in the sprawling Intermountain West — mule deer country — most states and provinces remain rich in ecosystem-sized expanses of public land. Here, long-term management for balanced biotic systems — including natural, balanced, sustainable, and healthy ratios of predators and prey — is not merely attainable, but mandatory if we want healthy mule deer numbers and herd dynamics tomorrow.

But warns Tom Beck: "Even if the last coyote in the universe were killed, without the support of hunters for increased habitat protection and enhancement, quality mule deer hunting for future generations is only a field of dreams."

As good a summary as any comes from hunter and predator/prey research biologist Jamin Grigg. As a young research assistant, Grigg (who now works with wolves and elk near Yellowstone National Park) spent more time "on the ground" with the mule deer of the Uncompahgre Plateau than anyone, and his recollection and summation of that intensely personal learning experience is this:

"I don't think we'll ever again see muley numbers as high as those of the 1950s through the '70s, for three main reasons. The first, and probably the most important, is development and exploding human populations. Muleys are far less adaptive to changes in home range than are elk. Radio telemetry has shown that the home range of deer is essentially 'hard-wired' into them. Here on the Plateau and elsewhere, muleys don't simply move when they lose their traditional home range. Rather, they will continue to try and live where they always have. Consequently, we see more and more deer trying to live in and around subdivisions and their numbers eventually fading out.

"The second issue is roads. I think we are vastly underestimating roadkill impact and the splintering of habitat caused by roads and traffic.

"Finally, muley numbers were probably greatly inflated during the middle of the last century by the abundance of agricultural fields throughout the animal's range and the plentiful, but unnatural and temporary, nutrition these manmade feeding grounds supplied. Increasingly, tying problem three back to the first two problems, those fields and the deer food they once supplied no longer exist, replaced by subdivisions, roads, and other deer-lethal forms of human development."

Scapegoating — whether aimed at our fellow humans, or at our fellow natural predators — has always been, and will always be, the realm of small mean minds, cowards and paranoids; a counterproductive approach to solving subtly complex problems. No matter our affinity and superficial justification for blind hatred of any stripe, it simply doesn't work.

David Petersen

Chapter Thirty-One

Let's Use the Quads God Gave Us

"Use the Quads God Gave You!"

Thus proclaims a downright clever, walk-the-talk bumper sticker distributed by the booming young sportsmen-conservation group Backcountry Hunters and Anglers, or BHA. Founded and headquartered in Oregon, BHA is a 501c3 approved nonprofit organization with members in thirty-eight states and two foreign countries. BHA is dedicated to quality ethical hunting and fishing opportunities in North America, and the aggressive protection of wilderness and roadless backcountry habitat, upon which America's outdoor tradition depends.

For the examples of traditional-bowhunter influence in BHA, consider ...

I am privileged to serve on the board of directors, and to chair the Colorado chapter as well ...

For the past two years, BHA volunteers have manned (and womanned) a booth at *TBM's* Expo West, receiving gratifying support from the crowd and heading home with huge bundles of new-member forms ... The entire *Traditional Bowhunter Magazine* family — publishers T.J. Conrads and Larry Fischer, their better halves Robin and Belinda, and co-editor Don Thomas — all are BHA members and strong supporters ...

And it's likely you've seen BHA's color ads in the magazine.

Even so, BHA is not a traditional bowhunters' group, per se. Nor, given the massive mouthful of challenge we're biting off nationwide, can we afford to be.

What BHA is, what *we* are, is a diverse congeries of thoughtful traditional-values hunters — from "primitive" bowhunters who make all our own gear, to scope-sighted riflemen; and from dry-fly "elitists" to bait casters — outdoorsmen and women who respect, embody, and strive to uphold the traditional values of outdoor sport in North America. By "traditional" here I mean allegiance to wholly democratic and distinctly American sporting traditions and values that depend absolutely for their survival and prosperity on an abundance of road- and motor-free, truly *wild* and *public* lands. Let these go, and hunting in America will inevitably shrink to the tragic Texas model, where only the privileged can play and rarely fairly. Nor do all BHA members necessarily hunt and fish exclusively or even frequently in the backcountry; that is not a prerequisite for membership, so don't let the name mislead.

The only requisites for BHA membership are:

(1) that we cherish and want to assure for future generations the ongoing availability of the uniquely American, traditional (that is, muscle-powered, quiet-use, fair-chase) sporting experience;

(2) that we understand that public lands wilderness and roadless areas provide clean, cold water, and therefore quality fishing far beyond their borders, while also acting as population stability and trophy production areas for all our most prized big game species — which means that unroaded, unmotorized backcountry public lands benefit even those "downstream" hunters and anglers who never get out of sight of a road, and/or who hunt and fish exclusively on private lands; and

(3) that we are willing to fight some damn tough odds in order to protect American backcountry values and habitat from increasingly numerous, well funded, highly organized "me first" invaders.

Simply put, BHA practices enlightened self-interest. How can any thinking outdoorsman or woman *not* be passionately in favor of assuring the long-term health of the delicate high- and mid-altitude watersheds that assure abundant clean water for drinking, irrigation, wildlife, and fishing? How can be *not* be for protecting the vast natural landscapes that shelter and nurture healthy big game populations and produce a disproportionate percentage of trophy animals, at the same time providing the biggest, wildest, most exciting and all-around best hunting grounds left on the continent today, essentially free and equally available to all ablebodied Americans? As Woodrow Wilson Guthrie reminds us, these lands

211

lands. To be used and shared by all. But to be spoiled and ruined

.

kcountry Hunters and Anglers came into being a handful of years
a rallying point for selfless and enlightened sportsmen and
no matter the type of weapons we choose to use. We are quiet-use
and anglers who are offended by the growing number of befud-
)uld-be sportsmen we encounter on public lands today — even
e don't see them, we darn sure hear them! — who've bent obedi-
) the amoral outdoor industry's dictum to abandon lungs, legs,
manners, ethics, and the American outdoorsman's historic con-
)n conscience, in favor of fossil-fuel engines, annoying noise, and
)ften an overtly "To hell with you!" attitude toward everyone and
ing but themselves and their adolescent addiction to motorized

tainly, there are places and uses for OHVs, such as riding fence,
ng, and other routine chores on private property. But *not* for
ional use in public lands wildlife habitat, especially during hunt-
son. Nor is this merely a problem of abuse, as bad as it is. It's
a matter of *over*-use, no matter how well-behaved the users.
:oo many hikers threaten a delicate landscape, the Forest Service
limited, permitted entry. When too many boaters threaten the
nes and riparian corridors of the streams they float, BLM goes to
, permitted entry. Why haven't these two public lands "protective"
:s done the same for ATVs in at least the most hammered "wild"
inder their jurisdictions?
iditional hunters are embarrassed and angered by the rude words,
tless actions, and myopic "We want *ours* and *yours* too!" politics of
ie Ribbon Coalition, the ATV industry, and a growing majority of
zed users who buzz endlessly along forest backroads and trails,
o often illegally cross-country, in search of new camping sites to
ind easy targets to pot-shoot, and who leave erosive tire ruts and
)les, mountains of trash, spooked wildlife, and severely damaged
t everywhere they go.
's just a few bad apples among us," ATV spokesmen chant. But
on what we're seeing out there today, the whole damn orchard is
If the responsible public lands agencies can't or won't effectively
the bad apples, which clearly then can't or won't, then self-
imed responsible ATV users need to … starting with telling the

industry to quit running magazine ads showing their products in the process of destroying wild landscapes, as if that's how it's supposed to be. And clearly, shamefully, a lion's share of the worst offenses are perpetrated during hunting seasons.

As one crusty Colorado elk outfitter and BHA member puts it: "Motorized huntin' ain't no *huntin'* a'tall."

And where's the *joy* in it? The *challenge?* The stories to be told around campfire and to grandchildren? Nor are motorized hunters as successful in bagging game. The whole damn mess is logically inexplicable.

And yet, year by year and leaps by bounds, the smelly menace metastasizes among us.

For an example of the harassment and harm roads and motorized trails bring to wildlife, wildlife habitat, and the traditional hunting experience, let's consider the impacts one of the most popular, tough, and adaptable big game species on the continent, an animal that's been the subject of intense long-term studies in relation to road impacts and vulnerability — you guessed it — our beloved North American wapiti.

On heavily roaded landscapes, which most Forest Service and BLM lands are (in Colorado, for example, only 8 percent of FS lands lie more than a mile from a road, and only 4 percent of BLM lands!), elk find themselves lethally sandwiched between aggressive harassment by motorized invaders during hunting seasons, and decreased hiding cover. Expanding on the well-known Big Three, the "big four" survival essentials for elk are food, water, cover — and room to roam. This fourth element, expansive legroom, is essential to elk (a highly mobile and migratory species) not only to meet the first three needs through all the seasons, but also to allow females to "shop around" for the fittest males to father their young. In heavily roaded, logged-over, gas-well-pocked, or otherwise heavily roaded and disturbed habitat, this essential ability to roam must be bought by elk at the usurious price of greatly increased stress and greatly reduced survival. Either way, move or sit tight, wildlife too often lose. Moreover, scientific research and personal observation document that elk and other wildlife often suffer stress, behavioral disruption, and forced displacement due to motorized traffic noise alone — the roar and engine-rattle of big diesel road rigs, the mosquito-whine of quads, dirt bikes, and snowmobiles — even should they escape more direct motorized harassment including getting shot at, run down, or chased around.

Ostensibly to reduce the risks to elk in considering the ecological impact of new roads and timber sales, the Forest Service has long employed a "vulnerability paradigm" called the Blue Mountain Habitat Effectiveness Model.

This working rule of thumb, developed through studies conducted in the fecund but criminally clear-cut forests of the Pacific Northwest, proclaims that "good" elk habitat consists of 60 percent forage (whose requirements are generally and falsely considered by forest managers to be satisfied by clear-cuts) and 40 percent hiding and thermal cover. But the radically varying quality of forage and cover across all the many western states occupied by elk is inadequately addressed, and over-represented by the Oregon studies. Moreover, cow-burnt clear-cuts and arid rangelands offer radically inferior forage (not only in calories per acre, but in digestibility and nutritional variety) compared to ungrazed riparian (streamside) corridors and rich aspen understory. Likewise, the harsh artificial edges between clear-cuts and bulldozed road edges, and standing timber, do *not* equate to rich natural ecotones, where natural forest segues into natural forest opening; quite the opposite in fact as well as ecological impact, as preeminent conservation biologist and bowhunter Dr. Michael Soulé and others have unimpeachably demonstrated, time and time again.

The Blue Mountain model goes on to specify that satisfactory elk cover should consist of 20 percent hiding, 10 percent thermal, and 10 percent "either thermal or hiding cover." In the small print, effective hiding cover is decreed to be "vegetation capable of hiding 90 percent of a standing adult deer or elk from the view of a human at a distance equal to or less than 200 yards." Which leaves one to wonder: Is that with the naked eye, or through a riflescope?

Such substantially hypothetical and incomplete models and definitions would be laughable if they weren't so potentially tragic for the animals they purport to protect, and those of us who hunt those animals. Yet, even these obviously inadequate minimums have traditionally been subverted when they threaten to interfere with bureaucratic business as usual. According to retired Montana Forest Service elk biologist Jack Lyon, as quoted in *Bugle* (the journal of the Rocky Mountain Elk Foundation): "We had a lot of trouble recognizing the distinct difference between habitat effectiveness and habitat security for a while. Many wildlife biologists would say, 'No [the 60/40 model] doesn't necessarily provide security,' but district rangers would say, 'Yes it does; we need to get the cut out.' I can't describe how rash the interpretations were. And it was very clear why the interpretations came about, and it didn't have a damn thing to do with elk."

Another former FS biologist, Alan Christensen, who specialized in elk vulnerability, summarized his career findings and feelings (also in *Bugle*), when he proclaimed flat-out that "Roads are the single biggest problem on the landscape for elk. It's well documented and everything else pales in comparison."

Citing long-term studies in Idaho, Christensen points out that bull elk survival and average age (which determine trophy status) decrease radically with increased road access. "It's simple biology and common sense. Roads are the delivery system for people to invade habitat. If a wildlife population is weakened by land management decisions — in this case motorized access — you'll have higher losses from everything: winterkill, predation, hunting, accidents, and disease."

What goes unsaid by all these experts (though all of them, I'm confident, will readily agree with), is that elk and ecosystems don't know the difference between a dirt bike or quad on a narrow forest trail, and a pickup on a dirt road. So when we hear of say "roads," we should be saying and thinking "roads *and* motorized trails."

This is no "liberal tree-hugger voodoo," no matter how forcefully some right-tilted bullies try to make us believe that it is. Rather, the facts that roads and motorized trails damage wildlife habitat, harass and drive away game, and ruin and displace the traditional, quiet-use, muscle-powered hunting experience are scientifically documented and personally observable *facts*. Even the most exhaust-intoxicated of motorized sports should be able to understand the basic logic that if you want to hunt elk, you need some elk to hunt. And to have and hold elk — and particularly to produce trophy bulls — you need large tracts of unmotorized habitat to support and shelter them from over-hunting and harassment, in all seasons and forever.

Through the motorized community's harsh words and care-less actions, we are led increasingly to the stark conclusion that they just don't give a damn.

And so it is, by eroding the effectiveness of wildlife habitat in pursuit of a personal preference for effortless motorized access *everywhere* (No more wilderness!" read the signs they bring to public meetings), all too many fake sportsmen and women, speeding all too comfortably on motorized wheels blithely along (and just as often, illegally off) tens of thousands of miles of public-lands roads and trails, are quite arguably *the* most threatening enemies of traditional, quiet-use, democratic, muscle-powered hunting. On a personal note, while I've never had a hunt disturbed by the big bag Antis, I've repeatedly and consistently had hunts ruined, and entire hunting areas denied to me for traditional quiet-use access, by motorized invaders.

Bottom line and perhaps most tragic of all, by foregoing the healthy and sustainable pleasures of using the quads God gave them to interact with wildness in meaningful, satisfying, and sustainable ways, these smug sit-down folk are shortchanging themselves and their own hunts, even while molesting us and ours.

I'll end this rant as it began, with another bit of BHA bumper-sticker wisdom, to wit:

"The Backcountry: Where Roads End & Adventure Begins."
Backcountry Hunters and Anglers.
Check us out at www.backcountryhunters.org.
And join us, won't you?

A Man Made of Elk

David Petersen

Postscript

Thomas Aquinas Daly
Bowhunter, Bowyer, Artist

"Dave ... come check this out!"

Upstate New Yorker Tom Daly and I have just spent a gorgeous but fruitless September morning hunting elk near my Colorado cabin, in the San Juan National Forest near Durango. So when my bearded buddy whispers urgently for me to come see whatever it is he's so excited about, I assume he's found fresh sign.

"Check this out," Tom repeats as I draw near, his voice quiet but brimming with excitement as he runs a hand up and down the chalky trunk of an aspen, tracing the vertical shadow-line of the sun. *"That* side of the tree is in light. *This* side is in shadow. *That* side is one color. *This* side is another. The difference is subtle, yet it's *everything."*

No, Aquinas isn't crazy ... he's an artist.

Matter of fact, this rough-talking, hard-walking traditional bowhunter and bowyer is one of America's most important contemporary painters. Now, having made his latest artful point – which I'm instructed to pass along to my hobby-artist spouse – Tom takes up his handmade recurve – he also fashions bamboo fly rods, carves duck decoys, and builds sneak boats for hunting waterfowl, all in his "spare" time between painting and farming – and we move on.

Thomas Aquinas Daly was born in 1937 in Albany, New York. He grew up in Niagara Falls, graduated from the University of Buffalo, worked twenty-three years as a commercial lithographer and art director, fathered six children, lives today with his wife, Christine, on a working farm, and has been painting professionally since 1978.

Watercolors are Daly's traditional passion, though increasingly he produces stunning oils, etchings, and aquatints, and is one of a select few contemporary sporting artists whose work is embraced by the fine arts community as well. Tom's paintings have been featured in *Gray's Sporting Journal, Bugle, Traditional Bowhunter,* and other artful outdoor magazines, and also celebrated in such fine arts periodicals as *Arts, American Artist,* and *Southwest Art.* The winter 2000 issue of *Watercolor* honored Daly with both a cover and a feature story. Additionally, more than two hundred of Daly's paintings – selected from a lifetime output of nearly a thousand – are reproduced in two books: *Painting Nature's Quiet Places* (New York: Watson-Guptill, 1985; now a collector's item with price to match), and *The Painting Season* (1998), self-published by Tom and his writer/editor/artist wife. *Season,* by my lights, is the finest art book in print.

Daly's work also appears frequently in major galleries throughout the U.S., and in 1987, his solo exhibition at New York's Grand Central Art Galleries won that prestigious institution's Gold Medal, presented personally by President Gerald Ford. When James Cox, Grand Central's director, boasts: "Daly is being increasingly endorsed as a legitimate successor to Winslow Homer," he's accurately reflecting Daly's growing praise in the fine-arts community. But a more apropos compliment, to my hunter's sensibilities, comes from Anthony Bannon, director of New York's Burchfield Art Center, who muses that "If churches were built for the adoration of the sportsman's landscape, the works by Thomas Aquinas Daly would be appropriate altarpieces."

In addition to Winslow Homer, other artists whose influence shines in Daly's work, and to whom he is often compared, include Charles Wilson Peale, George Inness, John La Farge, Georgia O'Keeffe, Jean-Baptiste-Simeon Chardin, Andrew Wyeth, and James McNeill Whistler. Yet all this acclaim has failed to fatten Daly's hard head. Art scholar Cassandra Langer nails it perfectly when she calls Tom "a quiet, unpretentious, taciturn and very private man" whose paintings are "as intimate and unpretentious as he is."

In a coincidence of timing that would help shape his life, Tom Daly became interested in painting and outdoor sport simultaneously, in the

1950s, while he was still in high school. His favorite writer then was Ted Trueblood. In Daly's recollection of a Trueblood tale of a family elk hunt, we see the roots of the artist's personal hunting ethic, which are anchored in respect and humility, rather than ego and acquisition. The Truebloods, as Tom recalls, "made a family vacation of their hunt in the Idaho mountains, enjoying the total camping and wilderness experience. Yet they never lost sight of their goal. Contrary to the trophy-hunting mentality so common today, their quest was for meat, preferably from a barren cow. That humility and clarity of intent had a lasting influence on my thinking."

But young Tom's most significant outdoor mentor was his father. "One of the fondest memories I own," he told me, "is when my dad learned how much I wanted to hunt. He was not an outdoorsman, and would have rather seen me go crazy over baseball. Yet he put my desires above his own, helped me get a good shotgun and enrolled me in the first hunter safety course ever held in our area. I'll always be grateful."

In 1963, Tom Daly moved from Niagara Falls to a rural setting where hunting and fishing were closer at hand. Throughout the 1970s he enjoyed wilderness river floats in southern Canada, fishing for trout, salmon, and adventure. This was also Tom's self-described "all-consuming" waterfowl period, when he refined the sneak-boat technique to a lethal art and duck hunting scenes to a fine art.

In 1987, the same year he won the Grand Central Gold Medal and shook hands with a president, Tom bought a working farm near East Arcade, in upstate New York, and took up elk hunting in Colorado. It's a long old haul from New England to the southern Rockies, yet most years, before whitetail season opens at home, Tom drives the distance to tent-camp and bowhunt for elk, often as not alone and generally for a full two weeks.

In fact, in Tom Daly's life, time is kept by sporting seasons. Deep winter means ice fishing. As an "unrepentant meat fisher" with a taste for perch, Daly practices "catch and devour" ice angling. For years, waterfowling shared the frozen months, and while he still occasionally hunts ducks, "because I still like to eat them," he has largely satisfied that particular hunger. The same for trapping, which he practiced most of his life but has recently put aside, explaining only "I'd rather go fishing."

The manic gobbling of wild turkeys heralds springtime and Tom Daly responds with vigor. In contrast to his subsistence fishing philosophy, he views turkey hunting as an "almost spiritual quest," which he honors by hunting only with self-made bows and arrows. As Tom explains, "killing a turkey doesn't motivate me nearly so much as the woodsmanship required to bring these wary birds in close. In the murky, gray-blue woods of dawn, an approaching gobbler is a neon apparition. The wild, depraved music of his gobbles renders the experience all the more surreal. While I love to eat wild turkeys, I love to hunt them even more."

Summer brings more fishing, which for decades meant teasing trout, salmon, and steelhead with hand-tied flies. But more and more of late, rather than wading and casting, Tom sits in small boats on lakes and ponds, pestering perch. "After fly-fishing most of my life, I feel I know something about streams," he explains. "Lately, I've become enchanted by the mysteries of deep, quiet water – a new world to explore."

And come again September, "in good years," Daly repeats his ritual drive to Colorado to commune with the wily wapiti. Which brings us back around to our adventurous week together.

A weird and frustrating year for elk, this one, with winter drought and summer monsoons teaming to scatter the wapiti far, wide, and mostly high. Because my usual hunting haunts, lower down, are largely elkless, Tom and I decide after a couple of days to move up in the world by a few thousand feet.

And so it is that one rosy dawn midway through our week together, on a high lonesome saddle in the San Juan Mountains, we meet legendary local outfitter T. Mike Murphy, whose TBarM base camp is nearby, and for whom I occasionally guide. Mike is leading a muzzle-loading client, and after a brief whispered conference we hatch an equitable plan. Tom and I will stay high, hunting along the timbered ridge, while Mike and Russ drop off the far side – down and down – into a blowdown-tangled abyss known respectfully as the Black Hole.

Tom and I haven't gone fifty yards when a bull roars just ahead – not a bugle, but a ground-shaking bellow that tells me the animal is huge and hot to trot. Tom goes to his knees behind the nearest bush and strings an arrow, focused and ready. My part is to drop back a bit, hide, coyly cow call ... and the artist will take it from there.

But there is an awkward catch. "We can kill this bull," I whisper to Tom. "But I think we should give Mike first crack. This is his stamping grounds, his livelihood, and we're here, so far as I'm concerned, as his guests." Tom nods, whispers "no problem" and visibly relaxes. I scurry after Mike and Russ who, from their location a hundred yards down the far side of the ridge, heard the bull but thought it sounded small and much farther away. I convince Mike otherwise and as they slip in as Tom and I slide out. Moments later, we hear two quiet mews –silence – then the signature boom of a big-bore smoke pole.

The rest of the morning Tom and I spend helping Mike disassemble the biggest-bodied bull I've ever laid hands on, carrying a massive 6x5 rack. "What a privilege it is to help field dress such a magnificent animal," Tom says repeatedly, like some feral mantra, as we struggle with the beautiful monster, bloodied to our elbows. Music to my ears, this, as I've frankly been concerned that Tom might begrudge my having given away "his" bull (and frankly, I doubt I'd do it again today). Quite the opposite in fact, exemplifying the process-above-product outlook that sets mature traditional bowhunters apart from the "get it done the fastest and easiest way" high-tech mob.

In the end, Tom and I finished our week together tired, elkless, and happy. As I headed back up the mountain for more wapiti-inflicted abuse, Tom pointed his rig east, home to New York, where he'd conclude his sporting year with a profitable two-month whitetail season. Although he doesn't consider himself purely a "meat hunter" – a label suggesting a coldly utilitarian attitude toward wildlife – Daly hunts and fishes not just for the joy of it, but for the eating pleasure it brings. Likewise, while he honors antlers as nature's most elegant sculptures, Tom the traditionalist remains admirably free of rack addiction.

Autumn is also Daly's season for shotguns, pointing dogs, and upland birds. "With deer, elk, and birds to keep me busy," he confesses (or boasts), "I lock the door to my art studio for weeks at a stretch in order to direct my full attention to hunting. For me, big game hunting is an all-consuming passion that can't possibly coexist within the same time frame as painting. Although each feeds the other, these distinct endeavors demand individual fidelity."

Which brings us to a fifth season in the annual unfolding of Tom Daly's life: the painting season. "When I'm not hunting, fishing or doing farm chores," he says, "I'm painting. When I return to my studio after a hunting or fishing trip, I'm refreshed and eager to tap the flow of ideas and emotions the experience has generated. It's never my intention merely to *describe* the physical attributes of a place. Rather, I strive to capture its *essence* – to reproduce for others the gut-level feelings wild nature stirs in me."

By including human figures – hunters, fishers, trappers, berry pickers – in his landscapes, Daly enables us to inhabit his scenes vicariously, placing ourselves, as he says, "into the landscape, into the *experience itself.*" To further facilitate this viewer participation, Daly's most effective scenes (in my opinion) render his human figures small and essentially faceless – via distance or orientation – allowing us to imagine our own faces onto the amorphous figures and, thus, into the scene. "Dark Timber," the original oil Tom painted to grace the cover of this little book, is a sterling example of this artful everyman technique.

In addition to landscapes and sporting scenes, Tom Daly paints striking still life portraits – sometimes the familiar flowers in a vase, but just as often the *nature morte* – still life portraits of artfully arranged, distinctly dead game animals, birds, and fish. In defending this un-PC form, preeminent outdoor art and literature critic Stephen Bodio explains that Daly's boldly graphic wildlife stills "come from a long tradition; one unafraid to face death even as it celebrates the richness of food."

As Tom points out, that "long tradition" is long in fact, stretching back "at least to the upper Pleistocene, when primal hunting peoples paid homage to the animals that sustained them by immortalizing them on the walls of Lascaux, Chauvet, and countless other European caves. At least since then, and probably long before, hunters have expressed a *spiritual need* to honor their prey, in death as well as life. My still lifes celebrate and continue this tradition."

"Spiritual need" indeed. My own semi-scholarly investigations and hunter's logic suggest that cave art was the first holy text, recording humanity's first, most universal, and longest-running religion, animism, which divvies-up the power, mystery, and magic of "God" more or less equally every living thing on Earth, creating a diffused and democratic spirituality that places humans snugly within both nature and godliness.

For those of us who share Thomas Aquinas Daly's love for wildlife and his comprehension of the natural beauty of the predator-prey relationship, his "dead animal" portraits are not only poignant, but brimming with respect. Yet Daly's audience extends beyond the bounds of traditional sporting art patrons to a much broader and more diverse viewing public dominated by nonhunters. Which leads one to wonder: Aren't many urbane fine-art patrons turned off by Daly's *nature morte* scenes, which, being ingenuous in the ways of natural life and death, they perceive as reflecting a barbaric fixation on "the murders of innocents"?

When I put this question to Tom, he shrugged and said, "I am what I am, and I do what I do. And one of the things I do with my art is to challenge the nonhunting viewer's preconceived sense of moral order."

Flipping that coin, to challenge the often narrowly preconceived expectations of sporting art collectors, Daly frequently paints landscapes visibly devoid of animal or human figures, yet which, to viewers with sufficient outdoor experience and aesthetic alertness, nonetheless are exhilarating "sporting" scenes. In such wildly "uninhabited" Daly landscapes, you can *feel* the wildness of the place itself, as if you were swimming in it — "see" the unseen fish holding just below the water's mirrored surface, "spot" the invisible quail within the brush, and sense the certainty of deer or elk lurking back in the shadowy woods.

And that mysterious, magical power arises from metaphor, which is one thing – a word, image, or idea – that calls to mind another and entirely different thing, not merely physically, but essentially, even spiritually. When Shakespeare declares that "Love is a rose," he's not talking about a literal, physical resemblance – which obviously does not exist. Rather, he's suggesting a whole universe of subtly *parallel*s (which I'll leave to you to enjoy discovering). Similarly, when Thomas Aquinas Daly paints a wild landscape devoid of people and wildlife, he's relying on subtle similarities between that painted landscape and actual landscapes you and I have known, to suggest on a *personalized* and *individualized* level the intriguing *possibilities*.

Such symbolic thinking — the ability to create and perceive metaphor; to reason and imagine beyond the currently visible and thus merely literal — is a distinguishing quality of human intellect. For our deep-time hunter/gatherer ancestors, animal tracks were the original metaphors and the precursors to written language, evoking not only the image of a thing unseen — the beast that left the track — but a whole universe of associated feelings and intuited possibilities as well: danger, beauty, challenge, food, clothing, sounds and smells, acclaim by the tribe should the hunt arising from trailing the tracks be successful. Nor has this changed much. Even today, the sight of a fresh deer or elk or bear or even turkey track can be more gut-stirring than actually seeing the animal that made it. That's because tracks, like fine art, literature, and lingerie, are metaphorical and mysterious, teasing our imaginations to run wild and free ... while seeing the actual deer or naked body, while certainly a thrill, leaves nothing to be imagined, stifling the magic of mystery.

Thus, the metaphorical magic of Tom Daly's art.

Or one important aspect of it, at least. There is more.

Like another eminent modern landscape artist, Montana sportsman Russell Chatham, much of Daly's most moving work embraces the luminist theme, comprising a moody, diffused, often darkly somber background highlighted by a mesmerizing point or streak or smear of brightness. For Daly, a recurring expression of the luminist icon is a full moon or twilight sun hung low above a wild horizon, its buttery glow glimmering ethereally on quiet water. The effect is hypnotic and deeply emotional, even when "nothing much is going on" by way of overt action.

Which is entirely as it should be, in that Daly says his paintings "evolve from emotion, not from calculated logic. Most sporting art aims for the fleeting moment of high drama, the peak of the action – a flushing grouse, say, or a leaping trout or running deer. While I appreciate and sometimes paint such exciting moments myself, my preference is to evoke the more subtle and prolonged pleasures of outdoor adventure and sport."

And of such patience and subtlety, masterful magic is born — in hunting as in hunting art.

Facilitating the realistic surrealism that distinguishes Tom Daly's work is a technique I call "purposeful ambiguity," a kissing cousin to metaphor and equally effective in art and literature. To illustrate: One print in my own humble collection, from an original oil by a well-known wildlife portraitist, is a bust of a golden eagle. The anatomical detail in this work is so strikingly precise that most viewers mistake it for a photo. And that's high praise indeed. Yet, exactly *because* of its precise realism, coupled with its unnatural isolation – posed against a sterile studio background – the fullness of its far richer potential magic is denied.

Were Tom Daly to paint an eagle, I'll wager that he'd hang it in a brooding sky, caught in lifelike flight in a natural setting, rather than frozen out of context in statuesque stillness. Moreover, Daly would provide only enough detail to suggest the *idea* of an eagle interacting with the *idea* of its environment, leaving the rest to individual imagination and ... *Eureka!*

Magic is made.

Which is all I can say, and more than I probably should, by way of impersonating an art critic.

Long ago, in the only art appreciation class I ever took, we were challenged with the classic conundrum: "Does art imitate life – or the other way around?"

For traditional bowhunter Tom Daly, *neither* is an imitation: art *is* life ... the sporting life.

David Petersen

About the Author

David Petersen has been a Marine Corps helicopter pilot, a college writing instructor, a magazine editor, and a wildlands conservation activist. Since 1980, David has made his home in the rural San Juan Mountains near Durango, Colorado, where he hand-built the cabin he still lives in today. David is the recipient of numerous conservation awards, founder of the Colorado chapter of Backcountry Hunters and Anglers, former Colorado Public Lands Conservation Field Director for Trout Unlimited, and served on the Governor's Roadless Areas Review Task Force, representing the interests of hunters and anglers. Along the way, David has written a dozen nonfiction books, all having to do with humanity's relationship to nature. Additionally, he collected and edited the journals, correspondence, and poetry of Edward Abbey, and the environmental essays of Pulitzer Prize-winning novelist A.B. Guthrie, Jr. Most recently, David and his wife Caroline were the subjects of the documentary film *On the Wild Edge: Hunting for a Natural Life,* by Belgian filmmaker Christopher Daley. That film and all of David's books are available at www.davidpetersenbooks.com.

David Petersen

A Man Made of Elk

David Petersen